The Essenes

Children of the Light

by
Stuart Wilson and Joanna Prentis

OZARK
MOUNTAIN
PUBLISHERS

P.O. Box 754
Huntsville, AR 72740

For permission, or serialization, condensation, adaptions, or for our catalog of other publications, write to: Ozark Mountain Publishing, Inc., P.O. Box 754, Huntsville, AR 72740, Attn: Permissions Department.

Library of Congress Cataloging-in-Publication Data
Wilson, Stuart - 1937 –
Prentis, Joanna - 1943 –
    "The Essenes - Children of the Light" by Stuart Wilson and Joanna Prentis
    Eyewitness accounts of the secrets of the mystery school of the Essenes at Qumran; and Jesus' and Joseph of Arimathea's connection with the Essenes. The information was gained through regressive hypnosis, conducted by Joanna Prentis. Includes Bibliography and Index.

1. Essenes 2. Jesus 3. Hypnosis 4. Reincarnation 5. Joseph of Arimathea 6. Mary Magdalene 7. Melchizedek 8. Druids

I. Wilson, Stuart, 1937 - II. Prentis, Joanna, 1943 - III. Essenes IV. Title
Library of Congress Catalog Card Number: 2004117349
ISBN: 978-1-886940-87-1

Cover Art and Layout: www.noir33.com
Book Design: Julia Degan
Book Set in: Times New Roman, Agaramond
Published By

PO Box 754, Huntsville, AR 72740
800-935-0045 or 479-738-2348 fax: 479-738-2448
WWW.OZARKMT.COM Printed in the United States of America

Acknowledgments

We would like to say a big "thank you" to all those who took part in the groups at the Starlight Centre, and particularly to those whose regression sessions form the core of this book. This is very much your book, and we feel privileged to have been part of this process which has renewed so many links of friendship. Sadly our friend Martha, one of the seven regression subjects, died before this book was published. Our thoughts are with you, Martha, and the whole group misses you.

Joanna writes: I would like to acknowledge my daughter Tatanya for her help and supplying information for this book. My thanks also to the rest of my family, Larissa, Katinka and Chris, for their patience and for putting up with me whilst I co-wrote this book. All of you, thank you. Our special thanks to Dolores Cannon for her help and support during the development of this book. In particular we are grateful for her advice on extending the manuscript, and her help in identifying areas that needed more research. By going back to the regression process much new and interesting information emerged.

Our thanks to Anne MacEwen, President of the Essene Network International, for tracking down sources and for reading the manuscript and identifying mis-typings. We are grateful to Anne and to Sylvia Moss for their encouragement and support, especially during the Network's Summer Gathering in July 2001. This convinced us that it was worthwhile making one final effort to access the Melchizedek material.

Many thanks to Maggi Fielder for suggesting sources, reading the manuscript and making many useful comments; to Ann Ross, Dechen Powell and Felicity Bartlett for suggesting sources; Martin Holyoak for letting us see the book by Gaura Devi; and Jackie Dixon for reading the manuscript and identifying mis-typings.

We are grateful to the following for permissions to quote from copyright material:

The quote from *The Isaiah Effect* by Gregg Braden is reprinted by permission of Random House (©2000 by Gregg Braden).

The quote from *Poetical Works of Robert Browning* edited by Ian Jack and Margaret Smith is reprinted by permissions of Oxford University Press (© Ian Jack and Margaret Smith 1983).

The quotes from *Jesus and the Essenes* by Dolores Cannon are reprinted by permission of Ozark Mountain Publishing, Inc. (©2000 by Dolores Cannon).

The quote from *Fire of Transformation: My Life with Babaji* by Gaura Devi is reprinted by permission of Nymet Press (©2001 by Gaura Devi).

The quote from *The Emerald Tablets of Thoth the Atlantean* translated by M. Doreal is reprinted by permission of Source Books (©M. Doreal).

The quote from *Mary Magdalene: Christianity's Hidden Goddess* by Lynn Picknett is reprinted by permission of Constable & Robinson Ltd (©2003 by Lynn Picknett).

The quote from *The Lost Magic of Christianity: Celtic*

Essene Connections by Michael Poynder is reprinted by permission of Green Magic (©2000 by Michael Poynder). The quote from *Summons to a High Crusade* by Sir George Trevelyan is reprinted by permission of Findhorn Press (©1986 by Findhorn Press). The quote from Sir George Trevelyan's Foreword to *The New Essenes* by Sophie Edwards is reprinted by permission of Sophie Edwards (©1983 by Sophie Edwards). The quotes from *The Complete Dead Sea Scrolls in English* by Geza Vermes (London 1997) are reproduced by permission of Penguin Books Ltd. (©1962, 1965, 1968, 1975, 1987, 1995, 1997 by Geza Vermes). The lines from *St. Matthew's Gospel* quoted on page 195 are from *The New Revised Standard Version of the Bible*, Anglicized Edition, copyright 1989, 1995 by the Division of Christian Education of the National Council of the Churches of Christ in the United States of America, and are used by permission. All rights reserved.

Our thanks to Ashian Belsey for permission to quote from her book *Beyond Fear: Teachings from the Ascended Masters*, published by Excalibur Editions in Munich; to Anne Hughes for her quotes; and to Anne MacEwen for permission to quote the Essene Network version of the Prologue.

Contents

Preface by Stuart Wilson   i

Introduction by Joanna Prentis   iv

Part One: The Process Begins

1. First Meeting with Daniel   3
2. Rowena   8
3. Joseph and Daniel   12

Part Two: The Founding of the Essene Brotherhood

4. The Kaloo   21
5. How the Essene Way Developed   26

Part Three: The Essenes

6. The Essene Communities   35
7. Life in the Essene Communities   53
8. The Essene Children   62
9. John and Roberta   70
10. Traveling and Contact with Strangers   77
11. Skills and Powers   84

Part Four: Essene Knowledge and Belief

12. Exploring Essene Knowledge   95
13. The Essene Libraries   104
14. A Lay Brother's Credo   110

Part Five: The Secret Core of Essene Life

15. Secrecy and Security   119
16. The Core Group   124

Part Six: Jesus

17. Jesus as Student and Teacher   131

18. Jesus in Britain   135
19. Being With Jesus   139
20. Teaching and Healing   148

Part Seven: The Drama Unfolds

21. Essene Meeting in the Cave   155
22. The Energy System   158
23. The Crucifixion   164
24. The Empty Tomb   169

Part Eight: New Perspectives

25. Mary Magdalene   179
26. Jesus and Mary Magdalene   184
27. Time and Timelessness   188

Part Nine: The Truth Within

28. The Foundation Prayer   195

Part Ten: The Essenes Disperse

29. After the Crucifixion   203

Part Eleven: Joseph of Arimathea

30. Joseph in Perspective   211

Part Twelve: The Celtic Connection

31. The Druids   219
32. Joseph in Britain   224
33. The Mother of Mary and Joseph   229
34. Connections between the Essenes and the Druids   233
35. The Significance of Joseph's Work in Britain   238

Part Thirteen: A Deeper Understanding

36. The Projection of Consciousness   243
37. The Balance of Priests and Lay Essenes   251

Part Fourteen: The Coming of the Light

38. Stepping into the Light 257

Part Fifteen: The Melchizedek Heritage

39. The Order of Melchizedek 269
40. The Way of Oneness 278
41. The Diversity of the Melchizedek Teachings 286
42. The Triumph of the Light 290

Part Sixteen: Towards Completion

43. The Final Gathering 299
44. Completing the Process 305
45. Farewell to Qumran 309
46. The Last Days of Daniel 312

Part Seventeen: Summation

47. New Light on the Essenes 319

Part Eighteen: Overview

48. The Continuing Story 329
49. Conclusion 334

Glossary 340

Further Reading 343

Index 350

Authors 358

Front Cover Picture / Feedback from Readers 363

Preface by Stuart Wilson

I am a writer on new perspectives and the author of a best-selling name dictionary called *Simply the Best Baby Name Book*. I moved to mid Devon in the English Westcountry in 1990 to work on the development of the Starlight Centre with its co-founder Joanna Prentis. The Centre focuses on healing and the transformation of consciousness.

This book is the result of our collaboration in the field of past life regression. Joanna is a qualified hypnotherapist and past life therapist, and conducted the sessions. I transcribed the tapes and edited the material into book form.

We have each contributed an introductory section, and we wrote commentaries where appropriate in the text. I also wrote a summation putting the project into perspective.

The regression process which forms the core of this book involves a number of sessions with a total of seven subjects:

Subject's name	Essene name
Stuart	Daniel Benezra
Rowena	Joseph of Arimathea
John	Luke
Roberta	"The Silent One"
Martha	Name not given

The two other subjects, Nicky and Carol, were followers of Jesus, but we did not find an Essene connection.

We are not saying that Rowena is the incarnation of the

entire higher self of Joseph of Arimathea. One higher self may incarnate in several simultaneous soul "aspects" and we regard Rowena as an aspect of Joseph. This means that other people now living could also be aspects of Joseph. However, as individuals go through the regression process, it feels to them as if they are the entire being.

The first four subjects knew one another during that life: three lived in communities to the west of the Dead Sea, whilst the fourth (Joseph) traveled frequently and visited all three communities. The close links between these four people formed a key which enabled us to penetrate the Essene veil of secrecy. It made it possible for us to access information in a number of areas including some quite sensitive material concerning security issues. This information, including the location of Essene communities and the existence of a Core Group, has not previously been revealed, and advances our knowledge of the way in which the Essenes functioned. So does the material on Essene philosophy and the balance of priests and lay Brothers. The information emerging from this process both confirms previous regression work, and opens up an entirely new understanding of the lives and thought world of the Essenes.

The Essenes did not refer to Jesus by that name. For reasons of secrecy and security he was referred to either as Benjoseph (literally, 'the son of Joseph') or as Yeshua, another form of this name being Jeshua. We realize that these names may well be confusing to the reader, and whenever he is referred to in the regression sessions we have altered this to read "Jesus".

When Dolores Cannon visited the Starlight Centre in the autumn of 1999 we gave her a copy of the original manuscript, and having read it she was kind enough to say that "It does contain more information that adds to the information I discovered." Dolores encouraged us then (and

ii

later when we met her again in 2002) to return to the regression process and extend the manuscript, which we did. Without these further stages of development we would not have the deeper understanding of Essene life which emerged from the new material. Thank you, Dolores, this book has been transformed through your most helpful involvement.

Other friends – notably Anne MacEwen, Sylvia Moss and Maggi Fielder – contributed to the further extension of the text, and we are most grateful for their help.

One further comment on the structure of the book: after the first three introductory chapters, I have arranged the information according to content. The reader should be aware that presenting it in this way inevitably mixes material from early sessions (when the subjects were experiencing their lives) with later sessions (when they were reviewing their lives in the Interlife).

We realize this book is only a beginning. Despite the problems of secrecy the Essene story is now being told. And judging by the flood of articles, books and internet websites it is a story whose time has come. We hope others will be inspired by what they read here, and will come forward to tell their part in the Essene story. It is with this thought in mind that we send this book out into the world.

Introduction
by
Joanna Prentis, D.Hyp.

I am a healer, counselor and past life therapist. People come to me for many reasons: to remember past skills, to get more understanding of their current relationships, to overcome fears and phobias (as so many of these are caused by memories from the past), and to deal with health problems (so often the reliving of a past memory can release aches and pains in the body). All past life memories are stored in the emotional body, and in the cellular memory. Clearing these memories can release energy blocks to enable the client to go forward lighter and clearer. Life is a learning process: we keep repeating the same patterns over and over again till we understand the lessons.

All in all it is fascinating work, and a good way to learn history first hand – though as so much of history has been distorted by the passing of time it is not necessarily the same story we learn from textbooks! Most of my clients have fairly ordinary past lives, but these can be most important for them. It is very rare for me to encounter someone who was well known, or indeed had any place at all in written history.

It is also not often one finds a person who goes into a deep hypnotic state and remembers nothing when they come out. A light altered state of consciousness is much more common. It's as if the normal personality stands aside and they become temporarily the person they were, and will talk as that person. They are usually half aware of what is going on, but will rarely be able to remember exactly what they have said, so I always tape the sessions.

I had no belief in reincarnation when I started doing this work. I came from a conventional background and it was only when we went to farm in Western Australia that my horizons started to expand and I began to investigate new perspectives. I am now convinced of the validity of reincarnation, but I feel that everyone should make up their own minds as to whether we do indeed return life after life. And I would never expect anyone to believe in reincarnation who hadn't had some experience of a past life.

Many people have these experiences as part of the normal process of living. Do you remember the feeling that you recognize a certain place, you know it so well, and yet in this life you've never been there? Or meeting a person for the first time and you immediately feel you have known them all your life? Or very vivid and life-like dreams of another time-period?

During my time as a past life therapist I have learned that some past lives are significant only to the client, whilst some seem to expand and connect with the experiences of others. It was exactly that kind of connection which happened here, and it is a truly amazing story. When I started to explore an Essene life with Stuart, never would I have dreamed it would disclose such a wealth of information, involve so many friends, bring in new ones, and also be very relevant to today. However, I am aware the same groups of people tend to reincarnate together lifetime after lifetime, and it has been a great joy to watch these old friends meeting and recognizing one another.

Luke, for example, was in tears when he remembered Daniel Benezra, which was very touching. He didn't have such fond memories of Joseph! But then Joseph had been an older man, and sometimes responsible for disciplining the young Luke, who was quite a handful. Luke even showed us how Joseph used to wag his finger when he was disciplining him, which caused Stuart and myself much amusement as Rowena makes exactly the same gesture today!

At no stage did anyone see a transcript of these tapes before they relived their own life with Jesus. Nor did Stuart read *Jesus and the Essenes* by Dolores Cannon until the main regression process was completed. This was to ensure that no one was influenced by prior knowledge. The outstanding thing that emerges from this process is how much of Daniel's story was confirmed by other accounts. Of course there are some areas of disagreement, but these are simply a difference in perspective.

It has been a real adventure for us putting this account together, and we know there is much more yet to come. What seems to be happening is that those who lived and served with Jesus have reincarnated to tell the world about these original teachings – teachings which are very relevant to this time.

In this account the Essenes emerge both as rooted in a historical period and in some respects surprisingly modern. Two thousand years ago they were familiar with the dynamics of the higher self, and were exploring multi-dimensionality. I believe everyone now has the chance to get in touch with their higher self, recognize the Divine Self within, and become multi-dimensional beings. More and more I'm meeting people who have made this leap out of heavy density. A leap that gives you access to a much broader range of knowledge, and to all the gifts and skills you have developed in past lives. This is one of the reasons behind the many wonderful healings we hear about. The manifestation of oils and sacred ash, being able to make crystals sing, being able to communicate with dolphins and fire-walk unscathed. Jesus was able to do many wonderful things, and he said that we would be able to do "even greater things". What has been revealed to me as the absolute core of his ministry is Love – unconditional love – and that is what we need to return to.

We hope this book will trigger in you that feeling of being with Jesus, a feeling of completely unconditional love that is difficult to describe in words. But it is this feeling and energy of unconditional love, this state of blissfulness to be in his presence, that has made this project so amazing for all who were involved. It has created even greater bonds of love and friendship with those we have worked with, and I offer them my gratitude for making it all possible.

All I ask is that you read this account with an open mind. Take from it what is acceptable to you in your heart and enjoy your time with Daniel and the Essenes.

Part One:
The Process Begins

Their lifelong purity, their avoiding of oaths or falsehood, their recognition of a good providence alone showed their love of God. Their love of virtue revealed itself in their indifference to money, worldly position and pleasure. Their love of man in their kindliness, their equality, their fellowship, passing all words.

Philo of Alexandria,
writing about the Essenes in 20 CE

1

First Meeting with Daniel

I had been working with Stuart for over four years, and we had explored a number of his past lives. In each case there had been detailed recall, as he is one of the best subjects I have worked with. He has the ability when regressed to talk for some time with very little prompting, which makes the process much easier for me. Although we worked intensively on the Daniel sessions, the main story still took over six weeks to work through, and we returned for more regression at four later stages to add more detail to the text.

Stuart had already explored one Essene life in the Damascus community around 100 BCE. This is his brief summary of that life:

"In the Damascus community we were preparing for the coming of a great Teacher. It was a simple life, a balance of physical work in growing crops with a study of the works of the great sages as contained in the scrolls. In the evening we would eat together, then gather around a large fire and share our thoughts and feelings about the day.

"We did not know when the Teacher of Righteousness would come, but we wished to be well prepared so we could help in his work. To that end we also helped other communities to establish themselves, partly by writing down our experiences of running our community in the form of general instructions and guidance. There were rules, and these we had developed over a period of time. We thought it was important to share our experiences in this way, for groups setting up a community would not know what kind of structure might work, and what rules were necessary to help the community become a cohesive whole. There is no replacement for practical experience.

"We felt that if other groups of people following our way could be established the Teacher would be able to find willing hearts and helpful hands in many places, and that would benefit the work as a whole."

This account is fascinating because it seems to be a description of how (and why) the Damascus Document, a key Essene text, was written. Here we get the feeling of being in at the very start of the whole Essene experience.

I knew it was possible that Stuart might have had another Essene life, so I put him into an altered state of consciousness and asked him to connect with the life immediately following the Damascus one. I began by asking him his name.

Stuart: My name is Daniel. Some say that Daniel is not a good name, because it means "God is my judge". They say it is a hard name, but they do not understand it. It means you will only be judged by God, and God knows what is in your heart. So to me it is a comfortable name, it means you will be judged with a

4

full knowledge of your being, what is in your heart, not what seems to be on the outside.

This was a piece of luck – Daniel certainly sounded like a Jewish name, but was he an Essene? I decided to go cautiously and ask first about his father.

Joanna: And what is your father's name?
Daniel: My father's name is Ezra, so I am Daniel Benezra. My father was an elder in our community.
Joanna: Is your father still alive?
Daniel: No. He died before I had thirty years.

He seemed to be interested in names so I asked him what his father's name meant.

Daniel: My father's name means "salvation". We see salvation as a continuous thing. We are always being protected from those things that lead us away from the truth, away from the Light. So we see it as a step by step, day by day thing: we are always being saved.

I noticed he had said, "We see" rather than "I see". Maybe it was just the closeness of his community, but I decided I would be bold and follow this up in quite a direct way.

Joanna: Is your community an Essene one?

There was a long pause. At last Daniel answered, "Yes". I realized from the length of the pause that I had to tread carefully here, so I tried to reassure him.

Joanna: We are interested in the Essenes, have sympathy with their beliefs and wish them well.
Daniel: That is good. There are many people who do not wish us well.
Joanna: Is your community a large one?
Daniel: No, it is not the largest.
Joanna: How many people live in your community?
Daniel: (quite sharply) *It is not permitted that I speak of this!*

That was another signal for me to go carefully. Although I knew the Essenes were highly secretive, I was not at all sure what subjects they were sensitive about, so I just had to feel my way. I thought I had better stay away from the subject of the community for the moment and ask Daniel about himself.

Joanna: Are you married?
Daniel: No, I am a single one. It is only a small sacrifice for me, and I have many friends around me.

I made some more tentative inquiries in this first session, but nothing more of interest emerged. By the end of the session I was already feeling the restrictions of Essene secrecy close in around me. If there were many forbidden areas, how were we ever to progress properly? I was beginning to think that, despite a promising start, this life might never add very much to our knowledge about the mysterious Essenes.

The conventional view of the Essenes is recorded by the historian Josephus, and by Philo of Alexandria and the elder Pliny. They described the Essenes as gathering in rural communities and balancing hard work in agriculture with communal study of moral and religious questions. They paid much attention to ceremonial purity, and held property in common. These writers give a general picture of the Essenes as an ascetic, pious and pacifist group, quite detached from political issues and commercial pressures. More modern writers have taken a broader view of the Essenes, seeing them as a widespread movement of anti-Jerusalem non-conformists. Here the Essenes become a fluid, ill-defined and changeable group in contrast to the more structured and organized conventional Jews. In this perception the Essenes might embrace a wide range of views from the pacifist and the pious to the most extreme and violent anti-Roman militancy.

2

Rowena

A week after the first session with Daniel I had arranged another appointment with a client who had already explored several lives. We will call her Rowena, although that is not her name. She has asked for her identity not to be disclosed. Rowena is middle-aged – on the surface a fairly outgoing person, open-minded and with a keen sense of humor. But there is also a deep and secretive side to her, and the reasons for this will become apparent as her story unfolds.

She is a very different type of subject to Stuart, who seldom shows emotion but often has detailed memories. I will let her describe her process in her own words: "I seem to feel everything. My recall is a blend of seeing, hearing and feeling."

As usual with Rowena, I simply asked her to go back to the most significant life. Once she was into an altered state of consciousness I began by asking her to describe whatever she could see, hear or feel.

Rowena: It is hot, and the sun shines in a blue sky. We are journeying by camel across the desert. It has been a

difficult journey and I am tired. My camel is a bad-tempered creature and I will be glad when this day is over and I can rest.
Joanna: What is your name?
Rowena: I am called Joseph.

(Now that Joseph has identified himself I will use that name rather than Rowena.)
I thought I might be able to establish his identity by asking his father's name. Daniel after all, was not just Daniel but Daniel Benezra.

Joanna: And what is your father's name?
Joseph: It is not necessary that you know that.

I was beginning to think we might not get too much out of this life, as Joseph was clearly very cautious. However I persevered.

Joanna: Do people just call you Joseph, then?
Joseph: No. (There was a pause). *I am called Joseph of Arimathea.*

At this point I almost fell off my chair. This was not simply any old Joseph, but one of the key players in the story of Jesus. It was Joseph of Arimathea, the rich man who asked Pontius Pilate for Jesus' body after the crucifixion and who prepared the tomb. In Luke chapter 23:52, 53 we read:
This man went unto Pilate, and begged the body of Jesus. And he took it down, and wrapped it in linen, and laid it in a sepulchre that was hewn in stone, wherein never man before was laid.

9

The unexpected introduction of such a major figure from the Biblical record had clearly moved the whole project onto quite a different level. However, for the moment I had to hold down my excitement, and keep going with the questions.

Joanna: Do you live in a community?
Joseph: No, I travel about.
Joanna: Why do you need to travel?
Joseph: I am a merchant. I deal in tin and other metals.

And then a thought struck me. If Joseph was close to Jesus he was probably an Essene, and we'd established that Daniel was too. Did Joseph and Daniel know one another? I took a deep breath and went straight into the big question.

Joanna: Do you know Daniel Benezra?
Joseph: Yes. He is my friend.

I had to stop myself from whooping with joy! We had stumbled upon two people who knew one another at the time of Jesus, and one of them was a character recognized in the Bible narrative. All I had to do was put these two subjects into regression together, and let them dialogue with one another. There was a good chance that I had found a way around the whole problem of secrecy which has been such a major issue in all recorded Essene lives.

This session with Rowena was the first of a series of breakthroughs I made while researching these Essene lives. At first I put it down to good luck, but as the breakthroughs kept piling up we came to see them as gifts of the Spirit. If the Essenes wanted their story told now, the right people would come at the right time to add their part to the jigsaw. Just how big a picture it would become I had no idea then, and looking back perhaps that was just as well!

3

Joseph and Daniel

I looked forward to the next session with a great feeling of excitement, a sense of making a fresh beginning. The session took place in our house which overlooks the beautiful valley of the river Burn in a quiet and rural part of Devonshire. I first ensured that my clients were comfortable, switched on the tape recorder and settled in my chair. I put both Rowena and Stuart into an altered state of consciousness, took them back to their lives as Joseph and Daniel, and made sure they each knew that the other was present. After one or two general questions to relax them and get them going, I began to move towards the Essenc material.

Joanna: What about the Jews who are not Essenes. Do you feel you have much in common with them?
Daniel: *We have a little in common with them, yes, but we feel like Essenes first and Jews second. We don't feel much sympathy for most of the Jews outside our Brotherhood. They have chosen what we consider to be a wrong path. We see them as sons of darkness, whereas the Essenes are Sons of Light.*

I noted the reference to Light, which was to prove a recurring symbol throughout these sessions. The term "Sons of Light" seemed a very apt name for the Essenes as a group, and underlined the root of their struggle with some of the more conventional Jewish groups, such as the Pharisees. The Pharisees were one of the groups vying for power within Judaism. Their strength lay in their control of the developing rabbinic stream of Judaism. This functioned through the synagogues which were meeting places but also places for prayer and instruction in the Law. The Jewish Law (also known as the Torah) governed many aspects of individual and family life. It was highly structured and codified, and laid down detailed observances including rules on what food was permissible and what one could (and could not) do on the seventh day or Sabbath.

The Pharisees were aware of the public interest, and although always a minority group, wielded power out of proportion to their numbers. Coming from the middle and artisan classes, they had some understanding of the problems of the common people. The Pharisees stressed ethics, rather than theology, subordinating Temple worship to the fulfilment of all aspects of the Law.

But to return to the session with Joseph and Daniel. I wanted to know how they saw themselves in relation to the rest of the world.

Joanna: Do you think of your land as being in the east?
Daniel: No, it is in the center of things, neither east nor west.
Joseph: It seems to me as if we are in the middle of the world, with all the trade routes flowing past our door, so we're very much in the center.

13

Daniel: Of course, the Romans think Rome is in the center of things!

Joseph: When you say that my whole being sighs. What arrogance they have!

Daniel: Yes. And the strange thing is they don't believe they're doing anything wrong. It seems quite natural to them to go out and conquer people.

Joseph: Heavy feet and everything done in straight lines. Too rigid for my taste.

Daniel: Violence is a habit with them; they strike first and only use their minds afterwards.

Joseph: Hmm, muscular people much given to the wearing of leather, and in the heat here that's not very wise! (Daniel laughed).

Joseph: I'm sure your keen nose remembers....

Daniel: Hmm... (He chuckled).

Joseph: Mind you, in comparison to camel... (They both laughed).

From this it was clear they shared the wariness and distaste of the Roman army of occupation which many Jews felt at that time. After all, the period of the Roman conquest (in 63BCE) was only a generation or two away, and the collective Jewish memory of that event, and the restrictions on Jewish life that followed it, must have been quite vivid for both Joseph and Daniel. At that point the Jews would still have been adapting to being a subject people, and it was clearly not a role that many Jews relished.

Even from this first exchange it was quite evident that they had the easy familiarity of old friends. Their relationship seemed light and humorous, as if they had known each other for years. Much later in the sessions I was to find out that Daniel and Joseph had grown up together as children. During a session with Daniel alone I was able to ask him about this.

Joanna: When did you first meet Joseph?
Daniel: I saw him first when we were both quite young. A great friend of mine called James was related to his family, so we wandered around together, a little group of us. You see, our parents were also pursuing the Essene Way so it was natural that we should meet the other young Essenes.

I was also able to ask Daniel if he had a favorite story about the younger Joseph.

*Daniel: Well, when he and I were young fellows, there was a time when we had too much wine to drink...(*He chuckled). *We were visiting one of Joseph's relatives in a little town, but we had too much wine* (he laughed) *and returned, ah, yes, a little the worse for wear, to the house of his relative. I think he was a cousin, rather older than we were, and more earnest. He did not approve of the drinking of wine, and he locked us out.* (He laughed). *So we had to go away and find some stable somewhere, and sleep it off in the straw, and no great harm came to us. We were young and foolish, but I became more abstemious in my old age. I liked a little wine, but Joseph was able to hold his wine better, maybe due to much practice in traveling and being polite to many a host upon the way.*
  So Joseph was not always solemn, you see. He also was young, yes, and I led him astray and his cousin did not like that. (He laughed again). *That*

15

cousin was old before his time and set in his ways. He was fond of quoting from the Law, and had many quotations to cover drunkenness. (He chuckled). *So, yes, it is good for the elders to remember when they were young. This Joseph said to me many times, so that when they think they are altogether wise they remember their younger foolishness. Indeed a little foolishness is good because it rounds us out and shows us when we deal with others that all are human.*

Joanna: How would you sum up your old friend Joseph?

Daniel: Joseph is a great friend and a wise man, but also a man who is careful in his speech. He is quite strong physically, and there is a calmness and balance about him which impresses people.

He listens to people, and has a quiet charm and a keen sense of humor, but that's deceptive. He's really quite a clever man, but he hides his gifts. People don't realize the extent of his knowledge. He seems to be just an innocent and shallow pool, but he's really a deep lake, deep and secretive.

The ease of their relationship also emerges in another exchange between Joseph and Daniel:

Joseph: I had a bigger view of things than you, for my travels took me to many places to talk with many people. But then, you were more versed in the detail than I, for I never had much heart for studying, whereas you my friend....

Daniel interrupted him: "I had my nose in the scrolls from an early age, that is true!"

The laughter which Daniel and Joseph shared on that occasion seemed so typical of their friendship. It was a friendship built to survive the test of time.

Part Two:

The Founding of the Essene Brotherhood

Your Father is the Cosmos.

Your Mother is Nature.

Your brothers are your fellow men.

Live in harmony with the laws

and forces of the Universe,

and Nature and your own being.

The Essene Master Banus,
as reported by the historian Josephus

4

The Kaloo

Thanks to the work of Dolores Cannon I knew that much of the Essene knowledge came from a mysterious people called the Kaloo, and I was interested to see what Daniel might say about them. First of all I asked him if the Kaloo were called by other names.

Daniel: They were also called the Ancient Ones and the Wise Ones. They were from a very ancient race. It is said that we also are descended from them, but I am not sure of this.

The Kaloo came from far in the west. They stopped for some time in Egypt and then traveled on to our land and beyond. But their original land was far away, we call it the Old Land in the West. This was once a very large land, and there were islands in the main body of it. There were many peoples in this great land, and the Kaloo were only one of these races. Eventually parts of the land began to sink into the ocean, many thousands of years before my time. The Kaloo saw that their land was sinking, and went by ship to Egypt, although some went farther to the east.

They had great wisdom and were most skillful in the

making of things, like the jars that gave light without fire. Many of the precious things which the Essenes had were passed down by the Kaloo. There would have been skilled craftspeople who made and repaired such things at the height of the Kaloo civilization in the Old Land in the West, but centuries had passed since some of these things were made. I think the Kaloo who visited us were mainly messengers and teachers, not skilled craftsmen, so they could not tell us how to repair these things when they ceased to function.

This makes fascinating reading alongside Suddi's account of them in *Jesus and the Essenes* by Dolores Cannon. The jars he mentions are particularly intriguing, as they seem to have been an early form of electricity. Examples of these jars could at one time be found in the Berlin Museum (see *Jesus and the Essenes*, pages 51-54).

Joanna: Did the Kaloo gather in one place?
Daniel: No, they were scattered and became wanderers. They traveled all the time, and this was their protection. Before any could become too curious about them they would have moved on.
Joanna: Were the Kaloo a dying race, then?
Daniel: Yes, a dying race. As far as the mass of the Jewish people were concerned, this was a race of distant myth and legend which was now dead, and that was a good thought to foster, as the Kaloo did not wish anyone to be looking for them. Those ones in positions of power would have liked to gain the knowledge of the Kaloo, for it would have made them still more powerful. So it was important to spread the idea that the Kaloo were an ancient race, now long dead.

Joanna: And the Kaloo gave their knowledge to the Essenes?

Daniel: *Yes, because they knew we would not misuse it. Those who first gathered to set up our communities had peace as their aim, so when the Kaloo first founded our Order they knew the knowledge would be in safe hands.*

Joanna: How did the Kaloo store their knowledge?

Daniel: *Both in crystals and in scrolls. The crystals were secret, and most Essenes saw only the scrolls which had been copied by our own people.*

Joanna: Were you able to talk to any of the Kaloo and have discussions with them?

Daniel: *I talked to them when they came to us, but they were a law unto themselves, and so far beyond us that we revered them as holy beings. Their race was most ancient and most revered. Just a few last remnants of this dying race could be found in my day, a few scattered wanderers upon the face of the Earth. We did not know from whence they came or whither they went. They came from time to time, and visited our communities to encourage us and see how the knowledge was being stored and passed on.*

Joanna: Did the Kaloo also visit the Druids in Britain?

Daniel: *I believe so. My friend Joseph told me the Druids recognized the Kaloo, but by a different name. Different branches of this one great family might call them by different names, but they were the same beings, the same messengers, the same weary travelers connecting all these scattered ones, these ones who held the knowledge. Joseph told me that sometimes he would meet the Kaloo in his travels, for they were linking with the same places, the same communities and safe places where there were people who thought as we did.*

I wanted to ask him some more about the possibility that the Essenes were descended from the Kaloo. It was certainly a startling idea, and I had come across it first in *Jesus and the Essenes* by Dolores Cannon.

Joanna: Could you tell me more about the Essenes being descended from the Kaloo?
Daniel: There is so little information on this. I did try to make some inquiries but it was regarded as a most secret area. In the complete absence of any real information I concluded that it might be a legend. But there is another possibility: we may be their children in the sense of being their spiritual successors, their inheritors.
Joanna: Did the Kaloo ever inter-marry with the Essenes?
Daniel: No, they kept themselves apart. They gave us their gifts and came to see how we used those gifts from time to time, but they were on a different level from us. They were masters in dealing with consciousness and energy in most subtle and complex ways. We respected and preserved carefully what they gave us, but we could never really understand them.

So in the end the Kaloo were a mystery even to the Essenes who were lucky enough to meet them from time to time. Yet one thing Daniel said did shed some light on the Kaloo: he said they had come from "the Old Land in the West". To me that sounds very much like Atlantis, and his description of it certainly seems to bear this out. If the Kaloo were an Atlantean people they would have been ancient indeed, even two thousand years ago. The date normally assigned to the sinking of the last fragment of the Atlantean continent is around 9600 BCE. If the Kaloo were Atlanteans that would account for their very advanced technology, including the use of crystals, and for the depth of their wisdom. The Essenes were fortunate indeed to have such teachers and benefactors as these.

There are inner and outer founders of any esoteric Order, but although Daniel would talk about the Kaloo as the outer founders of the Essene Brotherhood, he would not talk about an inner founder. However we were able to return to this and get information at a later stage (see Chapter 39).

5

How the Essene Way Developed

The sessions with Daniel were now progressing smoothly and easily. There is one in particular that stands out in my memory. In this session Daniel did not wait for me to ask a question, but went straight into a general statement about his contact with us.

Daniel: I have attuned to the Brotherhood as a whole regarding these dialogues with you. They have looked at your being and know that you wish us well. They tell me that through this dialogue time can be overcome and a new light can be cast upon the Essene Way in future time. I feel it is important that I give you all the help that is necessary if it will assist those who were our people, and who may be known to you in another time.

This was remarkable in several ways. Daniel had clearly been checking us out, and we seemed to meet with his approval. By saying "the Brotherhood as a whole" he seemed to be talking about the existence of some kind of Essene collective consciousness. From this point on we got the impression that Daniel was sometimes speaking, not only for himself, but for the whole Essene movement. But most interestingly of all he seemed to recognize that from his viewpoint we are "in future time", and the reincarnating Essenes, "those who were our people", may need this information now. I really felt Daniel reaching out across time to us here, and I found this very moving.

Daniel seemed to be putting the whole contact on quite a new basis. We had certainly been focusing very much upon him, but here for the first time Daniel seemed to have focused clearly enough upon us to understand what we were about. The last sentence I found particulary significant. We were aware that others who had Essene lives were beginning to come to us and could already see that this was all part of a greater process of connection.

Since Daniel had made such a positive start I felt bold enough to ask him what his areas of special interest and training were.

Daniel: The history of the Essenes, and in particular the part played by the Kaloo; star lore and star cycles; and the mysteries.

The Mysteries included teachings which regarded myths as sources of great symbolic power. Only through the insights of modern psychology (particularly the work of Jung) have we begun to understand the profound impact of archetypal energies on the psyche. Many of the greatest minds in the ancient world were initiates of the Mystery Schools which spread throughout the ancient Mediterranean. All Mystery Schools followed a similar basic structure of Outer Mysteries, involving ceremonies in which all could take part, and Inner Mysteries, accessible only through a deep and transformative initiatory process.

Because Daniel had mentioned history, I decided to ask him about the development of the whole Essene movement. We will return to some of the points he touched on here – like the communities and the energy system – later in this book.

Daniel: What became known as the Essene Way began about a hundred and fifty years before I was born. The founders of the Essene Way were the Kaloo, the ancient ones who came from the Old Land in the West, first to Egypt and then to our land. They brought with them many secrets, much knowledge and wonderful machines. They began to spread out over our land, looking for ones who might set up communities. There was a central place, a place in which much of the knowledge was gathered, and smaller outlying communities. The central community was Qumran on the edge of the Dead Sea, a remote and harsh area, but chosen as such, so that it would not attract too much attention.

The "wonderful machines" which Daniel mentions include that most remarkable model of the solar system described in pages 82 to 85 of Dolores Cannon's book *Jesus and the Essenes.*

Daniel: When Qumran was set up, the Kaloo began to found other communities amongst those open to the inner truth. Those who were open in their minds and hearts. One by one the communities were established. Not all of these flourished, and some had a most difficult time. Much work was done upon the energies of the Earth in

28

*preparation for the time when a great Teacher would
come. The Teacher would need much support through
a well-founded energy system. The Kaloo did all this
and much more: they helped us, advised us, and visited
the communities from time to time.*

We shall return to the energy system he mentions in a
later chapter.

*Daniel: So the communities were set up, but because we
were so secretive and kept ourselves to ourselves we
began to arouse suspicion and hostility, especially
among the Pharisees and Sadducees. These ones
heard reports of our knowledge and feared that this
might outstrip theirs, and be deeper and more profound
than any knowledge they had. They feared that we
might displace them from the position of power they
held and they became intent upon acquiring our
knowledge. That knowledge at any rate would remain
safe. We guarded it carefully so that they would not
get their unworthy hands upon it.*

The Sadducees were a Judaic group drawn from the
wealthy and aristocratic families. Many of the Sadducees
were priests, and they dominated the Temple in Jerusalem.
They were rigidly conservative in religion, severe in
judgment and had no popularity amongst the people as a
whole. They exercised power outside their stronghold of the
Temple mainly by collaborating with the Pharisees.

*Daniel: The whole Essene effort was centered upon the
coming of a great Teacher, a Teacher of*

Righteousness. At first we did not know his name, we only knew that a great Teacher would come, and he would lead us to the Light. The Spirit would be strong within him, and many would follow him and listen to his teachings. So it was to be a supportive framework for him, and all would be ready for him when he came. We would be able to take care of him, nourish and protect him, feed his mind and inspire his soul. But although we would guide his early steps, he would soar up far beyond us, for he had a new teaching to bring, and a new way to establish.

So that we could provide the broadest and most effective learning foundation for the Teacher, the Kaloo ensured that our minds were never confined to one religion. They gathered the best knowledge from Egypt, Persia, Greece and elsewhere, and through their traveling were able constantly to challenge us with new ideas and new perspectives. As they came into our land through Egypt it was Egyptian ideas, together with our home-grown Hebrew concepts, which formed the original base of our communities. But through the Kaloo's travels in Persia we came into contact with Zoroastrian ideas, including the duality of Light and darkness, and purification rituals with running water which influenced us greatly. Later on the Kaloo gained the confidence of the Pythagorean Order, and from that point on we were inspired by the ideas of the great sage Pythagoras on harmony, living an ethical life, and the proper ordering of communities.

Zoroastrianism is the ancient religion of Iran, and focuses upon a supreme deity named Ahura Mazda ('the Wise Lord'). It was founded in Persia by the prophet and reformer Zoroaster in the 6th century BCE. Zoroastrian concepts of dualism influenced the Greek philosophers and may also have had some impact on the development of Judaism. In Zoroastrian cosmology, Good (symbolized by Light) and Evil (symbolized by darkness) fight an unequal battle in which Good is certain to triumph.

Pythagoras was a Greek philosopher and mathematician who lived from about 580 to 500 BCE. He founded a system of thought which influenced Plato and Aristotle. Pythagorean philosophy united an interest in mathematics and harmony, and Pythagorean communities spread rapidly throughout the ancient world. The Pythagorean Brotherhood, which observed strict loyalty and secrecy, held that the soul can rise to unite with the Divine.

Daniel: Over the course of our history these four major strands came together to create the Essene Way: Egyptian, Zoroastrian, and Pythagorean ideas, and the Jewish Law. The merging of these four sources took place over the century before I was born, and was the result of constant flux and development over this period. Some Essenes preferred one strand to another – for example, many of the priests clung to the Torah. And for most of this time there was no general consensus which the majority of Essenes would accept. Yet by the time I reached maturity these four elements had fused and combined to create a powerful and flexible system, which – though diverse – had gained its own stability and balance. Somehow out of this seething cauldron of experiment and debate there had emerged a new unity, a powerful and broad pathway to the Light. This was the perfect platform for the Teacher of Righteousness to push forward into new and

31

transformative areas, taking still more advanced and daring ideas out into the greater world.

It is also important to understand that Mystery Schools existed in most of the ancient traditions, and through a study of the mysteries we gained insight into the universal aspirations of humanity and Universal Law. This knowledge gave us a much bigger perspective than that of the conventional Jews around us. The Kaloo had encouraged us in these studies, and nourished us with information from many sources. Without knowing the part the Kaloo played in our lives it is impossible to understand the breadth and depth of our knowledge. To view the Essenes (as many conventional Jews did) *as simply an offshoot of the main tree of Jewish thought is to ignore the whole pattern of our development, and this can only lead to a distorted view of us.*

We were beginning to glimpse the breadth and depth of Essene knowledge here, and the Essenes were starting to emerge as much more universal and significant than we might have expected. I was also aware that we were steadily pushing back the boundaries of secrecy. Daniel had mentioned Qumran for the first time, and although he had not named Jesus as the Teacher of Righteousness he was beginning to talk about a "great Teacher" and his central position within the Essene movement. Given the unexpected blessing of the Essene Brotherhood on this project, it was beginning to dawn on us that a whole raft of significant information might emerge. It was with a rising sense of excitement that I now continued the sessions and watched to see where all this process might take us.

Part Three:

The Essenes

The working day of the Essenes gave a balanced discipline of practical work, creative craft and art, exercise of the body, a period of study of great masterworks, a time of teaching and learning and of recreation. And through it all is the sense of working closely with the nature spirits and the angelic worlds, with all activity dedicated to the glory of God, and with joy in the heart.

Sir George Trevelyan,
Summons to a High Crusade

6

The Essene Communities

Our first enquiries about the location of Essene communities were not very successful. Daniel was very reluctant to be specific. It was only when the cycle of that life was completed and Daniel could talk to us from the Interlife that we were able to make a real breakthrough in this area. We had a number of sessions with Daniel in this Interlife state, which he also called "the space between lives". In one of these he seemed to become quite abstracted; he paused, breathed deeply, and after a little while said this:

Daniel: I have asked the Brotherhood about giving the most secret levels of knowledge. They have told me that because you live in future time there is no danger for our people, and therefore information can be given on the location of communities and the inner Essene structure.

Encouraged by this quite extraordinary statement, indicating a further level of approval by the Brotherhood, I decided to go straight into questions about where the communities were.

Joanna: Which communities were set up first, Daniel?

Daniel: There were communities which were central to our work, and I shall talk of these first. When the Kaloo came from the Old Land in the West they settled first at Lake Mareotis near Alexandria. Here they established the first major community which we think of as our Mother House. Then they traveled on to found Qumran by the Dead Sea, and went on up the trading route to Damascus. These three communities were like the main stem of the plant, and all others were like side-shoots leading off from them. Along this stem our people could travel from one safe place to another from Egypt up into Persia and beyond. When the Kaloo set up other communities linked to this main stem, none of them were in towns or villages, but always outside in remote areas.

Joanna: And Qumran had a special place amongst all the communities?

Daniel: Yes, Qumran was the Father House, the center of it all. At Qumran many very ancient scrolls were stored, and most of the precious machines also. Qumran was like Father Sun to us, shedding the light of knowledge upon us all. As it is in the heavens, so also upon the Earth. The Kaloo, who were wise in these things, have told us that it should be so, and that there should be one central foundation that sustained us all.

A good deal of information on Qumran has already been gathered through past-life regression. See Chapters 5, 6 and 7 in *Jesus and the Essenes* by Dolores Cannon.

Joanna: And how were the communities arranged? Were they in groups or clusters?

Daniel: *We grouped our communities in threes, not only to provide necessary support for one another but to form triangles within our overall energy system.*

What Daniel is referring to here is a system for channeling and directing earth-energies (see Chapter 22).

Daniel: *So to the south and west of Qumran there was a triangle formed by communities at Ein Gedi and Arad, and my own community at Hebron. While to the north of Qumran there were communities at Rama, Jenin and Mount Carmel. The one at Mount Carmel was an exception to the general pattern because it had teachers, priests and students only, no families or craftspeople. It was more severe and ascetic than any other community. And from Rama the route extended north and east to Damascus, our most northerly outpost.*

What emerges from this information is a list of the main communities. None of these was actually in a village, and if a village name is given here the community would be some way outside it, often on the poorer and more rocky land. The list is interesting, and there are some surprises:

The main stem communities:

1. Alexandria (at Lake Mareotis)
2. Qumran
3. Damascus

The southern group:

4. Ein Gedi
5. Arad
6. Hebron

The northern group:

7. Rama
8. Jenin
9. Mount Carmel

Before we began to think about the communities, we assumed that all would be within the boundaries of the present State of Israel, but Alexandria is in Egypt and Damascus is in Syria. We had also assumed that all the communities would be near the Dead Sea (see Diagram 1). Certainly the southern group were near the Dead Sea, but the northern group were well to the north of it, including Mount Carmel, which is west of the Sea of Galilee and quite close to the coast.

Confirmation of these community sites may come from two main sources: archaeological evidence and the regression of other Essene subjects. However, the stones used to build these communities could have been removed for use in other structures elsewhere – a common practice in many countries. Fortunately there is another factor – the water supply. This is what Daniel said about that:

Daniel: The Kaloo told us much concerning the use of water, and over time we became expert in this area. Our buildings were fashioned so that the walls were

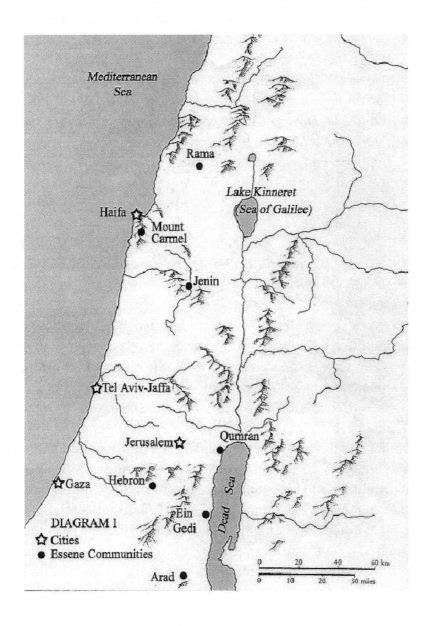

Mediterranean
Sea

Rama

Lake Kinneret
(Sea of Galilee)

Haifa ☆
Mount
Carmel

Jenin

☆Tel Aviv-Jaffa

Jerusalem ☆   Qumran

☆Gaza   Hebron

Ein
DIAGRAM 1   Gedi
☆ Cities
● Essene Communities

Dead Sea

Arad ●

| 0 | 20 | 40 | 60 km |
| 0 | 10 | 20 | 30 miles |

continuous, one flowing into the other. Using common walls and adjoining roofs enabled us to channel the rainwater down into great storage tanks. Where there was a nearby wadi the waters from this were also directed down into the tanks. So we preserve every drop of water, and this enables us to survive in arid areas that are considered too poor for any other people to farm and settle. Water is one of the most vital things, and we respect it and preserve all the water which comes from the heavens. There is a special quality about rain which has fallen through pure air in a good place.

These are the essentials of life: pure air and pure water. Without these how can we be at ease within our bodies?

A wadi is a rocky watercourse which is dry except during the rainy season. At Qumran there is a water tunnel about three feet square carved through solid rock to direct seasonal water from the wadi into underground storage tanks. (See plates 32 to 35 in *The Dead Sea Scrolls Deception* by Baigent and Leigh). Even if all the stones from a site have been removed, and the underground tanks filled in, the existence of water tunnels should still be able to provide useful clues to the location of these communities.

In January 1995 some members of our group (including John Armitage, Roberta Shewen and Judith Clough) went to Israel. During their time there they were able to verify the exact location of the community site at Ein Gedi. At that time this site had not been excavated, but that is not surprising. Israel is full of sites of archaeological interest which await excavation. A country so rich in antiquities will inevitably have a backlog of sites awaiting research.

Judith Clough, a friend who is an astrologer and Reiki Master, wrote an account of their trip at the time, and we give some extracts from it here:

"We departed for Israel at dawn on the 17th January, 1995. Once we had arrived, we spent some days tuning in. We explored the desert, took in its beauty, the huge variety of rocks and plants, the incredible colors of the landscape. We drove up to the Dead Sea, all the time feeling increasingly our connections with this land. The whole area between the Dead Sea and the southernmost tip of the Negev is crystalline and full of minerals – a perfect transmitter of energies! We visited old sites, named and un-named. We found sites marked as prehistoric, many along the present-day borders with Egypt and Sinai, which we immediately felt familiar with from Essene lifetimes."

We also asked John Armitage for his comments on the trip, and this is what he said:

"I was in the Ein Gedi area a lot during the 1960's. I always felt drawn to that area, but never knew why at the time. I have done a lot of work on earth energies since that time, and when we got there in 1995 I found the site of the community by following the energies. There is a vortex of energy there which is quite powerful and I just tuned in to it.

"We found just a few stones visible at the top of the hill, behind the kibbutz building by the spring and waterfall. Many of the other buildings on the Ein Gedi site have been excavated and restored, but not the Essene part of it. That still remained untouched at the time of our visit.

"At Arad it was more difficult to fix the site of the Essene community. The town has been built over the site and has obliterated all traces of the community. Some traces may still be down there under all the buildings, but it's difficult to say exactly where."

Comment by Stuart: We are still at a very early stage as far as the excavation of Essene sites is concerned. We await future archaeological digs in this area with interest.

But to return to the session; I was curious about the size of the Essene communities, and asked Daniel about this.

Daniel: Qumran was the biggest, I would think about two hundred people, although it varied in size from time to time. The others were smaller than this: seventy would be a good-sized community.

In addition to those I have spoken of there was also a community at Mount Horeb in Sinai, but I hesitate to add it to the list. I visited it, but was not comfortable with it. The intensity of the Father energy in this wilderness place gave it an almost Zealot-like quality, and you might argue that it was a community which both Essenes and Zealots could claim as their own. A number of the more extreme Essenes had Zealot-like tendencies, and they made me feel uncomfortable. They saw themselves as Warriors for God, ready to fight one last battle against the forces of darkness. But like the great majority of those in our communities I saw the Essenes as bringers of peace. We oppose the sons of darkness by letting our Light shine, not by taking up the sword. It is not the sword that conquers wickedness but the Truth shining in the hearts of the Children of Light.

Comment by Stuart: Hippolytus, the third century historian describes two groups of Essenes: the traditional one and another of a more Zealot-like nature which he calls "Zealot-Essenes". With the benefit of hindsight it might appear that the Jewish groups at the time were quite separate and distinct, but for those living through this era it might have seemed very different, with much more overlapping at the edges of each group. This is illustrated by the finding of Essene texts at Masada, showing that this was not exclusively a Zealot stronghold.

Joanna:Did all the Essenes live in communities?
Daniel: No. As in all things Essene, there is an inner and an outer here. The inner form was the communities, while the outer was the Essene families living in many of the towns. Sometimes two or three families would leave a town and move out to a more remote area and try to start a small community. Some of these communities prospered, but some did not, so the situation was always changing.

Here Daniel underlines the fluid nature of the Essene community structure. As well as those key communities he lists there may well have been others that only flourished for a short time and were then abandoned.

Daniel: In the towns our Brothers still kept what they owned and did not share all property in common as those in the communities did. On the other hand the town Brothers were expected to dispense charity widely, to both Essenes and non-Essenes. Many followed a single path in the communities, whereas in the towns most of the Essenes were married. It was a more demanding and committed path in the communities, and in the towns a less intense way.

When anyone entered one of our communities he gave all his property to the Brotherhood, so that eventually the Order had in this way acquired

43

dwellings all along the main trade route from Alexandria to Damascus. These acted as safe houses and resting places for the Brothers as they traveled along this route.

Our town Brothers were advised to follow a more traditional path than that in the communities. For them the emphasis was upon the Father alone, and they did not hold any scrolls or texts originating outside our land. We encouraged the openness of these town Brothers with their ordinary Jewish neighbors, and they might have friendly relationships with the synagogues nearby. This contrasted with the communities, where the Order as a whole had no contact at all with any synagogue. By dispensing charity through our town Brothers we built up some small degree of tolerance for our Order amongst ordinary Jews, and yet also deflected the attention of the Pharisees away from the work of our communities.

In the communities we knew that we had a special freedom, a freedom to study texts from Egypt such as the wisdom of the Isis cult and the Ascension Rite of the Sun; from Greece including many of their finest thinkers such as Pythagoras; and from Persia including the Zoroastrian texts. This freedom to range over the work of the great Sages and Master Souls of the world was bought at a high price — the discipline and restricted life led by our town Brothers. Yet they knew that in doing their work they were like a shield to us, as we were a shield to the Teacher of Righteousness.

Joanna: You mentioned the Ascension Rite of the Sun. Can you tell us some more about that?

Daniel: Yes. It was my favorite of all the Egyptian texts that I encountered. A few lines will give you some idea of it:

Father Sun, whose golden Disc
is the symbol of the Inner Light,
touch our hearts with your Sacred Fire
at the dawning of this new day.
As you ascend in the Heavens
inspire us to follow you,
so we may rise in Ascension
and dwell always in the Realm of Light.

Joanna: Daniel, this is a wonderful text. Thank you for sharing it with us. How old do you think it is?

Daniel: I am not certain. The Kaloo brought it to Alexandria many years before my time. Some of the teachers there thought it was linked to the cult of Ra, but others spoke of a heretical king who broke away from both Ra and Amun and pursued his own path.

I think Daniel is referring here to the Pharoah Amenhotep IV, who took the name Akhenaten, and died in 1350 BCE. He set up the cult of the Sun-god Aten (or Aton) in opposition to the priesthood of Amon-Ra, and was certainly considered heretical by later Pharoahs.

But to return to the subject of communities: I wanted to find out how many Essenes there were at the high point of the movement, and asked about this.

Daniel: At the height of our movement about three or four thousand people lived and worked as Essenes. The balance of inner and outer, the communities and the town Brothers, was a useful cloak and spread confusion in the minds of our enemies. We were open and yet secret, visible and yet invisible, known and yet unknown.

We thought this was a perfect way of summarizing the position of the Essenes within the Jewish society of that time. The balance of the known and the unknown clearly served the Essenes well.

Joanna: Were any crafts practiced in the communities?
Daniel: All our communities, except that at Mount Carmel, had some craftspeople. Many of our crafts were linked to healing processes. Thus we made oils and ointments, tinctures and incense, and mixtures of healing herbs. And we made the pots and jars to hold these things. Many of the craftsmen were not so much absorbed in Essene ideas; they chose to focus at a more practical level, but their work made a major contribution to the life of the communities.

This is an interesting statement by Daniel because it underlines the diversity of those who lived in Essene communities. Some of the literature on the internet puts forward a naive and simplistic view of Essene life, presenting the Essenes almost as pious medieval monks. Frankly the broad and human diversity described by Suddi (the Essene whose story is told in *Jesus and the Essenes* by Dolores Cannon) and by Daniel sounds much more credible.

Joanna: What crafts were practiced at Qumran?
Daniel: At Qumran they made fragrant balsam, because the conditions nearby were good for the trees which

*produced the resin for this. Some metalwork and much
pottery was also made there.*

Joanna: Is balsam a kind of perfume?

*Daniel: Yes. It suited us that Qumran should be seen just as
a place where people made perfume, and not as a
community. It allayed suspicion by allowing us to be
visible and yet invisible. It is hard to hide buildings
from the prying eyes of strangers, but to deceive them
as to the purpose of these buildings is much easier.*

The soundness of the Essenes' strategy emerges clearly
here. It would have been quite impractical to try to be
totally invisible, given the numbers of people involved and
the need to house and feed them. But this blend of the
visible and the invisible was much shrewder. The
conventional Jews must have thought they knew perfectly
well what the Essenes were up to, but they were only seeing
part of the picture.

Confirmation of the making of perfumes at Qumran has
come through the work of the Belgian archaeologist, Dr
Pauline Donceel-Voute. She identified the resin in a small
pottery jug found in a cave near Qumran as opobalsam, a
fragrant balm similar to myrrh. Her researches on the
Qumran site (reported in the BBC Horizon documentary
Resurrecting the Dead Sea Scrolls) confirm that perfume
was made there.

"Dead Sea Scrolls" is a general term used to denote
scrolls (or fragments of scrolls) discovered mainly between
1947 and 1960 at seven sites on the north-western and
western shores of the Dead Sea. These sites consisted of
eleven caves near Qumran, two caves in Wadi Murabba'at,
and caves at Nahal Hever, Nahal Mishmar and Nahal
Se'elim. Scroll discoveries were also made at Khirbet Mird

and Masada.

It has become customary, however, to use the term "Dead Sea Scrolls" in a narrower sense to mean only the Qumran material, which contained about 800 original documents present in whole or in part. The documents were written on skin or papyrus, with one embossed on copper. They are mainly in Hebrew, with some in Aramaic and a few in Greek. They span all the books of the Old Testament (except Esther) as well as many texts not previously known. The general scholarly opinion dates the Qumran scrolls to between 200 BCE and 70 CE, with a few texts from the third century BCE. As very little manuscript material in Hebrew or Aramaic has survived from this period, the Dead Sea Scrolls represent a discovery of unique importance.

But to return to our session with Daniel:

Joanna: So the craftwork acted as a cover, a cloak, for the communities?
Daniel: Yes, but it was also a useful way of getting money.
Joanna: But if you lived in a self-sufficient way, and Brothers joining the Order donated all their property, why would you need more money?
Daniel: Because the search for ancient scrolls was very expensive. The process of traveling to remote places to find the scrolls was costly, and the scrolls themselves were often expensive to purchase. We were not the only people interested in ancient scrolls. Many wealthy land-owners and merchants collected scrolls as they collected other antiquities, and we had to vie with them if we wished to acquire the best scrolls. Over the years we built up a web of contacts who kept a watch for any scroll which might be of interest to us,

and these contacts also needed paying from time to time.

We were now starting to get a picture of how the different parts of the Brotherhood related to one another, and wanted to explore how similar the communities were.

Joanna: Were all the communities very similar, apart from Qumran?

Daniel: No, all had their different character. Some were more practical and some were more scholarly or more priestly, more intense. And the people differed quite a lot. Many of the priests would be drawn to the more intense communities, where the fire of idealism burned strongly. In some of these a fierce idealism could be found, with priests who thought the answer to almost everything was to build the perfect Temple, perfectly designed, perfectly proportioned and perfectly made. They thought that to manifest God's will in such a perfect form would bring about an era of peace and righteousness. I'm afraid I thought this was a well-meaning illusion, and I found the intensity of some of the more extreme priests quite difficult to handle.

Information on Essene aspirations to build a perfect Temple is contained in The Temple Scroll, one of the texts within the Dead Sea Scrolls (see Further Reading entry under Yadin.)

Joanna: Apart from the communities and the town Brothers, was there any other focus of Essene activity?

Daniel: Yes. There were a number of retreat houses in

remote areas, places you would go to be alone, to forget about the burden of your community responsibilities for a while, and pursue your own inner path, your own connection with God. These places had to be remote, even by Essene standards. They would often be in hilly areas, and were sometimes physically quite difficult to get to, but that was deliberate. They were places where the deepest levels of peace could seep into the soul; places of profound refreshment and renewal. Only one of these retreat places was a full community and that was the one at Mount Carmel. The priests who lived at Carmel were severe and ascetic, but they were helpful to those Essenes who wanted a quiet space to meditate for a while. Sometimes the communities got very busy, and with young children it was not always as quiet as the elders would have wished.

The Mount Carmel community is described in some detail in *The Way of the Essenes: Christ's Hidden Life Remembered* (see Further Reading entry under Meurois-Givaudan.)

Joanna: And each of the communities had many different functions?

Daniel: Yes, that is true. Qumran, Alexandria and Damascus were like places of higher learning, of scholarly research, but they were also schools for the young ones. Most of the other communities also acted as schools, but in addition to this they were farms growing various crops, workshops with busy craftsmen, temples with dedicated priests, and places for people to build a family life with children. So if a place is a school, a farm, a workshop, a temple and a family home it attracts many different types of people with different interests and skills. So you would get a wide range of people, and sometimes the intense and mystical priests, the practical families, the busy craftsmen and the scholarly teachers had only the Essene Way holding them together. They were all such different people, doing such different work.

The remarkable range and diversity within Essene communities comes across clearly here, presenting a very different picture from the simplistic notion that the Essenes were like a closed Order of medieval monks. If the Essenes really were *this* diverse no wonder many people became so confused about them.

Daniel: This was not understood in my day. When I overheard conventional Jews in the towns talk about the Essenes, they usually talked from positions of complete ignorance. They assumed that we were all intense and ascetic priests, but I can understand how that came about. There were a number of Essene sayings circulating among the people, fragments of some scroll or other which had found its way out into the world. These fragments certainly gave that impression.

Joanna: It is an impression which continued for a long time, even into our day. And you wish to correct that view?

Daniel: Of course. It is always good to speak truth and tell of things as they are, not as they seem to be to the ignorant. A popular lie may continue for centuries, and only the truth can lay it to rest. In truth we are a most diverse people, and that should be recognized.

There were many illusions about the Essenes in my lifetime, and our need for secrecy was partly responsible for that. I fear that if the truth is not told the illusions will persist for a long time. That is why I have tried to speak the truth in this contact, for the sword of truth will bring Light into the darkness of the world. It is time for the Light to prevail and for many lies to be laid to rest.

We found this passage very moving. Daniel seemed to be reaching out across the barriers of time to us. It gave us the strong feeling that the Essenes as a whole wished to set the record straight, to be able to speak to the world in a way that was simply impossible at the time of Jesus. At that time secrecy, and the safety of Jesus, their Teacher of Righteousness, were paramount. But now we live in a different age, and it seems that it is time for the truth about Jesus and his Essene friends and supporters to come out.

7

Life in the Essene Communities

One advantage of moving to the Interlife stage was that Daniel was able to review his life from a different perspective. As part of this process he was able to give us an overview of what it felt like to be living in an Essene community.

Daniel: The communities were a balance of families, practical people, teachers and priests. The priests were respected as the guardians of the rules and ceremonies on which the community was based, but the real authority was the council on which priests and lay Brothers had an equal voice. In each community about a dozen elders, ones chosen from each area of study, played a major part in the council. These elders had the task of hearing the views of all members of the community, and if there was any dispute arriving at a balance which was fair to all. They also had to bear in mind the rules and aims of the community when reaching any conclusion.

Joanna: When we read the Essene texts which have survived to our day, some might think that the priests ruled the communities.

Daniel: (indignantly) *The priests do not rule us! We are a free people and rule ourselves. The priests may rule in Jerusalem, but we have chosen a different path. Any position of respect has to be earned. An old and wise teacher, or a very spiritual grandmother, might carry more weight in the community than any priest, for we would honor their attainment and their wisdom.*

I may have been an elder, but I had to work my way up to that. There was a great feeling of acceptance of how things were, a contentment with the whole life of the community. We were very reliant on each other, and it was a complete and satisfying system. A number of people in our communities had quite a high focus, and when you're working on that kind of level people are more balanced and the whole system works better. You sense that your worth is recognized in such a system, but also each recognizes the worth of the community as a whole, so the individual and the community support and reinforce each other, and each is stronger for this.

This seemed very significant to us, and we found an echo of it in the "Motto of the Social Ethic" in Rudolf Steiner's *Verses and Meditations.*

Daniel: There was a lot of feeling and sensing into how things were, how people were, so if someone was unhappy you knew right away and did something to help. A very ordered, serene life, with just the occasional drama. You noticed it particularly when you went out into the world and then returned again. You felt the measured rhythm of the community settle around you like an oasis of peace. In comparison the life in the towns was sharp and uneven, no regular rhythm to it, and very discordant. Most of the teachers traveled from time to time in order to pursue their researches, but we were glad to return to our own community and feel the peace of it enfold us like a comforting and familiar cloak.

Joanna: And were the teachers chosen by their star charts?

Daniel: Yes, and by where their interests lay. Even when young that would be clear.

Joanna: So it was clear where everyone was in the scheme of things?

Daniel: Yes, we all knew that different people had different abilities and different parts to play. We could see from the star charts where each one was, so it did away with a lot of jealousy. The strongest and oldest souls had the harder tasks and the more intensive training, and that was accepted. If they got more of the recognition we knew they had also done more of the work. So we didn't vie with one another, we just got on with our lives. But we were human so there was a gentle joking about people's foibles, yes. We had a lot of structure, but it was a gentle structure because it was arrived at by consent and agreement.

The term "old soul" is used to indicate someone who has had many incarnations on the Earth, and has hopefully acquired wisdom during that time.

Joanna: It must have been very different from the Romans' structure.

Daniel: Yes, they had a structure where the top families got most of the rewards, and only a small share filtered down to the rest. We shared everything equally, and gave out from the central supply according to the needs of each one. A single person would have different needs to a family, and so on.

Joanna: I suppose there were some who came in with quite good charts and didn't live up to their expectations, and others whose star charts weren't so good, but they worked hard and got more responsible positions in the community?

Daniel: Yes, it was a system of rewarding merit. All realized that each was in their position through merit, not simply because they were rich and owned much land. Our communities were run by the consent of all. Merit, consent and love formed the inner core on which our communities were founded. All three were necessary if the community was to live in harmony.

Joanna: Did you choose representatives to speak for you?

Daniel: Yes, each section within our community would have someone to speak for them at the council, and the chosen leader of each community would speak at the greater councils held at Qumran.

Joanna: And if there were human problems from time to time the elders sorted it out with discussion?

Daniel: Yes, but it was done quietly. If a marriage broke up it was between the two partners and the elders. No one else knew what caused the rift, and that was wise in many cases. The elders were trusted and that was enough. The elders were the link to the past, to the Kaloo, to the teachings. Although much was written down, it was also an oral tradition.

It was a healthy, harmonious life, but also quite a hard life, quite rigorous if there was much traveling. Yes, traveling was always a little uncertain for us. We were never quite sure whether we would reach the place we had chosen. But that was part of it, we treated it like one of the mysteries, for the traveling outside is linked to the traveling inside, the journey of the heart.

Joanna: Did you believe that a child is born with original sin?

Daniel: Well, there are original parcels of merit, positive merit and negative merit. Each one comes bearing some little gift or burden from past lives, but we did not see it as sin, or wickedness, just things to be worked out, lessons to learn, things to be balanced out in the harmony of the universe.

Joanna: So you believe the soul has many lives on Earth?

Daniel: Of course. People are born with such different physical and mental abilities. Only by a belief in rebirth can one explain these differences in a logical way. Then one can see the spiritual growth of a soul as part of a just, loving and harmonious universe.

Joanna: I'm beginning to see that the most important things you taught were loving your neighbor within the community, all getting together in harmony and teaching everything with love.

Daniel: Yes, the teachings were given out so that they would lead the people on the path of love. If they knew how to love truly, then they knew all things. We believed that God would preserve all that was important, and the rest would blow away into the sands of the desert.

Joanna: I feel there was great simplicity in your

communities.

Daniel: Yes, there was simplicity in our lives, but we did not strive for it. It arose naturally from our lives as the perfume arises from the flower. We strove for good things: peace, harmony, love, truth — yes, good things. And so even those of us who studied the complexity of the Law, the Torah, which was far from simple (he chuckled), *through other aspects of living together became well rounded in simplicity. So a sweet way for us to travel, a sweet path, yes. It was good. My only sadness is I wish we had been able to share this sweet fruit more widely with others. We shared as much as we could, as much as we dared, and still only a few, a very few tasted of the sweet fruit. That is perhaps my one sadness, but all ones have their own way, and must tread it in their own fashion.*

Joanna: So you tried not to judge others?

Daniel: Yes, it was not our part to judge anyone. We do not know the pattern that the soul has woven, for we can see only a few threads and not the whole picture.

Joanna: What kind of food was eaten in the communities?

Daniel: A variety of things: fish, the meat allowed by Jewish Law, fruit and food from other plant sources. As for myself, I chose to eat nuts, fruit, honey, grains and other plant foods, but no meat or fish. I did not see why any of God's creatures should have to die so that I might live. Animals are our younger brothers in terms of spiritual development. I do not believe that a loving God would create a universe in which a man must eat his brother in order to survive.

Those Essenes who did eat flesh were sparing in the amount of meat they ate, with the exception of those whose path drew them close to the Zealots. When I visited the community at Mount Horeb I found our Brothers there were eating large amounts of meat, some of it barely cooked, which I found disgusting even to look upon. When I took them to task on this, they said that if they were to be Warriors of God then red meat was needed to strengthen their bodies. Yet even those Brothers would not eat the unclean beasts, like the flesh of swine. I did not enjoy my stay at Horeb and returned quickly to my own community. There the fruits were especially sweet and I never missed meat at all in my diet.

Joanna: And did many of the Essenes in your community follow you in your choice of food?

Daniel: About a third of those at Hebron, and more began to do so when Jesus spoke about food. He said we should eat the fruits of trees, the plants of the field, honey and milk. All the good food spread out before us on the table of the Earthly Mother. Honey he praised highly, for it is made by the bees with such ritual care, each of their hives being like a temple in miniature, and their lives being ordered with perfect ceremony. Judging by what he said I believe honey is the most spiritual food one can eat upon the Earth. Every community kept hives, and we treated the bees with the greatest respect.

Joanna: And by "the fruits of trees" did Jesus mean also nuts from nut-bearing trees?

Daniel: Of course, for this is the fruit of that kind of tree. We grew two kinds of nut in Hebron, my favorite being almonds. I ate well of these and often thanked my Brother Trees for sustaining me.

The diversity among the Essenes emerges strongly from this part of Daniel's account. There was no fixed and standard diet, and the food eaten was an individual choice. The documentary evidence does seem to support the view that meat and fish were eaten. The Dead Sea Scrolls contain no general prohibition on the eating of meat and fish, but they do give – in the Damascus Document – an instruction on how to treat fish eaten on the Sabbath (see the section titled "Concerning the Sabbath to observe it according to its law.") It is difficult to reconcile this piece of evidence with a totally vegetarian diet.

The archaeology of Qumran has also contributed to our knowledge. The bones of goats, sheep, lambs and calves were found in 26 separate deposits on the site. They were carefully buried in pots, or covered by pots. In these circumstances these bones could be either the remains of ritual meals, or the result of animal sacrifice. However several writers of the period (including Josephus) noted that the Essenes abstained from all animal sacrifices, so the ritual meal alternative seems the more likely.

But let us return to our session with Daniel:

Joanna: And taken as a whole, was the experience in Essene communities a very balanced life?

Daniel: Yes, in many ways. We understood that there were many forms of balance which needed to be maintained in order to give a healthy life. The balance between movement and repose, for example was present in exercises for the body, in practical work in the fields and gardens, and in dance.

Joanna: And there was a form of Essene dance?

Daniel: Of course. Our teachers told us that dancing was

an essential balancing factor, especially for those of intense spiritual aspiration. We had slow, gentle dances and fast vigorous ones. Sometimes when we had lost someone in the community who was greatly loved, we could only come to terms with that loss when we had a gathering with many dances. Being able to move, all of us together, in slow reflective dances, thinking about the one who was no longer physically present, made it easier to bear the loss of a much-loved friend.

There was a strong tradition of dancing in groups, especially in lines, throughout this whole region. This tradition would have been established for many centuries before the Essenes, and so it is not surprising that this practice continued in the Essene communities. We can see echoes of these dances in those developed within the Israeli kibbutz movement. The dances pioneered in this movement have now gone out to a much wider audience as Israeli circle dances.

8

The Essene Children

As the Essene communities were not monasteries but a mixture of families and single adults (like Daniel and Suddi) we wondered how children fitted into Essene life. Knowing that Daniel was interested in the stars I began by asking about astrology.

Joanna: Is a star chart prepared for all Essene children?
Daniel: *Of course. The life chart is a most important guide to what the child has come to Earth to do, and indicates strengths and areas to be worked on.*
Joanna: I understand that when the children are born you are very aware of how they are still connected to their Divine Self, and that your whole preparation of young children is directed towards retaining that openness to the Light. Is this for all the children or just for the special ones?
Daniel: *No — for all children!* (Daniel sounded quite indignant here.) *But perhaps, yes, there would be more intense training in the case of those particular ones where the charts indicate that they have special work to do. But with all children, yes, the encouragement to*

keep the link with the Divine Self alive and active, that is most vital. The link is so easily diminished if the training is not good, or if the child is exposed too quickly to the heavy denseness of the world.

The child at the point of arrival on the Earth is like a spirit putting a finger down into the world, to see how life is, to gently explore and see if this is a good place to be. It is only a finger-hold at that point and there is much need of very gentle nurture so that the being is not alarmed or frightened. It should be a most friendly and welcoming and gentle place, hence also the emphasis on culture and beauty. Surrounding the child with beauty so that it knows that it is entering a world where the spiritual and the beautiful – which it sees as identical – are respected, as much as these are respected in the spiritual realm from which it comes.

The child is spiritual, but not in a religious sense. It is a spiritual being, and for it the spiritual, the beautiful, the harmonious are seen and felt as the same thing. And that is exactly what should surround the child in the early years so that it gains confidence and strength, and the ability to go forward in an open state. But so often there is no understanding of this, and the child is so roughly treated that it is not able to retain any real degree of openness, and when it comes time to teach meditation that openness has been lost. It is still possible to regain this open state, but it is much harder, so great gentleness in the nurture and care of children in the early years is the ideal.

Children become much stronger and more anchored in themselves at one point, but for the first seven years the soul is still descending and integrating with the new self. By the age of seven the soul should be securely anchored within the new self, but any great shock within the first seven years will impede integration and set the whole process back. The complete integration of soul and self is what we aim for, but it is hard to achieve. Life upon Earth is full of shocks of one sort or another.

Comment by Joanna: As my children were in a Steiner school for a year I find this statement by Daniel very interesting because it ties in with the ideas of Rudolf Steiner. It also echoes Maria Montessori's ideas about nurturing young children.

Joanna: Presumably some children will choose to be born into difficult circumstances which will make this integration hard to achieve.

Daniel: Because of their past lives, some have chosen to work this out by experiencing difficulties in the early years, yes. We place a great deal of emphasis upon accepting and consuming what is placed before us, whatever life presents. Experience is there for a reason, and to reject it and deny it is to fail to absorb it fully. It is better to accept the situation, learn the lesson and free oneself. So all our difficulties, our pains and troubles must be loved and embraced. They are the lessons that we have chosen to learn so we love and absorb them, consuming the whole fruit, and then we can move on to a different and lighter condition.

But those who rebel against a condition, who say, "This is not me, I did not make this, I reject this illness, this difficulty, and I will not accept it," these are the ones who are not learning their lessons. They have chosen to reject their past. All ones have aspects from their past which are painful, but by fully accepting them we can experience what we have chosen for ourselves. We have planted a tree and are now consuming the fruits of that tree. Whenever it was planted, in another life or in the early years of this life, the fruits must be consumed. If we spit out the fruit we are locked into that energy, and we will not be free to go on to the next experience.

Joanna: So you teach this to your children?

Daniel: Yes. Whatever happens, happens for a reason, for they have drawn this to them. No being ever experiences anything without drawing it to them, from a past life or from this life, or sometimes as a service to teach others; that also happens but it is much rarer. So we embrace what happens, knowing that it will be dissolved if we love it. By resisting we are giving it the energy it needs to continue. So instead we absorb it and love it into submission.

This matches up neatly with a good deal of the very latest thinking. There is a saying, "Whatever we resist, persists," and we have certainly found this to be true. But I wanted to find out if this attitude led to any neglect of physical symptoms of an illness.

Joanna: If a child had an illness would you still use any healing methods you had, herbs and salves and so on?

Daniel: We would do all we could possibly do, yes, but when all that was done, and still there was no easing of the illness, then we would know that it is the fruits of the past being consumed. And even if the child should die, we would love the child every day until it died (here his voice dropped to a whisper) *and the child would die in love and peace. Is that not better than to see it as a random happening in a chaotic universe? We do not believe in such a universe. A universe full of random events where people suffer for no reason would be a most cruel place. Would a loving God create a universe where people suffered for no reason? We do not believe so.*

Joanna: Presumably the children in your communities are aware from early on of some of the things they have carried over from other lives?

Daniel: Of course. And sometimes it is possible, for a teacher who is trained in this, simply to touch the third eye of the child and give him or her an experience, an understanding of the original cause of this affliction or this difficulty. When there is difficulty of any kind, there is a reason for it somewhere, in this life or in some previous life.

Joanna: So when the child has remembered the reason, would you support them with counseling?

Daniel: Yes. We would say, "This is why that is difficult for you. It is not because you are a bad person, it is not that God is rejecting you or we are rejecting you, nor that you are rejecting yourself. No, it is none of these things. It is simply there for a reason. Something happened in your past life and it is the cause of this thing. And now you understand how the tree was planted, now you see the fruits of it, you see the whole process. So now you are able to deal with the fruit, love it into submission, go beyond it, and then it will be gone."

Joanna: But presumably sometimes the child has chosen that pattern for the learning lesson it can bring for the parents?

Daniel: Yes, sometimes advanced beings come with severe physical limitations so this can be an opening experience of love for those around them. But we would say this is very rare; mostly it is the child working out what it set in motion before in the span of its lives.

Joanna: When there is a mother in the community who does not have this level of understanding can she ask advice from the elders?

Daniel: Yes, there is a continual process of advising going on in our communities. People will seek out the one who they most respect, and there are ones who also take on this advising role, but most often they will go to the one they most respect, are most in sympathy with.

Joanna: So when a child is born and a star chart is drawn up, is the destiny of the child explained to the parents?

Daniel: Of course. Each child comes with his or her own little history. The star chart is part of the history, but there is also the name and the vibration of the name. We believe that there is an Angel of the Name, and this Angel knows what name the soul has chosen. The Angel of the Name makes its presence felt by the mother, and if the mother is sensitive to the incoming soul she will know when she is in contact with the Angel of the Name, and she will recognize the name when it is presented to her. She will feel as if the right chord has been struck in music, and that is because she recognizes the energy of the incoming soul, and knows that the name reflects that energy. We would say it is more the mother's task than the father's to do this, but there are exceptions. In the case of a very practical mother and a mystical father, then the Angel of the

Name would come to the father. But generally it is the mother, and that is why the father should always listen to the mother's choice of name for the new child, even if she cannot explain exactly how she knows this is the right name.

Comment by Joanna: It is very interesting how Daniel confirms so much of what I have learned from taking people through their experiences of past lives. I was not born with a belief in past lives, though when I was a child I did remember part of my last life, and used to have nightmares about being in a concentration camp. This obviously was very frightening and I learned to suppress this experience because it was not acceptable to my family. Years later I was able to recall memories of other lives, so I have learned about reincarnation from direct experience. When I was puzzled about certain aspects I would ask my higher self for advice and this knowledge very much ties in with Daniel's account. Here was Daniel expressing in his own way so many of the lessons I have learned.

Daniel is also someone after my own heart in his view about the care of young children. I feel so strongly about the need for gentle and harmonious nurturing of young children, particularly when they are infants. So I was delighted to hear Daniel describe an ideal approach for children in their early years. I have worked for many years with small children, and also have rebirthed myself and others, so I know just how incredibly sensitive small children are. In an ideal world I would love to see every mother and infant teacher go through a rebirthing process before having children or teaching them! I wish I had had the opportunity to rebirth before I started working with young children, or had my own children. I would have been so much more sensitive, understanding and sympathetic to their needs.

My youngest girl had a natural, holistic Leboyer-type birth. It was extremely beautiful for all those involved and has been one of the great "highs" of my life. My daughter was very content and happy as a baby. When she was born, instead of wailing she gave a contented gurgle and seemed to look around the room.

If mothers had a better understanding and knew more about their children, they could have a far more harmonious and joyful time with them. I had the joy of educating my youngest two girls at home as part of Education Otherwise. It was wonderful to see these beautiful children unfold and explore their world in a natural and unpressured way. Teaching my children was also an education for me in many ways.

I am amazed at the wisdom of the Essenes with their children. All those years ago there were people educating and raising children in a way that is so close to my dream of an ideal way of teaching and nurturing children – but then, is it because I was an Essene and somewhere deep down I have remembered?

9

John and Roberta

We can now look at the sessions we did with John and Roberta, who is a shaman, healer and Feng Shui practitioner. John is a Reiki Master, healer and workshop leader who has been a friend and colleague for a number of years. He also works with crystal mandalas and earth energies. We had already established that he was an Essene called Luke, so let us now listen to a combined session with both John and Roberta. I began by asking both subjects what their work had been.

Roberta: We traveled at night mostly, stopping off at caves to hide during the day. That way we could cover big distances quite secretly. My main task was to be a messenger, traveling between communities. Sometimes the message would be concealed within a hollowed-out staff. It was very secret work so my name was not known. It was better that way. I was referred to as "The Silent One".

This reference to "The Silent One" intrigued us. As the Essenes were secretive by nature there were no doubt a number of them who were referred to in this way. A common name for the Essenes at that time was *hasha'im,* a Hebrew word meaning "silent ones".

Luke: I worked in healing people, and with crystals also on the energy lines.
Joanna: Which community did you both work in?
Luke: I was at Ein Gedi.
Roberta: And I at Arad near Masada.

As Luke had worked with crystals I asked him to tell me more about crystals in general.

Luke: The original knowledge from the Kaloo was stored in record-keeper crystals, and only later transferred to the scrolls. We were trained to read the crystals through using the third eye. From the Kaloo we also had lamps made from crystals. Some of the meetings in caves were entirely lit by crystal power.

This is interesting because it seems to indicate a different form of lighting to the basic electric lamps already mentioned.

I was also curious about the method Luke used to heal people, and asked him about this.

Luke: I used many ways to heal, including many strong and smelly ointments.

Roberta laughed when she heard Luke say this. *"I also remember the smelly ointments! I recall he spilled some ointment on a rock at the wayside, and everyone then passed that place rather quickly holding their noses!"*

After the session we looked at the map of Essene communities, and saw that Ein Gedi and Arad were quite close. It therefore seemed quite reasonable for Roberta as "The Silent One" and Luke to know one another. Over the years I have been regressing clients, I have noticed that the same group of people reincarnate together life after life, playing many different roles. In this present life John and Roberta are close friends, so this past link between them did not surprise me.

It also occurred to me that as Hebron was not far from the community at Ein Gedi, it was possible that Daniel also knew Luke, and at a later session I had the opportunity to ask him about this.

Daniel: Oh, young Luke, yes, I know him well. Always cheerful and bright, with a ready smile. A serious student of healing, and great skill I think in that area. It was not my area of study, but they told me he was skillful in these things. Yes, a ready smile and a hearty laugh.

Joanna: Was he able to charm and cajole sick people?

Daniel: Well, he was able to deal with many ones who were sick and cheer their spirits simply with his presence, and that was good, because when people are sick they often have a heaviness about them. So yes, that was useful to him, and he seemed always in good spirits.

Joanna: What methods did he use in healing people?

Daniel: Oh, many things, herbs, ointments, crystals, many things.

Joanna: Were the ointments powerful and smelly?

Daniel: (chuckling) Oh yes, he had some strange mixtures,

and some of these smelled terrible. They might do you much good in healing, but you didn't want to smell them. We used to say, "Watch out for this one! If he puts some of his ointment on you, you'll smell like a goat for a week!" (He laughed). *They were strong, yes, these ointments, but people weren't really worried about what they smelled like as long as it cured their ailments. There were a lot of skin problems, and people were frightened that any skin trouble might be the beginning of leprosy.*

Now we had established that Daniel and Luke knew one another, I was able to ask Luke about Daniel.

Joanna: Do you remember an elder called Daniel Benezra?
Luke: I know Daniel Benezra. I feel tears of joy in my eyes as I speak his name. He was a very holy and dedicated person. He stayed mainly around the communities and did not take long journeys with us. Daniel did some work on the land and the gardens in his community. He was a great lover of God and very committed to his service. He was an important person because of his commitment. We used to go to see him sometimes and tell him about our adventures: where we'd been, what we'd done and who we'd seen, and he was interested to hear about our travels. He was more of a stay-at-home type of person, but we all had our different work to do, and our places to be. No one's work was considered more important than others, so everyone knew that their task was as important as that of the next one. We weren't seen as the great teachers or healers puffed up with our own importance.

Joanna: So was Daniel one of your teachers?

Luke: Yes, he taught us. He knew many things that the old races had. The remnant of these old peoples would travel in our direction. They were called the Kaloo, or by some people the Koolas. Daniel had some knowledge of these people. He knew some things about using crystals for energy and for growing plants. He was involved in growing things. He also had some knowledge about the saving and correct use of water. He along with others could make plants grow with hardly any water. They used crystal teachings. He had many skills – a very humble man. Many people just see humbleness as weakness, but we knew that this was not so.

It was very moving to see the tears of John, as he relived Luke's remembrance of Daniel. It will not surprise you to know that John and Stuart are great friends in this life too, and that John is still a keen traveler to distant places, while Stuart prefers to stay more or less in one place as a writer. Although things do change with the passing of time, I have noticed that some character tendencies and lifestyle choices do persist over many lives.

The reference to Daniel working with plants was interesting too, for he never mentioned that. However he was fond of using similes based on trees, flowers and fruit, so I suppose we might have guessed he had some involvement in this area. It all helped to see Daniel as a rounded and balanced character, not simply a teacher, but also a practical man.

Luke also made one other important contribution. When talking about the communities he said, *"Our life in the communities was based on sharing."* Daniel expanded on this in a later session:

Daniel: In the communities we shared the space, the work, the knowledge and what was in our hearts when we talked about spiritual things and our inner experiences. We shared meals and times of celebration together – there were many levels of sharing.

We regard sharing as a spiritual process, although this is little understood. Through sharing there is a balancing. People have needs, people have resources, and sharing balances the two. And it balances needs and resources without calculation, without money and without counting the cost. To us, sharing is an affirmation of Wholeness, and from the greater perspective of the Whole one would naturally wish to share.

In sharing, the spiritual and material worlds are brought together and fused into one reality. Only through the heart can the two worlds of Spirit and matter be brought together to create this reality. When Spirit and matter merge together through the awakened energies of the heart, all things become possible for us.

This is echoed in Gaura Devi's inspiring account of her life in India as a disciple of Haidakhan Babaji:

"Babaji feeds everybody with immense love, and money comes from spontaneous donations. It's a natural exchange...a way of living life where everybody shares whatever one has to offer: money, work, spiritual or physical energy."

Gaura Devi, *Fire of Transformation: My Life with Babaji* (see Note 2 in Further Reading).

What Daniel has been describing here is a process of spiritual alchemy, something that has vast implications. Once again, he had surprised us by taking a basic idea and developing it into unexpected areas.

10

Traveling and Contact with Strangers

By now we were able to make some comparison between Daniel and Suddi Benzahmare in *Jesus and the Essenes* by Dolores Cannon. Whereas Suddi taught the Jewish Law, the Torah, and was generally direct and specific in his answers, Daniel showed a far greater tendency to digress into subtler areas. He seemed fascinated by the "why" of things, the ideas and philosophy that underlie human life. But in the light of his training, which included star cycles and the mysteries, this was understandable.

I could now see why many of his answers were long in comparison with Suddi's. Both his training and interests took him into subtle areas where precision might be harder to attain than in the teaching of a well-established area like the Jewish Law. In his answers Daniel often gave the impression of feeling his way, probing with his mind for a clear understanding and an accurate way of expressing the ideas involved. His training differed from that of Suddi, and he had a different perspective on things. He was not concerned with the established principles of law, but with concepts and perceptions which might shift and change and evolve over time. In dealing with these subtle and changeable things he tried to be as honest and precise in his answers as he could, yet we had the impression that often he was reaching out into his mind and intuition rather than simply restating what he remembered of some fixed and agreed principle.

Sometimes his efforts to answer our questions took him into areas that stretched and challenged him because he was exploring regions outside his usual familiar territory, yet despite that he was always willing to investigate these areas. And thus we got the impression of a restless and questing intelligence, continually probing to see what existed in human life, and in the universe beyond.

Very often we had the feeling that Daniel was speaking for himself, but also for others. Strangely enough, Dolores Cannon in the Preface to her book, *Jesus and the Essenes* makes a very similar point, saying that she felt the Essenes urging her to write, and bring out knowledge which had been hidden for too long.

Although Daniel had told us of his areas of special interest he had said nothing about how he was trained, and I wanted to explore this.

Joanna: Did your training extend over many years?
Daniel: Yes, many years. There was much to learn in my areas of interest. I sometimes felt that one life was altogether too short to encompass such a task. There were many written authorities to consult, much thinking and consideration, and many discussions with my teachers.
Joanna: Did you travel to meet and discuss with your teachers?

Daniel: Of course. My teachers were not all in Hebron, not all even at Qumran. I traveled to Alexandria and Damascus and to other places too, but all within the area bounded by the central sea. This is in the center of all the lands which concern us. Only my friend Joseph and a few bold travelers go much further. He goes out into the western ocean and up to Britain to visit the tin mines. I had no need to journey that far, for all my researches were focused upon our land and the lands around the central sea.

Joanna: When you travel do you talk much to the people you meet upon the way?

Daniel: I talk as little as possible. That is, I say pleasant nothings which reveal very little. Joseph has raised this to the level of an art. He can talk at length to a stranger without revealing anything about himself at all, and yet seem to be honest and open all the time in what he says. That is truly a most useful skill.

All Essenes are taught from quite a young age to be wary when talking to any stranger. As the guardians of great knowledge we know there are many who covet such knowledge, and would misuse it. We would like to be friends with all the world, indeed that would reflect our ideals very well, but we realize that much of the world is ruled by darkness and deceit. The sons of darkness are interested in power and greed, and not in the good of mankind. We know there is much selfishness in the world and our attitude is that strangers must prove themselves to us first before we talk openly to them. It is not that we wish to be selfish with our knowledge, but any knowledge brings responsibility with it, and we do not wish to see it misused by unworthy ones.

Yet we do talk to travelers who visit our communities, those who have been passed from friend to friend before they find us. But these ones prove themselves to us through their vibration, their aura. Their very being speaks to us. Where there is worthiness and integrity, this speaks for itself, without need of any words. We have shown hospitality to many visiting teachers and from time to time sages from other traditions. But these go quietly and do not make ripples in the pool as they pass. The mass of the people would not be aware of their passing, and that is good.

Joanna: When Essenes are traveling outside their community, how do they recognize fellow Essenes?

Daniel: Well, that depends upon the ability of the Essene. For those able to see the aura it is very simple. There will be the placing of colors in a harmonious way, and maybe also the blessing of God in a sprinkling of gold across the top of the aura.

Comment by Stuart: This was an interesting remark by Daniel. I recall that when talking to the leader of a Western esoteric Order he commented that a gold band across the top of an aura indicates that the person is an Initiate.

Daniel: There is also a way of tuning in to the resonance of the heart. Ones who cannot see the aura but are sensitive in other ways can tune in to the energy of the heart.

During another session with both Daniel and Joseph I had the chance to ask the same question again.

Joseph: By vibration and aura in my case.

Daniel: Even if you do recognize another Essene upon the road, you don't talk too much because you never know who may be overhearing you. There are many who would gain favor with the Pharisees.

Joseph: But we also have our web of information...

Daniel: Yes, particularly centered on the communities. You talk inside the communities much more freely.

Joseph: And you never talk very much to anyone outside the web.

Daniel: We speak little concerning ourselves and our beliefs unless we are amongst friends in one of our communities, or perhaps in a safe house upon the way. When we are on the open road, even if we recognize a stranger's essence, we are careful and do not say much. For me that is sometimes hard, but for you, Joseph, I think it was always a little easier. You were always a silent one, were you not?

Joseph: Hmm... (He chuckled).

Once again the easy and humorous friendship emerged here. In another session with Daniel alone I was able to ask him if there was any joke he shared with Joseph that stood out in his memory.

Daniel: Yes, many times Joseph likened me to Daniel in the lion's den. When I go to visit the towns I sit in the synagogue and listen to the conventional Jews. But I don't talk on these occasions, for it would be unwise to draw attention to myself. So I just sit there and listen to the lions of darkness growling a little. Amongst the younger ones who are being taught in the synagogues, sometimes there is an open mind here and there, but the older ones are too set in their ways. It is sad for me to think that the truth is not going to find a foothold in their minds and hearts, but that is also their choice to make. We acknowledge the right of each being to pursue their own path to the truth, however tortuous that path may be. So when Joseph comes to visit me he often asks whether the lions have been growling. (He chuckled).

The depth of the friendship between these two Essenes was very apparent. They had acquired a trust and an easy understanding. It all helped to bring Joseph to life for me as a real person. The Bible references to him are tantalizingly brief, but here a rounded personality was beginning to emerge: somewhat cautious and silent, certainly, yet also at times light and humorous. During a later session with Joseph I asked him about the ease and lightness of his friendship with Daniel.

Joseph: Well, I have known him for many years, and I can be quite outrageous with him because we both know he can get a little too intense and serious. And because he is an elder no one else in his community can joke with him in this way. He also helps to keep me with my feet on the ground with his jokes and that is good. We have to be careful when we go out into the world, but when we are alone together we can drink a little wine, and unbend a little and share a joke together. I look forward to these times, for when I travel I feel the burden of silence and responsibility fold around me like a heavy cloak.

That responsibility clearly weighed heavily upon

Joseph, and made him much more cautious in his communications with us than Daniel was. Joseph took the "burden of silence" very seriously, and as Daniel once said to us, *"My friend Joseph is a man of many secrets."*

To get a rounded view of the traveling done by the Essenes, I asked Daniel if either he or Joseph actually enjoyed any part of the traveling process.

Daniel: Joseph has told me he enjoys the sea voyages, when there is a light breeze in the sails and the ship is moving smoothly on a calm sea. I am not such a good sailor as he, and have traveled mostly overland. For me, the precious times are the quiet nights under the stars. Sometimes when the night is clear and the stars are bright, it is almost as if I could reach out with my hand and touch them. And at these times the everyday world and the Infinite seem to come together and merge as one.

11

Skills and Powers

We had already glimpsed some of the abilities of the Essenes, and were curious to learn more. Fortunately the later sessions in the Interlife presented an opportunity to follow up this line of enquiry. Once again, Daniel surprised us. We had expected brief references to a variety of skills, but instead got a system of classifying Essene powers. Daniel rattled through the list quite quickly, and we got the impression that this was the standard way of presenting the information to students in the communities. It certainly gave us a feeling of the overall scope and structure of Essene abilities, and how each skill fitted within the whole.

Daniel: The skills can be analyzed or perceived in a number of different ways. There are skills in:

> *healing,*
> *teaching,*
> *researching,*
> *traveling and*
> *defending.*

Also skills divide according to the beings you are working with :

human beings,
angelic beings or
star beings.
The skills are also divided by whether they concern:
consciousness or
energy.
And also whether they focus on:
number,
sound,
heat,
light or
color.
In other words, the aspects of vibration. The energy skills can be divided again according to whether you are working with:
earth energy,
solar energy or
star energy.
All these categories have different skills. The Kaloo taught us very much about the use of energies.

Some of these skills are quite complex and subtle. For example, in traveling skills, there is a method of moving quickly over distances by so lightening the physical body that you can bound along, only touching the ground here and there. There is also a way of traveling by entering a doorway which gives you access to another realm, another level, through which distant points can be easily and quickly reached. As to the skills required in the use of these doorways, there are skills in recognizing where these doorways are, keys to open them, and skills in using them. All these doorways need a key to open them. There is usually an opening process, not a physical key but a process to give you access to them. So there is a whole range of skills involved in the use of these doorways. These doorways were much used by the ancients, but were far less used in my day, and I think the skills to use them were becoming rarer.

This comment on traveling through doorways was interesting, and it seems that naturally occurring vortexes of energy have always existed on this planet. Apparently these were used as inter-dimensional doorways to travel vast distances in ancient times. This is the first reference to these doorways we had encountered in an Essene context.

Joanna: How did the Essenes choose which skill to teach you?

Daniel: Generally our aim is to teach only those skills which will be useful to a person in his or her present life. We analyze the star chart to see where the area of service is, where the skills have been developed in past lives, and where these are coming into play, and thus where they would be useful in service in this lifetime. So not all ones are taught all skills, but some basic skills are taught to all, yes. How to manage the energies on various levels, attunement and meditation skills, and basic skills in communicating with others, yes. But the more specific skills were only taught when it was relevant.

In my case I was taught how to project my consciousness into past and future time, but that was because my three main areas of study were the history of the Essenes, how the Essene Brotherhood was set up by the Kaloo; star lore, star wisdom, the stars and their impact upon human consciousness and human life, which involves star cycles; and the mysteries.

Those were my three areas of study, and although it was possible to study one of these areas and not have the need to project the consciousness, when you studied all three of these areas it was definitely a requirement because it was useful to you, and your researches would be quite limited without it. There were some who studied the stars and did not need to probe into the past or the future, but those who studied as I did the greater cosmic cycles and the impulses in the civilization of mankind were most interested to go either backward to see what happened and what were the roots of our present human condition, and also to go forward and see how various impulses worked out.

So the training was flexible in that it took into account the needs of the individual, and was adapted to that. Skills were given when they were required, but it was highly selective and not all ones were trained with all skills. The training in some of the most advanced skills was only given in one place, as there were only one or two teachers who could give this training. And towards the end of my life I began to notice gaps in the provision of some of the rarer skills, as the teachers of these had died and not been replaced.

The bit about Daniel projecting his consciousness made me sit up and take notice. I could not recall anyone writing about the Essenes and talking about this. If I could get Daniel to project his consciousness forward he might be able to give us an Essene perspective on the development of Christianity. I tried to stop my Geminian mind (I am Gemini rising!) from cantering forward too quickly along these lines, and fumbled to come up with another question on Essene skills.

Joanna: Can you tell us more about the healing skills?

Daniel: We saw healing as being on many levels. Of course there are well-established methods, many of these using herbs, ointments, clay and crystals, but on the highest level we saw healing as a reattunement to the essential note of the individual. In many cases illness is the result of a discord which has been set up within the being of the sick person, so that they are like a musical instrument which has got out of tune. If the healer can work with the healing angels they can assist in reattuning the individual to their note. Once they can resonate again fully to their note the physical level falls quickly into place and healing becomes much easier. So as part of the healing process we teach the individual how to recognize and sound their note. When you can fully sound your note, and vibrate and resonate to it, you become an active participant in your own healing.

Joanna: I believe many of the Essenes were powerful healers. When it came to the very advanced Essenes, did they use different methods?

Daniel: Yes, for an advanced Essene, a very strong and pure soul, it was possible to heal in a more direct and powerful way. But not even these advanced ones could cure all forms of sickness. Some people they would not attempt to heal, and would send away. They would first attune to the inner being of the sick person. If they discovered that they were not yet ready to learn their lesson and release the past, they would send them away. The advanced healers always attuned to the soul of each one before the healing started, and if the soul says, "No, there is still something to learn here. It is not the highest good of this individual to be healed now," the healer would always respect that. The soul is responsible for the spiritual learning of the individual, and all healing takes place within the orbit of the soul's consent. Only the soul knows the highest good of the individual, and that good must always take priority over the physical act of healing.

Joanna: Yes, we understand that the advanced healers would wish to consult the soul in this process. Providing the soul agrees to the healing, how would they then proceed?

Daniel: The healer holds the vision of the person before him as a perfect being, completely aligned with the Divine pattern. Whatever illness may be present, this pattern always remains perfect, and the healer affirms that perfection. Then the healer invokes the power of the Spirit to flow down into the pattern and to link it with the projection which is the physical body. Advanced healers are able to do this effectively because they have cleared away all the obstacles within themselves and have become perfect channels for this power. When the Spirit moves to manifest perfection, all else in the universe steps aside. The illness – whatever it is – simply gives way to this power. The perfect power-filled pattern and the physical body come together as one, and the person is healed, sometimes instantly. But this is not so much healing in the conventional sense as a restoration of Wholeness, the manifestation of the same perfection upon the physical level as exists upon the higher level.

Comment by Joanna: This account of the advanced

healing methods of the Essenes was a real gift for us, and is yet another example of Daniel's ability to take a straightforward question and lift it into fresh levels of insight. I don't know if Jesus used this technique, but it's certainly a fascinating possibility. Perhaps because I am a therapist I found this part of Daniel's account quite a moving experience, and could only manage a general question after this to keep the session going.

Joanna: Thank you for sharing that with us Daniel. And now can you tell us about any other special skills which the Essenes had?

Daniel: *There are a number of special skills, and I will mention only a few of these. There is inner vision, and the seeing of the aura. The aura is not seen by all who have the inner sight, but is an extension of that skill. There is also inner hearing, the ability to read the cosmic records, and the ability to attune to high angelic beings and high star beings and the energies that these beings focus. Then there is the ability to work with earth energies in practical ways, using crystals and sacred forms. These are only a few of the Essene skills. The Kaloo had many more skills also, but despite their efforts the knowledge and practice of some skills were beginning to die. The best teachers among the Essenes were no longer able to reach the highest levels in the use of these skills.*

I saw that as a natural progression. Certain skills are perfected in every age, every cycle, and when the cycle is over, the skills decay. They may be practiced still by the highest Sages, I don't think they are ever entirely lost, but the regular use of them passes out of human memory and experience. This has happened

90

before, and I see the signs of it again. In the Old Land in the West they perfected the working with crystals, for example. Whatever skills we now have are only a fragment of what was regularly practiced then. I do not mourn the passing of old skills, because for the Master Souls of mankind, the greatest Teachers and Sages, this knowledge lives on. But it may pass out of human experience for a while, and that seems to be the pattern of things.

As to the skills that we did practice in my day, I knew only the outline of many of them, and could not perceive all the skills clearly. To know the real extent of any skill one would have to practice that skill to a very high level. Those beginning at it, and within the middle range of mastering it, cannot yet see the full extent of it. One who has practiced that skill for many years and is adept in using it is in the best position to be able to determine the limits of that skill. We would say that all skills have limitations, and the wise master of that skill knows the boundaries and works always happily and harmoniously within them, not trying to exceed the inherent potential of that skill, what that skill is able to do, because that would be mere foolishness.

We were well taught and knew both the advantages and disadvantages of each skill. Some took much energy, or much out of the physical body, and some took from the etheric or emotional or mental bodies. So there was a price to pay for using each skill, and we were clear in knowing what the price was, and were able thus to work within our limits and not overstretch ourselves through ignorance.

Joanna: Was the price of your skill the frailness of your

etheric body?

Daniel: Yes, because to stretch your consciousness out in time was to stretch yourself thin, like a sinew is stretched thin. I was glad to pay the price and do the work, yes, but we all knew that for every form of work there is a cost. As my work progressed I found I was getting frailer at the etheric level. It was one of the problems with that work.

Joanna: And you would carry that forward through several lives?

Daniel: Yes.

Joanna: Was sound used in a number of ways?

Daniel: Yes, in defense as we have said, but also to balance and sustain the energies within the body, and in chanting, prayers and invocations. There were many ways to use sound.

The use of sound for the defense of the community is discussed in Chapter 15.

Joanna: And what training did Joseph have? Was it different from yours?

Daniel: Joseph had a fairly general training, because he had to know a little about everything. He was very focused on what was necessary down here on Earth, whereas he said I could fly off into the cosmos more easily (he chuckled). *And he had this underpinning of the work and the responsibility – a heavier burden than mine. So his training was more direct and practical, I think.*

Part Four:

Essene Knowledge and Belief

They are eminent for fidelity and are the ministers of peace...They also take great pains in studying the writings of the ancients and choose out of them what is most for the advantage of their soul and body.

Josephus

12

Exploring Essene Knowledge

I wanted to explore Essene knowledge, and knowing that harmony was an important part of their teachings I began by asking Daniel about that.

Daniel: For us there are many forms of harmony, the most important being harmony with the Heavenly Father and the Earthly Mother. We see harmony as the central Law of the universe, with all the other Laws supporting and sustaining it. So harmony is one of the key elements in our system, together with truth, and peace, and unconditional love. Harmony, truth, peace and love are the four pillars on which we build our house, and without any of those four pillars the house would not stand.

Daniel actually said, "pure and unselfish love", but we have translated it here (and throughout this book) as unconditional love, as that is the closest modern equivalent.

Joanna: You seem to be a very peace-loving people with

much patience. How do you achieve your patience?

Daniel: We realize that there is a right time for everything and that God knows this time and will present the gift, whatever it may be – the skill, the talent, the wisdom – at the most fitting time for us to receive it. So this gives us patience because we know that God is in charge of the timing aspect of our lives, and all we have to do is to trust and go forward, a day at a time. And if our hearts are open and we go forward in love, then the time is always right for us.

So we walk on in trust, accepting all that happens to us – even if we don't understand it – as the gift of God. Yet though we accept all, we try to choose from moment to moment the path of greatest good. We attune in our hearts to see if any course of action is having a good effect in our lives, to see if it is expanding our awareness and raising us to greater heights. We aspire to those heights, to the Light, for we believe that we are the Children of the Light.

Joanna: Sometimes your friend Joseph is referred to as a rabbi. Could you comment on this?

Daniel: Well, rabbi just means "teacher". Joseph teaches by example, I think, and by his presence. He has a quietness and integrity about him, so you feel he is securely founded upon inner wisdom, something beyond words. The Essenes have always known that words can be overvalued. We know that what happens in the heart is more important than all the ideas in the head. The business of the heart is the business of greater priority, we would say.

What is occurring in the heart is the key to how we are moving along a spiritual path, how we are moving towards the Light. The heart holds the essence of things, and as Essenes we are concerned with the essence rather than the outer husk. We have found that what really moves people forward is energy experienced in the heart, not words and ideas circulating in the mind. The mind might try to persuade you that ideas are all that really matter, but that is a lie.

Joanna: Still, if you're trying to teach people you have to give them some words, a story or something to hold on to.

Daniel: Yes, that is true, yet we try to go beyond words and convey the essence, the fundamental nature of things. We know the nature of the universe, through the wisdom of the Kaloo and others. We know that the universe is a web of consciousness founded upon harmony and sustained by love. It is like a great rocking stone which pivots on a single point: if you push the stone in any direction it moves back towards the center again to restore the balance, to restore the harmony. That is the process of it, consciousness is the intelligence of it, and the energy of it is love. The universe is sustained by love, by a great ocean of cosmic love, unconditional love.

Joanna: I've always felt that love, harmony, balance and wholeness were most important teachings.

Daniel: Yes, and what is more important to teach the young than these things? If our children are totally ignorant of everything else and yet know of these things, and use them to guide their lives, then they will live well, as truly human beings, and be happy. But if they know of all the other knowledge in the world and are ignorant of these things, then they will make many errors in their lives, and make misery for themselves and for

97

others also.

Our teachings gave us a balance, a wholeness that many others lacked. For example a rabbi in the synagogue might have a brilliant mind and be very strong in debating the Law, but be quite frail and as a child upon the emotional level of his being. In comparison to this we are balanced and whole upon many levels. Through our daily Attunements, and through living anchored within these energies, we harmonize our being with the greater whole.

Every human being is a microcosm of the universe, and within our bodies and minds the forces of the universe flow and resonate. By attuning to these forces and becoming conscious of them, we integrate ourselves into the universe and bring Spirit and matter ever closer together. When the universe and the human being are fully merged and integrated we become the Living Truth, an embodiment of wholeness, harmony, Light and peace.

Joanna: It seems very important that this information is handed down and not lost.

Daniel: Indeed, but the knowledge alone is only part of the key. To say the words of our Attunements in the morning and then to forget them and go about your work will not bring much result. Whilst we work we stay anchored in our being within that energy, within the grace of that angel, so that our being flows in oneness with the energy and unites with it. We find that working from this quiet and focused space has a healing aspect to it, and opens the heart to many possibilities.

Joanna: Is there any form of words you say before the Attunements?

Daniel: Yes, there is a prologue, but it varies from community to community. Qumran uses a simpler form of it, but my own community prefers an extended form.

Comment by Stuart: The best known version of a prologue is given on page 42 of Szekely's *Teachings of the Essenes from Enoch to the Dead Sea Scrolls.* This book also contains the Essene Communions, which Daniel calls "Attunements". It seems likely that it is the Qumran form of the prologue which has come down to us in that book. Szekely also gives an alternative form on page 12 of *The Essene Gospel of Peace,* Book Four. That form of words is the source of the Essene Network version of the prologue, which I have also adapted a little:

Let us enter the eternal and infinite Garden of Mystery,
our Spirit in Oneness with the Heavenly Father,
our bodies in Oneness with the Earthly Mother,
our hearts and minds in Oneness with each other
and with all of creation.

I think what Daniel said about the teachings will strike a chord with many people. The teachings of the Essenes were simple and yet so profound that they attune us to the very center of things, the Essence of all that is. I found his comment on taking the energies of the Attunements out into daily work most fascinating. The modern parallel here would be Karma Yoga, where the spiritual practice (meditation, prayers, puja, or the morning service in monastic orders) is taken out into the work of the day, and becomes the still center around which all the activities of the day revolve.

One can sense that the Essenes had developed a whole

science of handling energies, drawing parallels between human aspects and different energy sources in the cosmos. I wondered whether the Essenes distinguished between the universe and the cosmos. I got Joanna to ask about this, and here is Daniel's reply:

Daniel: The universe, the cosmos, the Heavenly Father, Celestial Man, Supreme Wisdom, the Totality of Knowledge, all these terms are used for the same. This is God manifested in Creation.

Joanna: So you see God as the universe?

Daniel: God in manifestation, yes. But God is also the Infinite Source beyond manifestation, the Eternal Mystery.

There are Kabbalistic overtones here, so I followed this up with a question.

Joanna: Did the Kabbalah influence your teachings?

Daniel: Of course. But that is a whole life's study in itself, I think. The Tree of Knowledge certainly helped me to see how high the Elohim were – even archangels are called Beni Elohim – Sons of the Elohim. The Tree of Knowledge reminded us that everything in Creation is balanced. There are resonances connecting every level, and there is always an inner and an outer. And of course we interpreted the whole of the Essene Way as a Tree of Wisdom.

Comment by Stuart: This balance of inner and outer was clearly important to the Essenes, for Daniel stressed it often. By this point we could see that his general method of dealing with questions was to answer first at a basic level, and then soar up into the subtle and the universal. Clearly moving from the outer to the inner was deeply instinctive to Daniel, and this was the way he habitually worked. By following this through Daniel's statements we got a real feeling of the way the Essene mind functioned. Although realistic and practical, it always seemed to be striving upwards towards the ideal.

Joanna: You seem often to be striving towards perfection. Do you see yourselves as consciously doing this?
Daniel: *Of course! I was greatly influenced by the Master Pythagoras, and one of his guiding principles was that the soul can rise in union with the Divine. I saw in this the best hope for the progress of the individual and the spiritual development of humanity.*

The depth and subtlety of Daniel's answers also served to underline how broad and universal Essene philosophy really was. Some scholars – judging by the written record alone – have characterized the Essenes as idealistic but also stiff and inflexible, locked into a rigid Judaic system. However Daniel was the living refutation of that over-simplistic perception. With all this information from him we were able to see that the Essenes had a very esoteric view of things, but also a very practical and pragmatic view.

Comment by Joanna: I find these Essene teachings very beautiful and I could really resonate with what Daniel was saying. When I was in my mid-twenties and working in an Australian kindergarten run on Montessori lines, I was very much drawn to Maria Montessori's methods and teachings, and years later I trained to be a Montessori teacher. Much of what Daniel said is so close to Maria's philosophy; I think

Maria must have been an Essene! Maybe I was drawn to teach in a Montessori way because it echoed old knowledge which I carried in my cellular memory. I know I was an Essene in Damascus (with Stuart) at a time when we both knew that we were preparing for a great Teacher to appear. This was just over a hundred years before the birth of Jesus, but the communities were steadily working towards the support of the coming Teacher at that time.

Comment by Stuart: When Daniel said, "We integrate ourselves into the universe," he was not making a philosophical point, but a practical one about the Essene system of balance. If any group of people were masters of living in a balanced way, that group was the Essenes. They were highly skilled at what Gregg Braden calls "internal technology". The balance between the chemical/atomic system of Mother Earth and the electro-magnetic system of Father Heaven was central to the whole Essene Way. There is both a chemical and an electro-magnetic basis for our existence and our consciousness, and we cannot function at peak efficiency if each system is not healthy and there is not a proper balance between these two systems. The Essenes understood this, and what they were developing was really a kind of Western yoga, a practical path of integration that brought balance into every aspect of their lives.

All the Brothers spent some part of every weekday in physical work, and that alone must have ensured that many of the ills which confront modern psychotherapists never had a chance to flourish. The Essenes knew well – as do Native American Medicine Teachers, and Shamans in every culture – that good grounding is absolutely essential if you are to work safely with high levels of spiritual energy. It is only the Christian perception of the physical body, seeing it both as unspiritual and unconnected in any way with spiritual development, which has hidden from us this basic truth of the human condition.

The Essenes blended the energies of mind and heart and hand in a way that revealed the true extent of human potential. Grounded securely by regular physical activity they were able to soar upwards into spiritual heights undreamed of by their conventional neighbors.

13

The Essene Libraries

We knew that Qumran had a fine library and wanted to get Daniel's impressions of it.

Joanna: Were you familiar with the library in Qumran?
Daniel: Yes, I visited it many times. As I was working on a general history of the Essenes my researches took me there quite often. The library at Hebron was limited and any serious research would have to be done at Qumran. My longest stay was for a period of about six weeks. That was a sweet time in the peak of my years and the time flew by like six days. It was high summer when I was there and the flowers in the gardens were particularly beautiful and heavily scented that year. It was a good year for the gardens, and for me also. Usually my visits were shorter – perhaps a week or ten days. I would complete my current area of research and go home to Hebron to absorb the new material into my work.
Joanna: Is it a big library in Qumran?
Daniel: Yes, in a large building with a number of windows. There was good light for the scholars and light is

important for those who work with the scrolls, some of which are old and faded and discolored so that reading them is more demanding on the eyes. The scrolls were arranged on shelves, some wrapped to protect them, and some not. Many had handles, some quite old and ornate, but some did not.

Joanna: *Was this library all on one floor?*

Daniel: *No, there was an upper floor, but this was only part of a floor, open in the middle with railings so you could look down and see who is below. It was a fine library, but not so fine as the library in our community near Alexandria.*

Joanna: Did you ever visit that community?

Daniel: *Yes, but I only managed to do so twice during the whole of my lifetime. The journey was a long one and I had other duties which made it difficult to be away from Hebron for so long. The library at our community at Lake Mareotis near Alexandria was the finest I have seen – even bigger than Qumran. It was a large building with windows right along the south side. Outside there were awnings, so you could adjust the amount of light coming through each of the windows. And all along the south wall were tables for the scholars to sit at. It was a most practical place to study. The tables had deep half-rounded channels in them, so that the handles of the scroll were put down into these when one had unrolled it to the desired place. This was a simpler arrangement to that at Qumran and I preferred it.*

The other three sides of the building were occupied with shelving, right up to the ceiling. There were special ladders, with broad platforms instead of rungs, so you could stand comfortably at any height. These ladders had wheels upon them so they could be moved along the line of shelving. The shelves were divided off so that five or six scrolls could be stored in each compartment. All the compartments were labeled and numbered, and a central index told you where the scroll you wanted was to be found.

Unlike Qumran, all the scrolls here had good handles, even the most recent copies. There was much copying in our libraries so that all the three main libraries had most of what was really important, in case any library was destroyed, or accidentally damaged by fire.

Joanna: You mentioned three libraries – where is the third library?

Daniel: At Damascus. I only visited it once, but it was a wasted journey. They had little that I had not seen before, except some minor Persian and Arabic sources. Nor was the library there as well-organized and as well-run as those at Qumran, and Alexandria. Altogether my visit there, after a long and tiring journey, was a disappointment to me. My only consolation was that it showed how thorough my researches had already been, since so little new material turned up there.

Joanna: So were all the three libraries more or less identical in the books they held?

Daniel: The main texts to which we all referred were common to all three, but each library had some local sources as well. Each of the other communities also had a small library of its own, except for Mount Carmel which had a large library. But this was a teaching library and not a research and copying center, so I did not consider it to be a main Essene library as the other three were.

I also wanted to explore the source of all this knowledge, so I asked Daniel where all these scrolls came from.

Daniel: Some from the Kaloo, but most we found ourselves. Most of the large communities had one person who traveled constantly in search of new scrolls. We put much effort into this gathering of knowledge, for it was most important to us. The Kaloo stressed that much knowledge was circulating in the ancient world in one tradition or another. We respected insight and wisdom from whatever source it came. There were no traditions that we were not willing to learn from. We might not agree with all their conclusions, but at least we were prepared to give them a fair and open-minded hearing.

The Kaloo also told us that things would change. Men would become intolerant, more focused on their own tradition to the exclusion of all others, and that the danger in this was that old and valuable knowledge from other traditions would be willfully destroyed. It was part of our task to overcome this tendency by gathering as many scrolls of real value as we could. And we copied the most important of these, and made summaries of every scroll so that we knew where all the knowledge was stored.

Joanna: Tell me about these summaries. What were they like?

Daniel: When a new scroll came into any of our communities it was read through and a brief summary made of what it contained. Any sources referred to were listed at the end of the summary. This gave us clues as to what to look for in the future if any sources entirely new to us were given. We would hunt down promising texts wherever we could find them. Copies of the summaries were regularly sent to the main libraries, so that all our scholars knew what knowledge we had, and where it was stored. That would make it harder for the knowledge to be lost.

Joanna: It sounds as if the hunting down of ancient scrolls was quite a major thing for you.

Daniel: Yes, and some of our Brothers were only hunters. They would travel and track down interesting scrolls, but never have time to study them. As soon as they had delivered the latest precious haul of texts, they would be off again to hunt down some more! This was not my way. I was the patient scholar, like a spider sitting in the middle of the web, and trying to make sense of it all. Yet I think they must have had more interesting and colorful lives than mine. They would tell me of their travels, and the excitement of being on the trail of something really old and rare. But they would also speak of the difficulties and dangers, and that made me value the quiet life I had at Hebron.

Joanna: Still, you did travel a little, to Alexandria and Damascus at least, and often to Qumran.

Daniel: It is true, but for most of my life I went to sleep at night in my own bed, and was glad to do so. There were rewards, though, on my journeys. The meetings with like-minded people who cared about the knowledge as I did, yes, that was good. Sweet times I remember in the summer evening in the gardens of Qumran, exchanging stories and meeting with old friends. And because so many Essenes did travel, there were always old friends visiting Qumran from all over our lands, and the meetings then were sweet, yes. And I loved the great crystal in the Qumran library also. I always took time to spend with it, like visiting a friend. Yes, a wonderful crystal, full of such power it was a blessing to be near it.

Joanna: Did you ever think what might happen to these great libraries in the future?

Daniel: Yes, and I was anxious about the survival of all these precious things, all this knowledge. We were few, and the sons of darkness were many. We knew the value of these things, but there were many superstitious ones who despised all knowledge from outside the boundaries of our land, and would destroy these libraries if they could. All these wonderful truths, these most marvelous pearls of wisdom, were quite impossible for them because their minds were closed. And that makes me very sad.

14

A Lay Brother's Credo

By now we knew that Daniel could be full of surprises, but even so the next session took us into new areas that we were not prepared for.

Joanna: Did the Essenes share similar beliefs? Did they all have the same perception of God, for example?

Daniel: You must realize that the Kaloo taught us that there are many perceptions of the Divine and many paths to God. I have already talked of the four main strands which made up the Essene Way. These strands gave us a broad and universal understanding that went far beyond the bounds of any one religion. Those who decided to become priests followed a more intense and restricted way, focusing upon Yahweh, but the lay Brothers such as I were much more free in how we chose to pursue our spiritual path.

All Essenes shared a great reverence for angels, and especially for the Elohim, very high angelic beings who stand above the level of archangel. The Elohim we saw as filling their places by reason of merit and not through being created great. We saw them as rising upwards from lesser angels or from the equivalent of human beings, through great ages of cosmic development until they reached that high level.

Though there are many ways of perceiving God, I found the symbolism of Light most helpful. I saw human beings as Children of the Light, dwelling perhaps for a while in the shadow of darkness, but coming home at last into the Light which is their birthright and their destiny. For in the heart of every human being burns the Light of God's Presence, and so at the deepest level we are Light, and returning to Light is returning to our own fundamental nature. Even though a human being may have fallen into error, still the Essence of God within longs for the Light. And forgiveness and love are the ways in which Light expresses itself within our lives and teaches us how to grow ever closer to God.

God manifests as the Light which illumines our path, and as the Spirit within which makes our inner development possible. As we live in joy and harmony and love, we live in the nature of God, and the Light steadily expands within us. This expansion of the Light anchors us in the true nature of our being. It nourishes us and allows us to unfold our talents and abilities as Children of the Light. Walking in the Spirit and inspired by the Light, we become expressions of God upon Earth. As Spirit merges with matter in us, we complete our task here, and prepare to ascend to the spiritual realms.

This is some of the most remarkable material that Daniel gave us. It places the teachings of Jesus firmly within a framework of Essene belief. The emphasis upon love and forgiveness and the Spirit are all here. Even the parable of the Prodigal Son is echoed in the words. "The Essence of God within longs for the Light."

The section on the Elohim was also a key passage in helping us to see the Essenes as a whole. From this we realized that they saw the universe as one vast meritocracy. That may not seem so dramatic to us, but we live in very different and more democratic times. Having these beliefs it is not surprising that the Essenes set up their communities in such a tolerant and merit-oriented way. However, to do so would have brought them into conflict with the rigid hierarchical society of their day. The Essenes were remarkably consistent. Their lives and social structures flowed naturally from their beliefs.

This whole statement gave us the strange feeling that time was being transcended here, and that the Essenes were speaking to us directly in a way which has a remarkable relevance for our life here and now. This feeling was reinforced when I asked Daniel about the Brotherhood.

Joanna: Was the Essene Brotherhood in touch with other Orders or ancient Brotherhoods?

Daniel: *Of course. That is why Essenes could move safely from our land to distant places, for example up through all the Celtic lands to Britain. Whatever Order you belong to, at the highest level all Orders become one, as the sides of the pyramid merge in a single point.*

All sages are of one heart, knowing that all life is One, and that all human beings share the same origin as Children of the Light, and the same goal, to merge with that Light. We saw the Triumph of the Light as something that must come, perhaps not for many years, or even many centuries. But however long it takes, we saw the Triumph of the Light, the victory of God and of love and truth as sure and certain as the rising of the sun.

All flows from the Spirit and from the Light. We are Children of the Light, Children of God, and Light is our source, our goal, and our destiny. This view of things has become central to my life, and was arrived at through study, discussion, reflection and attunement over many years. When I saw that this had become so important for me I fashioned a form of words to reflect it:

> *I believe in the Universe around me and in the Presence within,*
> *I believe in the Power of the Spirit,*
> *I believe in the Triumph of the Light.*

This is what I believe in; this is where I stand.

Joanna: And do the Essenes as a whole believe in this?

Daniel: I can only speak for myself, as each one can only speak for themselves. We enforce no common belief, no orthodoxy, and each one is free to choose their own perception of the Divine. Indeed each one has the responsibility of finding their own pathway to God. The heart can help us, can guide us, but no conformity of belief can direct our footsteps to the Light. Yes, there are universal meeting points within the Essene tradition, the Heavenly Father and the Earthly Mother, and the over-arching Peace. That is the foundation, but what each one builds upon this foundation is an individual choice. I have made my choice. This is where I stand.

We had a definite sense here of reaching the bedrock of what Daniel believed in. Whilst Daniel was very fluid and flexible in the way he used his mind, there were clearly some fixed stars in his world view, and this statement laid them out before us clearly and firmly. Many things in Daniel's life might be negotiable, but not this. His normal openness and flexibility made this statement seem all the more remarkable, especially the repetition of the words, "This is where I stand". Based on the written evidence, many people have perceived the Essenes as a rigid, dogmatic Judaic sect. What emerges from Daniel's testimony here is a very different picture. Yes, there was a "foundation", a shared tradition to build on, but it still remained essentially an individual choice, at any rate for the lay Essenes like Daniel. That choice in Daniel's case had thrown up an interesting credo, but we were aware that this was his own personal credo, and not one that could be taken as applying to the Essenes as a whole.

But to return to the session, I had spotted what I thought was an inconsistency, and wanted to follow this up.

Joanna: You say that all life is One, but how do the Pharisees, the "sons of darkness" fit into this?

Daniel: I see all human beings as Children of the Light, sons and daughters of God. Some have chosen to move away from the Light, and become sons of darkness, but this is only for a moment or two in the eternity of God. When these sons of darkness turn again to the Light they will fulfill their destiny as Children of the Light, and love and peace will embrace them as surely as it embraces each and every one of us. God never turns away and rejects us, even if we choose to turn our faces from the Light. And when we return to the Light there *is great rejoicing amongst the angels.*

Daniel's statement here shows remarkable tolerance, and represents a very different view to that expressed by the priestly scribes who wrote the Dead Sea Scrolls.

This whole section was a surprise to us. We had assumed there would be a conformity of belief among the Essenes, and certainly there were "universal meeting points", as Daniel put it. But ultimately what they believed in was an individual choice, and that was quite unexpected. However it is important to bear in mind that Daniel's experience was as a lay Essene, and the Essene priests, dedicated intensely to Yahweh, were clearly much more restricted.

Part Five:

The Secret Core of Essene Life

We had made the breakthrough
into the time of Christ
and had met one of the Essenes,
the most mysterious and
secretive group in history.

Dolores Cannon,
Jesus and the Essenes

15

Secrecy and Security

From the very beginning we were aware of the Essenes' need for secrecy, and their continuous concern for the security of their communities. Although our contact with Daniel got progressively easier, especially when he entered the Interlife stage, there was no corresponding movement in the case of Joseph. This was frustrating in a way, because Daniel, despite his position as an elder, was clearly a minor player in the Essene drama when compared with Joseph. When I asked Daniel about Joseph's secretiveness, he replied that on Joseph's mind there were "many gates and many latches". Although Joseph was able to give us a good deal of information about a number of things, we never found the keys to all these latches during the period of the regression process.

Daniel in comparison was much more relaxed and open, especially in the Interlife, and he even reached a point where he could be quite light-hearted about the whole security issue:

Daniel: You know, when you went to another community, there were three questions you knew you must not ask. First, how many people lived there; second, how they defended their community; and third, where the other entrance was. (He chuckled). *Usually there was only one obvious way in to the community, but there was always one other hidden entrance, and sometimes several. These entrances would go into tunnels, or through caves, depending on the land. But they were always hidden, and were ways of escape in case of attack. We could go down these tunnels, or into caves connected to these tunnels, and fade into the night. So that even if they had sent a small army they would not find us. The Kaloo taught us that this was necessary, and our skill in making these escape routes saved many a life.*

Joanna: Did you have gatherings with your neighboring Essene communities?

Daniel: Yes, especially those who were in our group. The communities were grouped together in threes, and we would share within this group, and support the other communities if they ran into trouble. It meant that you always knew there was a safe home for your people even if your community was overrun and all the buildings destroyed. So depending on the size of the communities, these group gatherings could be quite large, and a time of joyful sharing and celebration.

Joanna: And you sent messengers around the communities to link you all up?

Daniel: Yes, we sent travelers from one community to another. They went very carefully and traveled at night some of the time. We got snippets of news that way, and from other Essenes who visited us, and from the spokesman for our community when he went to the greater council meetings. But despite all that we were always hungry for news.

Joanna: Well, I can imagine, because there was much rumor and anxiety.

Daniel: Yes, many rumors and difficult to get reliable information. We felt like a minority in our own country, surrounded by the great mass of people who were either actively hostile to us or indifferent to our fate.

Joanna: And because you were so secretive other people would spread rumors about you?

Daniel: Yes, many false rumors, sometimes caused by ignorance, but there were also people paid good money to do this. People were spreading terrible lies about the Essenes, saying that we did all sorts of vile things, worshiping idols and so on. Terrible things they said. They felt that if they could blacken our name then it would be easier to persecute us.

Joanna: And the Kaloo helped you to set up the defense of your communities?

Daniel: Yes, and we lived very secretly in our own places, and even the ways in which we guarded our communities were secret. The Kaloo had given us many abilities, many skills. The use of sound was highly developed by the Kaloo. We could produce not only outer sound but also inner sound which would make a stranger who walked near our communities just uneasy. It would reverberate inside him and he would wish to go away; he would not know exactly why. The sound would vibrate inside him. We would set up vibrations which were different from his own note, and that would make him most uncomfortable. He would feel discomfort and even fear, and would wish to go quickly from that place. He would feel that it was a bad place full of spirits, perhaps he would interpret it

121

in this way.

Joanna: Could you also manipulate energy to make people fall over?

Daniel: Yes, we could shift their center of balance from the lower part of the body. We could shift it about and move it higher so that they would become unsteady on their feet and topple over. We would shift the focus of their energy. The Kaloo were very skilled in energies. Energy was a special study of theirs, and they passed much down to us.

At last I was beginning to understand how the Essenes managed to survive so long despite determined attempts by the Pharisees to dislodge them. By siting their communities in remote places where there was no competition for the poorer land, by being very careful and secret in their lives, by constructing elaborate escape routes, and having subtle defensive skills, they could cling on and survive for a long time. The choice of such a harsh and inhospitable site as Qumran now made perfect sense to me. If this was to be their "Father House", the place in which they kept their most precious things, a remote and forbidding place would be ideal.

I also wanted to explore the downside of maintaining all this secrecy.

Joanna: What did you see as the problems of being so secret and vigilant?

Daniel: The constant burden of secrecy would sometimes seem almost unbearable. Even my old friend Joseph, who was careful and secretive by nature, found it difficult to live in this way. But there is another aspect which troubled me: we were so secretive that the generations to come will not find it easy to know what is in our hearts. This saddens me, for unless you know what is in our hearts, how can you understand us? That is why dialogues such as this are valued by the Brotherhood. In these and in other communications of this kind yet to emerge we can speak freely, knowing that you wish us well, and standing in future time present no hazard to our communities. The Brotherhood wishes that the truth about us be told. We are surrounded by a sea of indifference amongst much of the people, and by many vipers who would harm us. Our enemies have been assiduous in the spreading of lies about us, and it is good that in future time the truth about us should be known, so that all may see that we have worked for the Light.

Once again, the feeling here is that the Essene Brotherhood as a whole was trying to communicate with us, a feeling shared by Dolores Cannon when she was working on her book *Jesus and the Essenes.* The words "yet to emerge" suggest that some of this story remains to be told.

16

The Core Group

By this time I had become aware that many of the greater secrets were known to Joseph and not to Daniel. Whatever Daniel knew, he was willing to talk about freely and at some length after he had the approval of the Brotherhood. Joseph, however, was quite different. His replies were often guarded and usually short. He never opened up in the way that Daniel did.

At first I put this down to a difference in temperament, and it was only during a session with Daniel when he was older that I stumbled across the first clue which led me to the real reason. Daniel was talking about the work that the Essenes were doing to support the greater work of Jesus. He said that this support was organized by something that he called the Core Group. This group would send messengers to the Essene communities, and there were meetings from time to time between the core group and a number of Essene elders.

I asked Daniel who the members of this core group were. At first he would not answer. Even the existence of this group was highly secret, he said, adding that, *"Only a few elders in each community knew of it. You could live and work in an Essene community for the whole of your life and never hear anyone talk about the core group.*" It was only when he had the approval of the Essene Brotherhood to talk about the "inner Essene structure" that I was able to get more information on this.

Daniel: There was always a core group in the Essene Brotherhood, ever since the Kaloo first established the communities. During my lifetime the core group included my friend Joseph, Mary his sister, Joseph her husband, their son James, Mary Magdalene and John. After the death of Mary's husband, an elder from Qumran held the focus, to be replaced later by Thomas, who became a disciple.

The seventh person was someone Daniel referred to as "The Silent One". I asked him if this person had another name.

Daniel: No. Nor has he ever come to any of the meetings with the elders, so I never met him.

This makes it clear that we are not dealing with Roberta's "Silent One", but someone quite different.

Daniel: There is always a place for him whenever the full core group gather, so that they sit three and three, with a space between. Joseph told me that he can feel his energy there, as if he is present on other levels, but it seems that he is never there in person. I know he is a close friend of John, who sometimes speaks of him, but even then he talks only of what he is doing on the inner planes to support the work, and never about him as a person.

Comment by Stuart: It is possible to speculate on the identity of "The Silent One", and here his friendship with John gives us a clue. According to the esoteric tradition John later reincarnated as St. Francis, and later still as the Master Koot Hoomi. C.W. Leadbeater's book *The Masters and the Path,* makes it clear that the Master KH had worked closely in a number of lives with his friend the Master Morya. For that reason it would certainly seem possible that Master Morya might be "The Silent One".

The esoteric tradition also casts some light on the previous lives of John, who had lived in Greece as the sage Pythagoras. Few writers have recognized the major part played by Pythagorean ideas in the development of Essenism, honorable exceptions being Martin Larson in *The Essene Heritage,* Gordon Strachan in *Jesus the Master Builder,* and Martin Hengel in *Judaism and Hellenism.*

The whole composition of the core group is interesting. The first four were related by blood or marriage, and the next two were disciples of Jesus (as the chapter on Mary Magdalene makes clear). The obvious omission here is Peter, who came to lead the Christian Church in the West. However Peter was the natural leader of the more conventional disciples, and for that reason it is unlikely that he was an Essene. I wondered if Peter realized that he was excluded from the inner council of those working to support Jesus, and whether this contributed to his irritability —something that will surface in a later chapter. It can't have been easy for a non-Essene like Peter to deal with the clannish closeness of the Essene Brotherhood.

We knew that Daniel was close to Joseph, but wanted to find out how well he knew the other members of the core group.

Joanna: So you knew the core group quite well, apart from
   The Silent One?

Daniel: We met them from time to time, but I'm not sure you
   could say I knew them, apart from my friend Joseph.
   Taking the core group as a whole, I would say we
   didn't understand them. They were on a higher level
   than us. They were like teachers, and we knew that
   they had been told many secret things, and could only
   reveal a little to us.

It was at this point that I realized the big difference
between Daniel and Joseph. They were close friends, but
Daniel knew Joseph was more advanced, and was a keeper
of many secrets. That was why Joseph was – and remained
during his sessions with me – rather guarded, while Daniel
could be more open because his information was less secret.

Of course, it would have been better if the talkative one
had been Joseph, because he knew so much more, but we
were getting a rich harvest of material from Daniel, and for
that I continued to be grateful.

Thanks to Daniel's vital evidence on the "inner Essene
structure" we were now in a position to assess the complex
layers of secrecy upon which the Essene organization was
founded. Even the communities like Qumran were not the
heart of the Essene operation. That was the highly secret
work of the core group. As the ministry of Jesus moved to
a climax, the work of this group emerged as a key element
in the whole drama, but that will become clear as the story
unfolds. For the moment we were content with this extra
piece of the jigsaw which enabled us to see the Essene
Brotherhood for the first time as one integrated whole.

The Essene Order had a complex structure resembling a nest of Chinese boxes:

Element:	Main loyalty to:	Level of Secrecy:
Town Brothers	The Essene Order	Most open
Communities	The Essene Order	
Core Group	Essene Teacher of Righteousness	Most secret

With these three layers of secrecy the Essenes managed to keep their enemies at bay. Each layer protected the one within it. No wonder outsiders became confused about who the Essenes were and what they were trying to do. The complexity of this structure illustrates how inadequate the written record can be in trying to assess a closed and highly secretive Order like the Essenes.

Part Six:

Jesus

All the children of righteousness are ruled by the Prince of Light and walk in the ways of light...And as for the visitation of all who walk in this spirit, it shall be...eternal joy in life without end, a crown of glory and a garment of majesty in unending light.

The Community Rule, a text in
The Complete Dead Sea Scrolls in English
by Geza Vermes

17

Jesus as Student and Teacher

We had explored the background of the Essenes and their lives in some detail. It was now time to move closer to the central figure of Jesus. Here we are putting together material from several sessions, some with Daniel and some with Joseph.

Joanna: I would like to ask you some more about your friend Joseph. Some say he is Mary's brother, and others that he is her uncle.

Daniel: *He is Mary's brother.*

Joanna: Is he older than Mary?

Daniel: *Yes, I believe by about four years.*

Joanna: And Joseph and Mary are very close?

Daniel: *Yes. If you were able to study their star charts you would see that they have many connections from past lives. They come with an understanding which has developed during these lives. That is why they are able to communicate upon subtler levels.*

****

Joanna: Did you see Jesus when he was a baby?

Joseph: After the birth Joseph and Mary went straight to our Brothers in Egypt, near Alexandria. It was not for me to see the babe.

Joanna: Did Jesus seem to be a remarkable child?

Joseph: Yes. It must have been hard sometimes because we had such high hopes for him. I remember him as a small boy being quite upset because he had been reprimanded. He only needed a stern voice or just a shift in your energy and he would notice it. We had never seen a child like this one before, so aware, so sensitive.

Joanna: What is your strongest impression about Jesus?

Joseph: The thing that comes over most strongly is that he was much better balanced than we were. And also that he was more pure and clear and light – just very much more whole. He was exceptional because he was very quick at getting to the heart of things, but in a very quiet way. He used to sit and listen a lot, and give everyone a chance to speak, but when he came in he had it summed up very quickly. In just a few words he could bring it all together.

He had a great range in his character, and would change according to who he was with. If he was with women and children he would be very gentle, and also with anyone who was suffering and needed healing. But then if he was debating with the men he would be acute and quick and there would be a strength and an edge to him.

Sometimes it would seem that he looked right through you, and that could be challenging for some people, and make them feel uneasy. But basically he was so well balanced that it's difficult to sum him up.

****

Joanna: What do you remember of Jesus when he was still a student?

Daniel: There were so many things. We talked and debated when he came to our community. By that time he was already well advanced in his studies and we talked long into the night on many things, yes. Our hopes for our people, also for all people, because there was a new opportunity now. A moving forward was possible through the energies of love focused in the heart. And the difficulties of spreading this message so that people would understand it, how it might be spread, and how the message might be received, yes.

It was such a joy to listen to him, it was all so simple to him. Many like me found it still complicated (he chuckled), *but for him it was so simple. It was as if he had stepped out of his own focus into the Light of the Spirit, and from that focus all was simple, all things so clear. Ah, yes, many a learned teacher almost despaired after hearing him* (he chuckled once more), *wondering how he could ever reach that level. And yet we knew he was also helping us to make that step, out of complexity into simplicity, out of confusion and darkness into the Light. So that is what I remember. And his eyes looking at you, like great pools of love, understanding and forgiving all you may have done. All your weaknesses were somehow forgiven, as if he were your best friend who understood all about you. Ah, wonderful eyes, yes.*

133

Joanna: But to have someone looking at you who seemed to know all about you, that would be uncomfortable for some people, surely?

Daniel: *It did not worry most of us because his love was so strong. There was a great clarity, a searching in the eyes, but the love was strong and his manner so gentle. He had clear eyes, all-seeing eyes, but much love in them and he spoke with great gentleness: great strength and great gentleness. It is said that many ones who had been Essenes for many years and thought they knew what it was to be an Essene, when they encountered Jesus, only then did they begin to realize what it was like to be an Essene to your fingertips.* (He chuckled again).

So Jesus was the ultimate Essene, the ultimate pattern of Esseneness. He was the exemplar for all of us. And when we looked at him – his power, his gentleness, the sheer radiance of this being who was nearer to God than any of us had thought possible – we could see our destiny.

Joanna: Well, he always said that others could do all that he had done.

Daniel: *Yes, that is true. But we saw the extent of his achievement, and valued him because of it.*

18

Jesus in Britain

We were fascinated by the prospect of getting some information on the visit which Jesus was said to have made to England with Joseph. There are a number of legends concerning this, and they center around two areas, Glastonbury in Somerset and various sites in Cornwall. The Cornish legends also speak of a visit made by Joseph of Arimathea with Mary and Jesus as a baby to Marazion in Cornwall. Whilst there are no ancient documents supporting these legends, there is a strong and widespread oral tradition. Lionel Smithett Lewis writes about this in Chapter 4 of *St. Joseph of Arimathea at Glastonbury*. Geoffrey Ashe, in his *Mythology of the British Isles* summarizes the legends of Jesus coming to Britain, and in *Jesus the Master Builder* Gordon Strachan gives a map marking twenty English sites where legends show a link with Jesus.

When I began the session with Joseph, I wanted to establish a contrast, so I first asked him to describe the landscape in his own country.

Joseph: Some places quite cultivated and green, with a network of water channels, but much of the land was

harsh with little vegetation, very rocky with just a few
vineyards and olive groves. And some areas were just
desert, where almost nothing would grow.

Joanna: So when you came to Britain did you find that a big
contrast?

Joseph: Yes, much greenness and many thick woods. And
many settlements in clearings in the woods.

Joanna: So when you visited Avalon when you came to
Britain, that would have been when Jesus was quite
young, and it would have been part of his education in
a way?

Joseph: Yes, he would have been around 15 years old.

Joanna: So Mary presumably was at home with the other
children when you were traveling with Jesus?

Joseph: Yes, but she did come on some of the journeys when
the other children were older.

Joanna: And did you meet the Druids at Avalon?

Joseph: Yes, they regarded it as an important place. There
was a circle of Druid sites around that area, twelve in
number, and the high ground in Avalon was the central
point.

At this period much of the land in the central low-lying
part of Somerset would have been flooded, resulting in a
number of islands of which Avalon (the modern
Glastonbury) was one.

Joanna: So the Druids had some links with the Essenes?

Joseph: Yes, they also traced their history back to the
Kaloo, so there were meeting points, there was some
similarity. The priests among the Druids knew much,
and they recognized the Essenes as another branch of
a wider family.

Joanna: So you were generally well received by the Druids?

Joseph: They said that we had something to offer, that we were people of knowledge and power, as the Druids were, and that helped us. There was sometimes a lack of understanding and that led to minor trouble. We were strangers, after all, but we were able to share much with them. They had knowledge about things which we did not, and we were able to share in return. By this time I had made several visits to purchase tin from the mines in the western part of Britain, so I was beginning to be known in that area, and made friends there wherever I could.

The Druids are a special interest of ours, and we will return to them again later in this book. But we were also interested in any information which Joseph may have given Daniel regarding these journeys.

Joanna: Did Joseph tell you anything of the journeys he made with Jesus?

Daniel: He did take Jesus away to travel from time to time, but he usually told me about these journeys afterwards. Joseph traveled a good deal in his trading, and that was a good cloak for his other activities in connecting up with our Essene Brothers. He preferred going by sea, but some sections of his journeys were overland, and that could not be avoided.

Joanna: What did Joseph trade in?

Daniel: Tin mainly, but sometimes other metals too. He avoided the precious metals like gold and silver. He said it would make his work too dangerous as many would then try to rob him. He collected crystals also, but secretly, and this was known only to the Brothers.

137

Joanna: I have heard that when Jesus and Joseph were traveling they would sometimes pick up a stone from a beach, put energy into it, and leave it there for people to find. Do you know about this?

Daniel: *Yes, Joseph told me of this. Jesus would imprint the stone with Light. So Jesus would awaken the stone a little, put energy into it, and leave it upon the beach for someone to find. Joseph said to me that Jesus had left these little blessings upon many a beach, and that if you placed all these stones together they would have made quite a little hill* (he chuckled). *Those with the inner sight could see the Light in them, so maybe they went around picking up the stones. But there were so many that perhaps some stones lie there upon the beaches still.*

We found this last section most intriguing. Are there actually some stones upon our beaches in Britain that Jesus held in his hand?

19

Being With Jesus

We were beginning to put together a picture of how it felt to be with Jesus, and wanted to pursue this. We now introduce sessions with three friends who enter the story for the first time, Carol, Martha and Nicky. This gives us four contrasting perspectives in this chapter: Daniel, quite elaborate and wordy; Carol, few words but very deep emotions; and Martha and Nicky, somewhere between these – deep feeling but quite freely expressed at the verbal level. These were quite separate sessions with Daniel, Carol, Martha and Nicky.

We became aware that any contact with Jesus occurred at many levels. It often had a powerful emotional charge which made a deep impression and helped the person to release, transform and move on.

Joanna: What was it like to be in the presence of Jesus when he was at the height of his powers?
Daniel: Well, by that time we were a little in awe of him. It's hard to describe. When we first knew him he seemed special, yes, but he became more special and more intense and more self-contained, because he was

139

containing and focusing these vast forces. It wasn't that he was remote and unapproachable, but he just had this enormous power around him, this energy. It was a very gentle loving energy, but it was energy, and it marked him as someone very special. In some ways he was like a high priest. Even if you had known him when he was young, becoming a high priest sets him apart. He carries a lot of energy, a lot of responsibility, and an inner knowing.

But that didn't make him heavy. There was a lot of laughter around him. Being with him was really a very joyful experience. It was sunny − being with him was just like being in the sunshine of a perfect day. But there was great power present too: it was like being with a very jovial and happy high priest. He was very light, he smiled a lot, but he was still like a high priest.

He was not jovial all the time, of course. Sometimes he was quite serious. But most of the time he was sunny, and being near him lightened people's lives. They were lighter as they went along the road with him, everything seemed lighter and brighter. He brought out the best in people − he brought the sunshine into people's lives, and their hearts expanded and glowed.

When you were with him you felt warm and comfortable. You felt that everything was going to be all right. You felt you were going to get to the conclusion of your own spiritual path in your own time, and it would all be fine. You just had to put one foot in front of the other, smiling gently as you went.

He wasn't heavy and solemn. People around him were happy and singing − there was a lot of singing, a lot of joy. And it was very light, the whole thing. It

*was like a merry group of friends, but he was also the
high priest figure. That was there all the time, too.*
Joanna: Did you see much of Jesus' disciples?
*Daniel: Those who were called disciples we only saw from
time to time. For example, when we went with Jesus
from village to village, but mostly they kept themselves
to themselves. They were a mixed bunch* (he chuckled).
*Some like Judas rather intense and morose and not
popular, some more amiable and some quite earnest
and serious. Some had been friends since they were
young, and some were strangers till they met Jesus. He
seemed to collect them from everywhere, a wide range
of people.*
Joanna: Was this so that the message could get through to
the widest number of people?
*Daniel: Yes, they seemed to have talents in different areas,
and they came from different parts of the country. I
suppose so that they could go back and teach their own
people in their own way. When they were being taught
by Jesus they remained with him, and did not speak
much to others. But sometimes he would send them out
on errands to go to this village or that, to do this work
or that, so they did not remain around him all the time.
And then there were also many followers. At first only
a few, and then more and more because of the healing
and the teaching, as his name grew amongst the
people.*
Joanna: So there would be many stories about Jesus going
about healing and teaching?
*Daniel: Oh, yes. When any traveler came to our community
we would always ask if he had heard reports of the
work of Jesus, and they told us many wonderful things.*
Joanna: It must have taken Jesus years of work to become

such a wonderful healer.

Daniel: He raised his consciousness so much that he was able to resonate with the power of the Spirit, and be a clear channel for that energy through his complete being. He was like a completely open channel down which all this energy flowed.

Joanna: Who were the people that Jesus seemed closest to amongst his friends, and relatives, and disciples?

Daniel: John, I think, who was a member of the core group and a most advanced being, and Mary Magdalene. But he was close to his brother James and Mary his mother also.

Joanna: And when Mary's husband died, your friend Joseph became almost another father to him?

Daniel: Yes, that is true, and Joseph helped him to travel, not only by taking Jesus with him, but he had many trading contacts and could help in planning Jesus' traveling when it was not possible for Joseph to go too.

****

Our focus now shifts to the session with Carol.

Carol: We are near the sea. I've just joined Jesus. He has taken my hands. I think we're praying...spirals of energy... he has recognized me as a friend...we've been giving thanks...for everything, life...I feel total acceptance. He's seeing everything but it's totally accepted...we're just standing at night time discussing...looking at the stars and talking, discussing many things...prayer and giving thanks for everything, the Earth and everything.

It is difficult to convey in words the impact this session had on Carol, as she was so overcome that not many words came out. Her body and her expression said so much, and because the energy was so beautiful in the room I did not wish to spoil it for her by asking too many questions. It was more important that she experienced the loving energy of being with Jesus. So we sat in blissful silence for quite some time. I found it very moving being with people experiencing their connection with Jesus, and I feel it was a real privilege to be allowed to share this with them.

****

There was this same loving energy in Martha's session too. Here the tape was difficult to follow because she spoke so softly. We didn't think we would be able to transcribe it at all, but by persevering we did manage to recover this piece of dialogue:

Martha: When I think of Jesus I hear the words, "The answers are in your heart." When he was with us he made it seem so easy....

Joanna: But after the crucifixion everything changed and it became much more difficult?

Martha: Yes. They took Jesus' body away, and it looked as if he was dead. I felt I should have protected him and stopped it from happening... (Weeping).

Joanna: So many of us felt like that.

Martha: I thought he would disappear into Light because of all the other magical things he could do. And then I felt as if I had been tricked, that he wasn't who he seemed to be. If he could die, was he just a man?

Joanna: You had put your faith in this being...

143

Martha: And I didn't know who he was because of this final twist, and because it was so dark and awful.

Joanna: There was a lot of fear and confusion around you?

Martha: Yes, a lot of confusion. We had all been given this gift of speaking the truth which was very powerful, so that the Word would continue. And then it all went wrong. It was all so dark and horrible, and we became afraid to speak. There were so many who opposed us, who wanted us to forget. And then there was this frantic writing down to try to capture what he had said. But it was speaking from the heart which had life in it: when everything was written down, in one sense the Word died.

****

We now move on to the session with Nicky. The interesting thing about this session was that it happened spontaneously during a Starlight Centre meeting, and it was not the intent to regress anyone at that time! Nicky was just in a very relaxed state, lying on a sofa bed. Suddenly there was a shift in energy, and Nicky started talking about a past life. I was totally unprepared for this, but quickly realized what was happening and went with it. When she started talking about Jesus I asked her this question:

Joanna: Tell us about Jesus. What was it like to be in his presence?

Nicky: It's like being transported to a different realm...it's quite remarkable... infinitely powerful and the love as well. It makes one want to get to one's knees and weep, the energy is so beautiful. It feels like going home...and it was such a relief that he was there. We have known him right from the start, beyond time, beyond space. It goes so deep that we can only get a glimpse of the depth, the connection that we had with him, but he also reminds us of our pain and suffering and it's all right. It feels that in his presence one can release it.

His eyes are like bottomless pools, deeper than space...they have a million things in them. He has total empathy with each of us...I don't want to leave him...I feel he has opened my heart...the love which he holds for each person is just beyond us. He accepts us as we are, whether we have done right or wrong...there are no boundaries and limits.

We keep on having to remind ourselves of who we are...we are part of Jesus. He came to show humanity what our Divine nature was like, to show us a part of our Divinity, a part of ourselves we had forgotten over time.

Again there was this very high loving energy in the room and again a very profound impact. I could observe this in Nicky's whole being. I could see that the other people around her in the room were also profoundly affected, and they confirmed this to me afterwards.

Our friend Ashian Belsey, channeling the Master Morya, writes:

Compassion allows.
Love changes.

Throughout the researching and writing of this book we have found this to be true. Everyone who was touched by the loving energy of Jesus was changed by that experience. The accepting and forgiving energy of unconditional love lays the past to rest and opens the door to a future in which fears and limitations fall away from us.

Now we return to Daniel's account of his time with Jesus:

Joanna: Did Jesus take a group of followers with him and go from village to village? And did you sometimes join these groups?

Daniel: *Yes. I was older of course, and could not travel with them as much as I would have liked, having responsibilities as an elder in my community. But I made a point of going with them as often as I could. From the very beginning when the group began to gather around Jesus I knew this was something very special. And when I was there I felt so very much more alive than I usually did, so that made me determined to go with them whenever I could.*

There was no fixed route on these occasions, and we went where the need was at the time. Jesus would attune and would realize that someone was ill, and we would go there, or that it was time to teach in a certain village.

It was very light, the whole thing, it was just a lovely thing to do, wandering along the paths to these villages. There was no great hurry, we just wandered along, maybe singing a little, and laughing and talking, and everyone so happy to be around him.

Joanna: When he taught in the inner groups, with just small numbers of people, was that different?

Daniel: *Yes, that could be quite challenging. Then he would be probing our beliefs, and making sure we were opening up and ready to move on. In those meetings, often in one of the communities like Qumran, he would be pushing our boundaries and encouraging us to change. But the journeys to the villages were just wonderful. It was very pleasant – a kind of divine wandering* (he chuckled). *We just had a wonderful time.*

Joanna: As you went along, I suppose parables would be told.

Daniel: Yes, Jesus was weaving stories much of the time. You would be listening to these stories, always something in them to make you think. And sometimes people would come to meet you from the next village. Word would spread that he was in the area, and they would come. Sometimes they would bring food, and we would all sit by the wayside and eat. When people began to realize how special Jesus was, many ones would come sooner, so as to be longer in his presence.

By the time of this session, Daniel was quite old and was looking back on his life. I was aware that while doing this he was becoming quite emotional. He was breathing deeply, and there was a long pause before he continued. I noticed that tears were beginning to trickle down Stuart's cheeks. When Daniel began again his voice was hoarse and subdued.

Daniel: It was just such a beautiful experience going out and visiting those villages with Jesus. It was so light...I'd forgotten how light it was, how happy we all were....

147

20

Teaching and Healing

By now we were wondering if we could get a new perspective on the teachings of Jesus. As we knew that Daniel had spent some time going from village to village with Jesus, we asked him to recall any outstanding memories of this time.

Joanna: When Jesus was teaching, what was his central theme?

Daniel: The need to reconnect with the heart energy, the energy of unconditional love. He not only talked about this energy, but demonstrated it in his life and his being. He gathered and focused the love energy, and because his energy was so strong within him, others were able to feel it and express it in the heart. This great cosmic energy of unconditional love, focusing through Jesus — and through him being made available to all. It was quite different from love as most people saw it. For many people it depended very much upon the response they got from the loved one. To love the person in front of you, however they act, whether they smile at you or snarl at you — that was quite a new idea for them.

Jesus understood the nature of a human being better than any of us. He understood that all ones are the children of the Creator, and is it not natural to love the children of a loving Creator? He understood the nature of God because that nature is essentially love and is expressed as love, focused as love and demonstrated as love. He understood all these things, and brought them together in his teaching.

Joanna: Were there several levels of teaching?

Daniel: Yes. For the people there were simple stories. For the disciples and the more advanced followers, there were higher teachings, and these were more direct, less wrapped up in the clothing of stories.

Joanna: And did some people criticize Jesus for his teachings?

Daniel: Yes, and for his attitude to people. Jesus accepted everyone. Many criticized him for this, and said, "Look, he is taking anyone as a follower, even the greatest sinners." But Jesus accepted anyone who left their past behind and turned towards the Light. Jesus lived in the moment, and when someone came to him truly repenting of the past, then Jesus lifted him or her into the moment, and it was as if the past ceased to exist for them.

Joanna: Which is good because it gives people another chance.

Daniel: Yes, a new beginning. All ones felt that in his presence a new beginning was possible. That was his great power, because there was nothing judgmental about him. No matter how much people had complicated their lives, with his help it could now be most simple, a turning to the Light. That was part of his power with the people, I think. They knew he would not judge them as the Pharisees did, because he lived from moment to moment taking no thought for what a man had done in his past. You know, it was as if he was teaching us to live fully in the moment, and we realized that none of us were capable of that. We all came trailing our doubts and fears and prejudices. All these things stopped us from living in the moment. Somehow Jesus had stepped out of all the rubbish of time, he had stepped into the living moment as he stepped into the Light. And he was able to convey the magic, the openness, the wonder of this to those around him. (Here Daniel's voice was reduced to a whisper). *It was wonderful and moving to see the effect he had upon people's lives.*

During another session with both Daniel and Joseph, I asked Joseph what part of Jesus' teaching he most remembered.

Joseph: I preferred the simple stories...
Daniel: Ah yes, Jesus was a great teller of simple stories, was he not?
Joseph: And who do you think he learned some of these from, my friend? (They both laughed).
Daniel: Yes, some of those well-honed parables had an ancestry in our common memory.
Joseph: Indeed they did, because that was part of our journeys, we could learn from the everyday things.
Daniel: Yes, he could take just the thread of an idea and weave it into a most simple and yet most profound story, which seemed to contain its own illumination.

150

Yet it was so simple – leading on to subtler things, yes, but of itself so simple and complete. A child could value it for the simple story that it was, yet a sage could also cherish it for its wisdom.

I remember that when we traveled from village to village, sometimes we would rest upon our way. Jesus would take some of the wayside grasses and weave them together to make simple little cups. And I could see this was his method, weaving ideas together to make a container for truth, yes, and all the stronger and better for being simple.

I also asked Daniel if he could recall any dramatic healings by Jesus.

Daniel: Yes, I remember he healed a man who had been blind for many years. Jesus laid his hands upon him, and when he took his hands away, he told the man to open his eyes. And he did so, and he could see. And this man had a child, and he had never seen the face of his son, and now he was able to look upon the face of his own child. (He sighed). *It was a wonderful moment, and there was a wonderful feeling in that village. It was as if healing was taking place for all those who were there. Not only were the bodies healed, but also the doubt and fear and disbelief were healed as well.*

It was as if the whole pattern of the universe had been leading up to that point, and the lives of all the people present in that village had been leading to that, so that it was a big opportunity for all ones who were present. And many people had a rebirth in their hearts, so there was healing on many different levels.

Part Seven:

The Drama Unfolds

The mind does nothing but talk,

and ask questions,

and search for meanings.

The heart does not talk,

does not ask questions,

does not search for meanings.

It silently moves towards God

and surrenders itself to him.

Francis of Assisi

21

Essene Meeting
in the Cave

We now moved forward in time. It was towards the
end of Jesus' ministry, and the Essenes were meeting in a
large cave, which was to the north of Jerusalem. Here is
Daniel's account of this gathering:

Daniel: It is a big meeting in this cave, in a remote and hilly
place and it's at night. The cave and the ways leading
to it are well guarded, so we will not be surprised by
anyone. We are sitting in a circle, maybe about thirty
people. In front of us are lamps, so that we can see the
faces. The only other light is coming from the middle
of the circle, where there is a huge round crystal. It's
pale purple in color, and is glowing. There are people
here from all the communities, as well as the core
group.

This is a special place, a sacred space, and we've
been meditating here for some time before anyone
speaks. Members of the core group are talking about
Jesus and his next step forward. They either call it his
ritual death experience or sometimes simply his

process. So we're discussing the preparations that have to be made, the effort which has to be put in, and the possibility of succeeding. And it's a very special process he will be going through, focusing on the use of the love energies through the heart. This is a new energy, a cosmic energy which is being brought in and demonstrated so that others can see how to use it. It is capable of taking people through a process of spiritual transformation in a direct way which is quite different from the complex methods used in the past. Jesus is marking out a new path, a broad new road into the Light. It is not certain that he will be able to achieve this, but the members of the core group are optimistic. They seem to talk from much deeper knowledge than we possess. We all hope it will work, we understand that it will help human development if it succeeds, but it's not certain. There are doubts, and some of us have more doubts than others. We can see it in theory, it's being explained to us. We hope it will work, and will do what we can to assist, but it's not at all certain.

So the plan is being laid before us: Jesus will go forward and act out in public the climax of the mystery school teaching. He will go through a mock trial, be crucified, and bring all the energies together into a synthesis. He will need a massive amount of support to sustain him while all this is proceeding. I just wish we had the certainty of the core group. We will go forward with high hopes but also much anxiety.

I could feel Daniel's anxiety and tension at this point. Clearly it was a very tense time for many of the Essene elders.

Daniel: So, there's a lot of support needed now, a lot of focusing and building up of the energy in order to help in this process. We're using the energy lines connecting the communities. We have been gathering crystals for some time, and working on the sites, linking them together and activating them. This huge crystal here in the cave is one of the focal points in this energy system.

The plan has been put forward and we've discussed it and it's generally agreed. There will be group leaders who lead the meditation in their communities. The meditational energy will be generated and directed to Jesus at higher levels, so he will have both this higher energy and the energy through the system with the crystals. There are crystals in patterns to hold the energy, and the energy of each of the community sites leads into the central area. Triangles flowing into a central triangle to make a complete energy system.

This proved to be a most interesting and revealing session. Daniel's references to an energy system are fascinating, and we will return to this in the next chapter. What emerges most strongly here is the sense of this group of Essenes planning towards, and preparing for, the process at the time of the crucifixion. This is seen, not as a sudden and unexpected event which overtook Jesus, but as the climax of a drama which had been carefully planned and thoroughly prepared for. Daniel's comment on the mystery school was particularly revealing. It seems that the events of Jesus' ministry, trial and crucifixion were a very deliberate acting out of the mysteries upon the outer stage of the world.

22

The Energy System

In a later session we were able to follow up Daniel's reference to an energy system. No other accounts of Essene life which we had read referred to this, and we had the sense of getting something entirely new here.

Joanna: When you told us about the meeting in the cave you mentioned a complete energy system. Can you tell us more about this?

Daniel: *Yes. There was an inner and an outer energy system. The outer energy, generated by the Earth, focused and intensified by crystals, was directed along lines of force running across the surface of the land towards Jesus on the cross. This enabled the energy levels in his body to be maintained. The inner meditational energy was fed by the communities into subtle levels for directing to Jesus. Together these two sources provided a complete system of support. The inner energy sustained and nourished the higher aspects of his being, and particularly their link with the physical body. It was essential that this link was strongly maintained until his energy process was completed.*

Joanna: And the outer system using earth energies – what points form the central triangle in this?

Daniel: The central triangle was formed by Jerusalem, the main focus of this drama, Qumran and the cave.

Joanna: And the cave was to the north of Jerusalem?

Daniel: In a hilly area well to the north. It formed a roughly equal-sided triangle with Qumran and Jerusalem.

This was a vital clue for us. It would place the cave almost halfway between Jericho and the town of Silwad, just to the north of the modern road which connects these two places. It is even today a remote area, and we could see that it would have served the Essenes well as the secret location for an important meeting cave. (See Diagram 2).

Looking at the overall pattern it was now clear what Daniel meant by "triangles flowing into a central triangle".

When we were able to step back and look at the whole system as identified on the map, we were amazed at the distances involved. This energy system runs for over a hundred and twenty miles. To work with what we would now call leylines in the establishment of such a system must have been a major undertaking. We are not experts in earth energies, but we have friends who are, and they tell us that working with the energies in this way takes a lot of time and effort. How could the Essenes have possibly been able to think that far ahead? When I asked Daniel about that, this was his reply:

Daniel: The original plan came from the Kaloo, and our people started working with the earth energies in alignment with this plan as soon as the communities were set up.

159

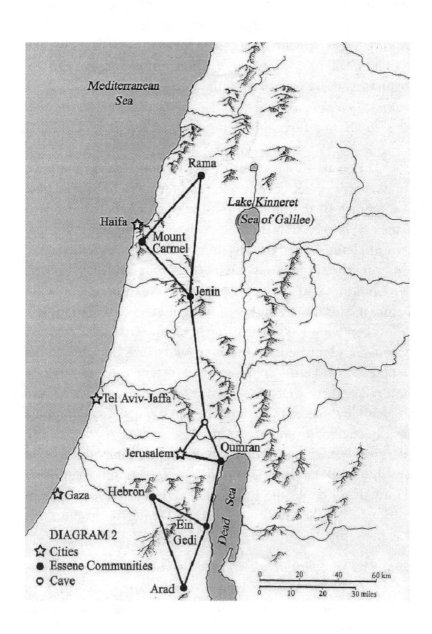

Mediterranean
Sea

Rama

Lake Kinneret
(Sea of Galilee)

Haifa ☆

Mount
Carmel

Jenin

☆ Tel Aviv-Jaffa

Jerusalem ☆   Qumran

☆ Gaza   Hebron

DIAGRAM 2
☆ Cities
● Essene Communities
○ Cave

Ein
Gedi

Dead Sea

Arad

| 0 | 20 | 40 | 60 km |
| 0 | 10 | 20 | 30 miles |

We found this quite extraordinary, and it led on to other questions. Why would the Kaloo have encouraged the Essenes to set up such an energy system, a system that would have involved years of work, the use of rare and expensive crystals, and the constant danger of discovery? Had they foreseen a specific need at the time of Jesus?

Joanna: This must have been a big undertaking for the communities to set up such a system.

Daniel: *Yes, it was a vast project. Most of the basics had been put in place before my lifetime. A lot of effort was put in over many years, strengthening the energy lines so that the power could be concentrated. The work had to be done very quietly and secretly so as not to attract the attention of the other Jews.*

Joanna: And how long did all this take?

Daniel: *The whole operation lasted about a hundred and fifty years. The Kaloo started assessing and developing the sites as soon as they arrived in the region. It was a priority for them to develop this energy system. The system was based on the natural energy lines that run along the surface of the Earth, with additions and strengthening of the pattern making a truer geometrical form through the use of crystals.*

Joanna: Did the Kaloo set up this system for general use, or were they making preparations for a specific event?

Daniel: *It was quite specific. They knew another Teacher of Righteousness would come, and this would be needed when his work reached a climax. The Kaloo were wise indeed; they knew what was to come and made preparations accordingly. We did not know the detail of their future knowledge, but they spoke of a great Teacher of Righteousness who was to come, and that all this work would support him. That was enough for us. We were content to carry out their plans. You do not question wise and holy beings who are far above you, and who can see the pattern of things more clearly than you can.*

So there it is. The Kaloo had foreseen the coming of Jesus and the need for a support system at the end of his ministry. And they worked with the Essenes over more than a century to put this support system in place.

We were interested to get some confirmation of work upon the energy system from another source, John reliving his life as Luke. I was asking him what his work was, and among other things he said this:

Luke: I was working with crystals, walking the earth energy lines to make them stronger, to build them up.
Joanna: You say "lines", where did these lines go to?
Luke: They connected the communities, and certain other power points. They worked together to form a complete system.

If the Kaloo came from Atlantis they would have had great skill in the use of crystals, and the construction of such an energy grid does not seem so remarkable in the light of Atlantean knowledge and technology. What was remarkable was the difficult conditions under which the Essenes had to work.

The inner triangle in the system was particularly interesting; it connected the large crystal in Qumran, the crystal in the cave, and Jesus on the cross. In a sense Jesus was the third crystal, the focal point for all these forces. A teacher who has been an inspiration to our whole group,

Anne Hughes, once said to us that "Christos is the crystal". We never understood this at the time, but that statement fits perfectly within this larger perspective.

23

The Crucifixion

We had been moving steadily through Daniel's story, and wondering when he would come to the events surrounding the crucifixion. He said he would be in his community near Hebron at this time, and we were curious to see what sort of impact it would have on him. We rejoined Daniel as the drama was moving towards its climax.

Daniel: We're meditating, bringing the power up, and Jesus is going through his process. We have a way of watching him without being there; it's called a clear-seeing chamber. Those with the inner sight can go into these chambers, and the clarity of their vision is strengthened through the use of crystals. There are five of us in this chamber. We're meditating, focusing power and observing Jesus.

The process is going through and it's getting heavy because there is quite a struggle going on. We are aware at this point of those who do not wish this project to succeed. They are trying to block the flow of energy so that the power cannot get through from the communities, and because of this it's becoming more difficult for us.

Although we saw the plan clearly we didn't see the strength of those who oppose us. They haven't succeeded yet, but it has diverted some power to hold them off. The Silent One is in the cave focusing much of this effort, but he's having a struggle.

It's getting very dark. Jesus is on the cross and going through his process. It does pass through my mind as I'm watching that maybe this attempt will fail. Those opposing it may overwhelm us and he may die before he completes the process, before the energies are resolved. He is gathering up and anchoring the energies. He is a great focus for energies, and if he cannot complete the cycle which the energies must go through, then the whole project will fail.

Time is doing very strange things. This whole process is not taking much Earth time, but because it's such a struggle it seems to be stretching out into eternity. (At this point Daniel's voice sounded very tired and strained). *I think we're starting to lose this battle...*

We've sent a mental signal to the core group that we've got to have more power. We're just holding it together and the meditators are getting exhausted...It's draining them...We can't keep this going for much longer... (Here Daniel's voice went down almost to a whisper). *We've got to have more power...*

The core group have sent out a request for help, to the angelic realm − I think to Archangel Michael...I don't know how long we can hold this group together. Some individuals are beginning to crack up with the intense concentration...it really is a battle...(Here Daniel gave a deep sigh).

Ah, the help has come, it's going to be all right.
Jesus has managed to complete the energy cycle. It's
all done...a great relief to us...(Daniel sighed again,
and there was a pause before he continued).

He's being taken down from the cross now, and we
are leaving the clear-seeing chamber. We had strict
orders from the core group to stop watching when
Jesus is taken down from the cross. Our part in the
process is over and we must report back to the rest of
the community who are meditating in another building.
They will be relieved to know that the work with the
energies was successfully completed.

Daniel sighed deeply and I could feel his tension
easing.

Daniel: It was a close thing. The whole plan could easily
have gone down. It was Archangel Michael who saved
the day. Without his help — who knows what might
have happened.
Joanna: I know you had to report to your community, but
afterwards, did you use your inner vision to see what
was happening to Jesus?
Daniel: (Emphatically) *No! It was forbidden! The core*
group strictly forbade it. Our part was done — we had
to continue with our lives and make no further
enquiries about Jesus.
Joanna: That seems hard.
Daniel: It was hard. He was like a brother to us — an elder
brother who had traveled farther than we along the
path. We listened to his wisdom and tried to live his
teachings, but now our ways are parting.
At this point Daniel sighed again. I realized that it

must have been a period of great strain for the whole Essene Brotherhood, and asked Daniel to comment on this.

Daniel: Many of our people gave all they had to give in supporting this process. It wasn't only Jesus who made a sacrifice. Two people died in the communities and some were very ill for years afterwards, reduced to a shell of what they had been. It was such a battle.

This was certainly a surprise to us, that others had paid with their lives and their health at that time. It underlined how much of a team effort the whole thing had been. By now we were beginning to see the events around the crucifixion in quite a new way. The drama was there, certainly, but it was a shared drama, and many had played a part in it. Paradoxically this does not diminish the achievement of Jesus. That he should have succeeded against formidable opposition remains a remarkable accomplishment.

I was also able to witness Joseph's perspective on the crucifixion in a separate session with him. It is impossible to convey the depth of emotion felt by Joseph, but I give here an excerpt from that session:

Joseph: Mary is here beside me, and I have my arm around her. Many years ago I was asked to support my little sister. I did not understand what that would mean then, but now I know. Mary needs someone to support and understand and protect her, and who better than her brother? (Speaking slowly as if in distress). *It is very hard today* (here he gave a deep sigh) *seeing Jesus on the cross. We had prepared for this. We knew much of it in advance, but however much you know, nothing* (he sighed again) *nothing prepares you for the reality of it...*(Joseph sighed once more) *...He was like a son to me...*(there was a long pause) *I find it hard to talk of these things....*

During a later session Joseph and Daniel were in dialogue together and were talking of the events following the crucifixion.

Joseph: I did not see you again, my old friend, to tell you of these things. Events moved very quickly then, and I had to leave in haste...I had to leave Mary...(here Joseph's voice sank to a whisper)*...and this created a great sadness in my heart...but it had to be thus.* (Joseph drew a deep breath and shed silent tears before continuing). *We had done our work in that place and there were many partings.*

Luke and Roberta had also been present during the crucifixion. In describing this, Roberta said, *"We both helped to hold the love energy at that time. Neither of us could afford to get emotional or we could not have held the energy, and that would have made Jesus' work harder."*

So all the Essenes in our story were helping at this time, but in different ways. Daniel was focusing the energy in his community, Luke and Roberta were holding the love energy on the hill, and Joseph was comforting and supporting Mary. Once again, the impression is of a team effort. We have seen the work of some members of the team, but there were many more, and some had been working for generations to prepare for this time.

24

The Empty Tomb

In the Interlife sessions with Daniel we were able to get more information on the events surrounding the crucifixion. I began by asking Daniel if he had investigated the drama around the crucifixion after his own death.

Daniel: Of course! The first question I asked when I woke up in the Interlife was, "What happened to Jesus?" I remember they laughed, the ones assigned to help me. They said, "All the Essenes are asking us this! Be patient, you will know soon enough." And indeed through the Angelic Record I was able to review it all.

After Jesus was taken down from the cross it was clear that he was far out of his body, for he did not move at all. I saw him being placed in the tomb, and the great stone being rolled across the entrance. Then I saw the Light around Jesus increase greatly. One part of that Light rose and ascended into the heavens, but the other part continued to focus around the body.

Then I learned how well the core group had prepared for it all. His tomb wasn't really a tomb at all, but a

169

healing chamber. If it was widely known that he had survived, there would have been many out looking for him, and not with good intent. So what appeared to be a tomb was a chamber into which healers could enter to do their healing.

Joanna: But surely the entrance to the tomb was sealed with a large stone and there were soldiers guarding it. How could anyone have got into the tomb to do the healing?

Daniel: (with a chuckle) *More easily than you might think! The Essenes had constructed a tunnel leading from the back of the tomb and running some distance underground to Joseph's house which was nearby. It was cut through the rock for a little way and then sloped down into the earth. One could walk along this tunnel, not at full height but stooping a little. It went through the earth, and then led up into a space behind the tomb. The door into the tomb was cleverly made of thick wood, but the outer side of it, which would be visible to anyone standing inside the tomb, was treated so that it looked like rock.*

The door fitted into slots so that as you went down the tunnel towards the tomb the door had to be lifted up in these slots, and then it could be pulled out and laid on one side. You could then crawl through a hole into the tomb itself. So even if someone stood inside the tomb with the door in place, they would see only rock.

The door and the tunnel were skillfully done, but remember that much time was available to prepare the tomb. We knew the Teacher would come, and would go through a ritual death experience, so the need for the tomb to act as a healing chamber was clear from the beginning. Under the direction of the Kaloo and the core group our people simply worked towards that need. It was a secret operation, of course. All the work had to be done most secretly, and very few even of the Essene Brotherhood knew about it. Certainly whilst I was living I heard no whisper of it. It must have been the most secret project in the whole of our land.

So *that's* how it was done! Everyone was watching the sealed entrance with the stone, and there was simply another way in. This underlines the big advantage the Essenes had over the Pharisees. They had the bigger picture and thought in terms of decades, while the Pharisees were just reacting to events and thought on a day-to-day basis. I don't expect it would ever have occurred to them that the Essenes might have painstakingly – and most secretly – dug a tunnel out of rock and earth, even if the operation had taken years to accomplish. With the secret tunnel in place, there would have been little difficulty in bringing in healers from Joseph's house nearby. But here we must return to Daniel's account:

Daniel: After the Light had hovered around the body for some time I could see he was breathing more deeply, but even so it was clear that he would need a lot of reviving. Although he had been far out of body, the shock of the crucifixion would have been immense. Jesus had trained himself for years in body and mind to withstand this massive shock, but we should not underestimate the impact upon him.

Luke and Clare, the sister of Jesus, led the healing team. These were the most powerful healers in all the Essene Brotherhood, and they worked day and night upon him. The great stone at the entrance to the tomb was designed to shut out every ray of light from outside, but it also made it impossible for any outside witness to see the light of lamps inside the tomb. And the great bulk of the stone also muffled any sound from within.

I was shown what happened during this healing process and I can describe it to you. I see the healers anoint Jesus in healing ointments, and there are huge crystals all around him. So he's being revived, it's taking some time to do, because he's far out of body, but the healers are confident that they can bring him back. And when he comes back into the body again he comes slowly, like one who has drifted off into a faraway place. And he comes reluctantly, because the pain from the wounds, even with all that healing, is still intense, and he gasps with the pain as he reenters the body. And then slowly he opens his eyes and sees Clare smiling down at him, and tears of joy are running down her face.

In another session I had the chance to ask Joseph about the difficulties of getting Jesus out of the tomb.

Joseph: After we revived Jesus he was not able to walk, so we used a simple stretcher and slid him down into the tunnel, and then along, and then lifted him when we reached my house. My house was close by, but it was still a difficult and anxious thing to accomplish. (He gave a deep sigh). *I feel the weight of the responsibility, all the secrecy and preparation. Only very few members of the Essene Brotherhood knew the extent of our plans, and the existence of the tunnel was revealed only to those directly involved. Even Mary*

*did not know of the tunnel while it was being made.
I told her just before the meeting in the cave, for the
fewer who knew the safer it was.*

How difficult it must have been to move Jesus after he
had been revived, and how big a burden it must have seemed
for Joseph to keep this secret from his beloved sister.

But what happened to this tunnel afterwards? Wouldn't
it have been discovered eventually?

Joanna: Surely the Pharisees would examine the tomb after
the body of Jesus disappeared. However good the door
was at the back of it, wouldn't they have found it
sooner or later?

*Daniel: Yes, and Joseph knew this. In the turmoil of that
time he had to act quickly. A prominent Essene at
Qumran had just died and he was laid to rest in the
tomb in some haste. The stone was rolled back again
to seal the entrance and then the work began in
earnest. A stable was hurriedly built on Joseph's land
at the back of the tomb, right over where they knew the
tunnel ran. Using the stable as a cover they broke
through into the tunnel and filled it up with earth at the
tomb end, removing all trace of that carefully crafted
door. By this time the Pharisees were demanding to
see inside the tomb, but that had to be agreed by the
Sanhedrin because the Essenes, led by Joseph, cried
outrage and desecration of a grave.*

The Sanhedrin was the highest tribunal of the Jews, the
supreme Jewish court, and it met regularly in Jerusalem.
This council of elders had wide powers, even under the
Romans, and its functions were both administrative and

judicial. It was also a place of religious judgment, with high priests (past and present) playing leading roles, and the current high priest presiding.

Daniel: By the time the Pharisees finally got authorization to open and inspect the tomb, the work had been completed and nothing suspicious could be found. As usual, the Brotherhood had covered its tracks efficiently, and by then Jesus had been taken to Qumran and thence from one safe house to another north to Damascus.

After he was safely out of our land the Brothers started to move our most precious things along that northward route, taking the most valuable scrolls out of harm's way. We knew that it was only a question of time before Qumran was destroyed, but our main task had been completed by then. When the outer work of the Teacher of Righteousness is finished, the whole structure around him can be dismantled.

Joseph's interventions to obtain the body of Jesus, and later to keep the tomb closed, cost him dearly. These were the first times he had spoken publicly for any Essene, as up to then all had been done quietly behind the scenes. From that point on, people began asking where Joseph's real loyalty lay. When the Pharisees found nothing amiss in the tomb their full fury turned upon Joseph, and he realized that he would very soon have to leave. If all traces of Jesus had eluded them, at least they had the living Joseph to vent their rage upon. From that time all the weight of their investigations centered upon Joseph and his connections with the Essenes.

The whole account of making the tunnel, reviving Jesus

and taking him covertly out of the country reads like some daring commando operation. This is an aspect of the Essene Brotherhood which has not been recognized so far, and it underlines the disciplined and dedicated nature of the team surrounding Jesus. Making this tunnel would not have seemed such a major operation for Essenes who were used to carving substantial water tunnels out of rock like those that have been found at Qumran.

By now we were getting a much more complete picture of this vital period, but there was another aspect of the drama that I wanted to check out. In *Jesus and the Essenes* Suddi says that the body of Jesus went through an accelerated process during which it crumbled rapidly into dust. This is not the only theory about Jesus after the crucifixion. In *The Essene Heritage* Martin Larson lists the eight main theories concerning the survival or death of Jesus and what happened to the body. Rudolf Steiner gives a ninth theory in his book *The Fifth Gospel.* In the light of all this controversy we thought it was important to give Daniel the opportunity to comment.

Joanna: It was said by some Essenes that the body of Jesus crumbled quickly into dust and that was why no body was found in the tomb. Could you comment on this please?

Daniel: Yes. Of course the news that the tomb was empty spread rapidly. There was so much confusion at that time that frankly I did not know what to believe. But when I talked to Joseph in the Interlife after his death the truth finally came out. He told me that this vanishing into dust was a rumor which the core group had spread in order to protect Jesus. To say that his body had crumbled into dust, helped by the angels, was

175

a most useful story. It explained why the tomb was empty, and also discouraged anyone from looking for the body. The core group did not want anyone looking for Jesus, alive or dead, and his security had to be considered.

Comment by Stuart: When Daniel says "the tomb was empty", he is of course referring to the time after Jesus had left the tomb, and before the Essene from Qumran was laid to rest there.

Part Eight:

New Perspectives

Pistis Sophia shows how the Magdalene – together with other women, such as the disciple Salome – constantly step forward to answer Jesus' questions with enormous enthusiasm, intelligence and not a little one-upmanship. This does not go down too well with the men.

Lynn Picknett,
Mary Magdalene: Christianity's Hidden Goddess

25

Mary Magdalene

We had noticed that Mary Magdalene was referred to as a member of the core group, and I was able to ask Daniel more about her.

Joanna: Was Mary Magdalene really a member of the core group?
Daniel: (Indignantly) *Of course she was! Why should she not be? Mary was a high being, an advanced being, but she was much misunderstood. Her difficulty was that she had gained much experience and training in Egypt. She had been a priestess of Isis and that was a problem for some of the more narrow-minded ones who gathered themselves around Jesus. Indeed that would have damned her in the eyes of most conventional Jews. For us it was not an issue — we had great respect for the Isis tradition in Egypt. And for most of the disciples it was not a problem, although one or two had reservations about her, and it caused ripples in the larger group around Jesus.*
It is important to understand that not all the disciples

were Essenes. That was deliberate, so that it would not be seen just as an Essene movement, but as something much broader, and so enable us to talk to all the people. But the problem was that not all the disciples had our breadth of vision, or our tolerance.

Joanna: So it was really a question of tolerance?

Daniel: Yes, many men could be tolerant of meek and mild women, but being tolerant of a powerful woman such as Mary Magdalene is another story.

Joanna: And did this cause trouble among some of the men following Jesus?

Daniel: Oh yes. Jesus and Mary Magdalene would have many deep and profound conversations, and this made some of the disciples feel uncomfortable, especially those who could not keep up with what was being said. Some of the disciples were quite traditional in their ways, and were not eager to see women have this kind of power. Mary was a person of real inner power and authority and I think that frightened some of the disciples. We Essenes realized that she had worked up to being where she was over many lives, some as a man, some as a woman. For that reason it did not concern us, but not everyone in the group around Jesus could see the bigger picture.

Joanna: Do you remember any moment of crisis between Mary and the disciples?

Daniel: Yes. I heard that after the crucifixion there was a very stormy discussion. James announced something that only the core group had known up to that point – that Mary Magdalene was to be the keeper of the inner mysteries for this New Way, the guardian of the highest wisdom. This caused much resentment and confusion amongst the disciples, especially those who were not

Essenes. It came as a shock to them that Jesus should have communicated much inner teaching to a woman. I think their pride was hurt by that idea and a group led by Peter tried to dismiss it. Tempers rose and hard words were said.

This underlines how paternalistic the Jewish society of the time was. It was simply assumed that the most important information and the deepest wisdom would be held by men. The idea that the highest wisdom could be entrusted to a woman would have seemed like an attack upon their authority.

We were interested to find confirmation of Daniel's account in *The Nag Hammadi Library in English*. *The Gospel of Mary* describes how, after the crucifixion, Mary Magdalene encouraged the disciples by telling them what Jesus had told her secretly, until interrupted by an angry Peter, who asked if Jesus had really spoken with Mary Magdalene without their knowledge. It was only after an intervention by Matthew that he calmed down.

The Nag Hammadi Library consists of 13 Gnostic texts discovered in 1945 near the town of Nag (or Naj) Hammadi on the west bank of the Nile north of Luxor. These texts are fourth century copies of second or third century Gnostic scriptures and commentaries.

But to return to the session with Daniel:

Joanna: Was the argument you mentioned resolved?
Daniel: Yes, I was told tempers calmed after a while, but ot all were reassured. I think this was the first real split amongst the disciples, and from that point on the two groups, the traditional group around Peter, and the other group around Mary, James and Thomas, started

to move apart. John somehow managed to keep the respect of both groups, but he was the only one to do so. He became the mediator and peacemaker between the two groups, but in the end their differences were too profound to be bridged, and they went their separate ways.

Joanna: So how would you sum up Mary Magdalene?

Daniel: Mary was a person of great virtue and authority, gained through many lives. She was like a priestess, a person of great intensity. We Essenes recognized her power and her lineage. We recognized what she had achieved. Not all ones did so. Some were very ready to dismiss her, especially when they heard of her connections with Egypt.

Joanna: Were there other female disciples of Jesus apart from Mary Magdalene?

Daniel: Yes, Mary his mother was a disciple, as were Martha and Salome. And there were others such as Clare, the sister of Jesus, who would have spent more time with him as disciples if their other duties had allowed this.

Joanna: I'm afraid that all these women disciples have been written out of the accounts of Jesus' life that have come down to us.

Daniel: That does not surprise me. Much resentment was stirred up against them by the more conventional male followers of Jesus. I could see Jesus working to restore the balance within the disciples in favor of feminine wisdom, but he had a difficult task.

The reference to Clare also intrigued me. She too has been written out of the Bible story, and I wanted to know more about her.

Joanna: Tell me about Clare. Did you see her many times during your life?

Daniel: Only a few times. She lived in another community, but we would meet when she was traveling with Joseph, or sometimes when she traveled with Jesus as he went from village to village. I remember she had intense eyes which flashed when anything annoyed her. She was already a renowned healer when she was only 16 or 17. Jesus had a strong link with her, and they could work together in healing without the need for speech, as they were in such harmony one with the other.

Clare had a perfect balance between joy and seriousness, between playfulness and a sense of the sacred. She could tell stories and parables almost as well as Jesus, and the depth of her wisdom and compassion was very moving. I have watched Clare and Mary Magdalene talk to a group of people, and together they were like two stars, perfect and bright in the heavens.

We were fascinated by Daniel's recollection of Clare, and we realize that Clare's perspective on these events would help to redress the imbalance in the accounts of that time. In most Christian texts the events around Jesus have been reported from a male perspective, ignoring the existence of women disciples. This contrasts with Gnostic sources which make it quite clear that Mary Magdalene held a leading position among the disciples of Jesus. Perhaps it is time that justice was done and the contribution made by the female disciples was acknowledged.

26

Jesus and Mary Magdalene

I still had the feeling that there was more to the relationship of Jesus and Mary Magdalene than had emerged so far, and in a later session I returned to this subject.

Joanna: So Mary Magdalene's relationship to Jesus was a very close one, something that went beyond his relationship to any of the other disciples?

Daniel: Yes, that is true. Mary understood the Kingdom of Heaven better than any of the other disciples – far better in fact, for the only one who remotely approached her in understanding was John. He knew how advanced Mary Magdalene was, and was glad to have her counsel. The more conventional disciples, however, were too proud to ask Mary for advice.

Because Mary's heart was closer to the Kingdom of Heaven than any other disciple, she was inevitably closer also to Jesus. Although Jesus was far beyond any of us, yet I saw that Mary Magdalene was more his equal than we were. Of course, both the masculine and feminine energies are aspects of the greater Divine energies, and as Essenes we knew the symbolism of the Father and the Mother very well. Yet I could sense that there was some even deeper mystery in their relationship, a mystery that went beyond my understanding. When they were together within one of the inner groups there were moments when great energies seemed to focus through them, giving even the simplest movement a special power and grace. I find it difficult to describe this effect, for it was so subtle. I can only say it was like watching the Mysteries unfold like a flower opening, or the performance of some ancient and sacred dance.

Joanna: And this only happened in the inner groups?

Daniel: Yes, the groups when only the disciples and some Essenes were present. Those were special times and I treasured them. I watched Jesus and Mary Magdalene closely at these times, for they seemed so much at the center of things, and the more I saw them together the more I marveled at this deep mystery.

Comment by Stuart: The authors Timothy Freke and Peter Gandy may be able to cast some light upon this mystery. In their book, *Jesus and the Goddess,* they speak of Sophia, the spirit of wisdom, becoming lost in the world through the process of incarnating upon Earth. In this perception, Mary Magdalene symbolizes the fallen Sophia, lost in ignorance, being awakened and redeemed by consciousness, symbolized by Jesus. Sophia can also represent the seed of the Spirit, the individual soul forgetting its own true nature, as it experiences the chaos and confusion of the world. Seen in this context, the relationship of Jesus and Mary Magdalene is revealed as an allegory of consciousness awakening the sleeping soul, a profound myth of archetypal power. If the relationship of Jesus and Mary Magdalene can symbolize *all of this,* it is little wonder that Daniel could sense a "deep mystery" within it.

But to return to the session with Daniel. There was one strand of information which had intrigued me, and which I wanted to follow up.

Joanna: So Mary Magdalene and John were good friends?

Daniel: Yes, they were very close, and these were the two most beloved of the disciples. Of course Jesus loved them all, but Mary and John were so closely in accord with him, in such deep harmony with him, that he could not help loving them a little more than all the rest.

Joanna: And this close accord with Jesus helped Mary rise in consciousness?

Daniel: Of course. Through her link with Jesus, Mary was able to ascend through many levels of consciousness into a state of being which some of the disciples could see was far beyond their own position, and which they envied greatly. This envy was the cause of a good deal of resentment.

Joanna: And this envy and resentment was not directed so much at John?

Daniel: John was so gentle and amiable a person, so full of tolerance and love for all of us, that it would be difficult for anyone to dislike him for long. And being a man, I suppose that protected him a little, whereas Mary was an easier target for that envy.

Joanna: And Mary taught the disciples, or at least those disciples who would listen to her?

Daniel: Yes, especially when Jesus was away, for he often took time on his own to commune with the Spirit in quiet places. Mary was in truth the supreme disciple, who became the teacher of teachers, for she understood the path to the Light so well. She came into her own after the crucifixion, when many of the followers of Jesus turned to her. Some were too proud or stubborn to listen to Mary, but I think that was their loss.

Comment by Stuart: Curiously enough, the assertion that Mary Magdalene was "the teacher of teachers" is not denied by the Roman Catholic Church. Within Catholic tradition she is accorded the title of "apostola apostolorum", which means "the apostle to the apostles".

Clearly the relationship of Mary Magdalene and Jesus is much more esoteric and profound than conventional accounts would suggest. There are other implications here, too. So far we have thought of John as "the Beloved Disciple". Perhaps this honor also belongs to Mary. And perhaps it is time to reassess the significance of Mary Magdalene and begin to see her within a larger context. We would not have to look too far for evidence to support Mary's unique position among the disciples. Gnostic sources like *Pistis Sophia* confirm that Mary's heart was focused on the Kingdom of Heaven to a greater degree than any of the other disciples. In this text she is presented as the most advanced of Jesus' pupils, and the one who plays the greatest part in the whole dialogue. The picture that emerges from this and other Gnostic sources is that of someone who was simply more open to Jesus' teaching than anyone else in the group around him at that time.

27

Time and Timelessness

I have never really understood what Grace is, and so I asked Daniel to tell me something about this.

Daniel: Grace is a gift of love and healing from the highest level. God going the extra mile to meet us upon the road of life. We considered that we were living in a time of Grace, and we felt that this Grace centered around Jesus. He was the bringer of our Grace because many cosmic energies focused around him, and made possible breakthroughs in consciousness, and a transformation in the lives of those who came into his presence.

Some ones, who had sight upon very high levels, told me that when they looked at Jesus they did not see only his aura, they saw this vast vortex of cosmic energy whirling around him. They said it was like the layers of an onion, an infinite number of transparent layers of energy moving out and out into the universe. So that he was the center of all things, the center not only of our drama but the whole drama of the planet. He was the center of all things, and forces were gathered around him that made many things possible. Others who were attuned to the higher reaches of the angelic realm said that around Jesus they sensed the presence of very high angels.

He was the bringer of Grace – who else could be a focus for all these energies? And because all these energies were focused together we could move through our experience faster. It quickened everything. You could not be anywhere near him and not move more quickly along your path.

Joanna: Tell me more about this vortex of energy surrounding Jesus.

Daniel: We were aware that a whole vortex of cosmic energy revolved around Jesus, and that anyone who encountered him stepped into that vortex. That was really the miracle for us. Not that he did this or that remarkable healing, but that his whole being was a focus of cosmic energy, and thus he could bring profound changes into the lives of all those he met who could accept these energies.

As his work flowered he became more a timeless being, talking about timeless things which would be relevant in any age. Time did not touch him, he escaped from time and that was part of his work and part of his gift. But we knew that in the end time might dilute and distort the message he came to bring. Once the Teacher is no longer physically present, the Teaching may become changed and weakened. What needs to go forward is the essential message that Jesus was trying to convey: unconditional love working through the heart, and the surrendering of the will to the Divine Presence within.

The more one surrenders one's will to the Divine Presence, the more one merges with that Presence which is within every human being, the more the path opens and the way becomes clear and straight. Then one can go forward and rise in consciousness and ascend into new frequencies of being. All of this was what Jesus was trying to teach his disciples and the groups around him. He was trying to teach this but many did not want to hear this message, and would much rather have rigid structures. The inner truth is of the Spirit and lives, and anything which is of the letter has its day, flowers and is gone.

Remember always that Jesus lived in a difficult and troubled time. Many people were frightened, and in their fear they clung to the comforting thought of a strong Father who would protect them. They preferred a strong external perception of Deity, a strong Father rather than the Divine Presence within. They saw the within as weak, and the external forces as strong and threatening. Jesus came to show them how strong the Divine Presence could be. How it could burn like a great Light within him and illumine the lives of all those around him, but many in their fear were not able to see this.

He was offering them a chance to step out of the child state and become fully adult in the spiritual sense, but this step was too much for them. They wished to be the powerless children of a loving Father for a little while longer. You know, he never blamed them for that. He used to say that we should have faith in the ability of every human being to awaken at exactly the right time, like a flower which opens in its due season. If we choose to awaken and become spiritually adult we can become creators with God, but many were not ready for that. They wished to slumber a little longer, to be the passive children of creation, walking hand in hand with the Father but unwilling to share in Divine knowledge and Divine power.

Joanna: And the vortex of energy around Jesus helped people to awaken at the right time?

Daniel: Yes. Because of all the vortex of power around Jesus he was able to pull people out of an obsession with the past and into the moment. When they were in his presence, the past disappeared. They realized that nothing was important but the moment, and that they were free to act within that moment.

This was one of the gifts Jesus brought for many ones, the ability to focus and act in the present in a way they had never experienced before he came. If you can forgive completely the past disappears for you. If you forgive completely you don't need to worry about the future either, you can function as fully aware beings, fully conscious beings, working and moving in the moment and focusing the energies of the Divine Presence.

Nothing else is important, nothing else will exist for you. That is why Jesus excited so many people, they could feel themselves being pulled out of time and into timelessness, out of the past into the everlasting present which is the only place in which you have power. The past and the future, if you are entangled with guilt or with worries and anxieties, rob you of your power. Only the present gives you power, and forgiveness is the key to ensuring you stay within that focus, expanding your awareness and living fully within the moment. This is living as God intended. This is joy,

191

this is freedom – and this is what Jesus taught. This is the most wonderful gift which he gave to us.

We feel that this section was one of Daniel's greatest gifts, too. It made us see the work of Jesus in a totally new light, and we realized that it is as much needed today as when he taught this wisdom two thousand years ago. Somehow in these words of Daniel all the dead weight of centuries of dogma and doctrine fell away, and the message – and the gift – of Jesus shone through.

Part Nine:

The Truth Within

Truth is within ourselves; it takes no rise

From outward things, whate'er you may believe.

There is an inmost centre in us all,

Where truth abides in fulness; and around,

Wall upon wall, the gross flesh hems it in,

This perfect, clear perception – which is truth.

A baffling and perverting carnal mesh

Binds it, and makes all error: and to KNOW

Rather consists in opening out a way

Whence the imprisoned splendour may escape,

Than in effecting entry for a light

Supposed to be without.

> Robert Browning,
> *Paracelsus*

28

The Foundation Prayer

Stuart wanted to know how widely the Lord's Prayer was used in Daniel's lifetime, and I got an opportunity to ask about this.

Joanna: Can you please tell us something about a prayer which is called the Lord's Prayer?

Daniel: There are many prayers, but I do not know one of that name. Perhaps we call it by another name. If you speak the words of it I may recognize it.

Joanna: Yes. I will read a modern version of it for you. (I then read Matthew 6:9 to 13 in the New Revised Standard Version). "Pray then in this way: Our Father in heaven, hallowed be your name. Your kingdom come. Your will be done, on earth as it is in heaven. Give us this day our daily bread. And forgive us our debts, as we also have forgiven our debtors. And do not bring us to the time of trial, but rescue us from the evil one."

Daniel: Yes, I recognize that, but we did not call it by the name you gave. Jesus used this prayer often when

195

beginning a meeting. When starting to speak to a large gathering of people, he would use this form of words: it focused the minds, it focused the energy. He sometimes used the form you have given, or sometimes a much shorter form about half as long. So it was not fixed, not rigid, sometimes the longer form and sometimes the shorter one.

Of course as Essenes we had our own prayers, and there were many forms of words used in the communities. The prayer that I preferred and used most often was the Foundation Prayer:

> *Divine Presence within,*
> *living in wholeness,*
> *moving in joy and love,*
> *I surrender to your Will.*
> *Bring the radiance of your Light*
> *into my heart and mind,*
> *and merge with me to manifest*
> *your Will upon the Earth.*

We were used to a concept of Presence. Shekinah is the Presence of God in the world. And wholeness, joy and love we saw as the nature of God, and the gifts of God when they manifest in our lives. The reference to Light is important: many Essene prayers focused upon Light. The Light inspires us because it is a symbol for the Spirit. Jesus taught us to go forward continually into the Light, letting go of everything that was not Light. And mark the line which says "I surrender to your Will." Continual surrendering of the will to the Divine Presence is the key. But we also need to merge and become fully one with the Divine Presence before we can manifest God's Will upon the Earth.

We can only merge with the Divine when we are

capable of true forgiveness. If we are able to take the leap of faith and forgive completely – and that includes forgiving ourselves – then everything is possible, and the future beckons like an open door.

Joanna: It seems a very important thing to the Essenes, this forgiveness.

Daniel: Yes, because forgiveness frees us. Without forgiveness we are locked forever in the past and we cannot reach the future. It was so central that Jesus spoke often of it. Forgiveness casts aside division and affirms Oneness, for it is only in a state of Oneness that we can rise into Eternal Life.

At the level of the Divine Presence there is no loss, only gain, and it seems natural to forgive. But at a limited individual level the view is different. Here many ones see forgiveness as a loss. They say, "Why should I give up my moral superiority over this person who has done something to hurt me?" So they hug the hurt to themselves, and then they are never free.

Joanna: And how do you feel or sense or perceive the Divine Presence within?

Daniel: It will vary from individual to individual. Some sense it as a great Angel, and some like a loving Energy which enters every fibre of their being. But the simplest way of thinking of the Divine Presence is as the Spirit. Jesus saw a clear difference between the Spirit and the soul. He told us that the soul is good, but limited, whereas the Spirit has no limits or boundaries, and links all beings in the greater Oneness. Jesus said that there are good qualities in the soul, but like reason they were limited and could take us only so far upon our journey. Whereas the Spirit, being one with the Light, contained all within it and was Infinite. Hence he urged us to lay aside the littleness of reason and become Spirit-filled, for when we are full of the Spirit, the whole universe opens to us and all things become possible.

This message was not well received by all, and many feared to cast themselves adrift upon the sea of Spirit. But Jesus counseled us to be bold and surrender ourselves to Spirit, for though we may not understand its ways it will inspire us to far greater things than reason could ever dream of. So he said, let reason be only your servant to be engaged from time to time when you require work of that level to be done. But let Spirit be your Master, and the Inner Voice to which you constantly pay heed, for Spirit is the Master of us all, and joins us all into one great Brotherhood/Sisterhood of Life and Light.

Joanna: Thank you, Daniel, that is a beautiful description.

We found confirmation of this in one of the Nag Hammadi scrolls. *The Apocryphon of James* talks of the need to be filled with the Spirit, saying that reason in comparison is merely something of the soul.

Joanna: And was this kind of experience of the Spirit possible in other traditions before the time of Jesus?

Daniel: Other traditions could only progress towards the Light by cutting themselves off from the mass of the people, in temples and other holy places. This allowed rapid progress for committed individuals, but denied the free spreading of the Light to the people as a whole. Jesus was interested in raising all the people, not just a select few. In that he went beyond the customs of our Brotherhood, for even we Essenes kept ourselves separate and apart. Yet we knew that the Essene Way, remarkable as it was, could only be a single step along the path. Jesus came to establish a more permanent way of spiritual development, and that centered upon this knowledge of the Divine Presence, the Spirit within.

Compared to the spiritual traditions of the past, this connection with the Divine Presence is a simple and straightforward way of moving to the Light. The work of Jesus was like a signpost pointing to this new way, but even when he taught this many did not understand him. They could not grasp that because the Divine Presence is within, knowing ourselves is also knowing God. I think this idea frightened them, and they would rather think of a perfect Father in the heavens, and themselves as miserable and imperfect creatures crawling upon the surface of the Earth. Yet the ancient sages had always said that knowing oneself is the key. The tragedy of the average person in my day was that this was a key they were too frightened to use, too frightened even to admit that it existed. This was the root of the confusion during my lifetime, and it is likely that in future time this confusion will only increase. Many people will not see clearly what is to be done, and will not have the commitment or the courage to surrender to the Divine Presence, even if it is a gateway to the Infinite. They will be like men starving when the richest treasure in the world lies neglected under their feet.

Joanna: But I know many people will find it hard to surrender to the Divine Presence, however rewarding that process may be.

Daniel: It is difficult for everyone. Many feel they are

199

leaving everything they have ever known, and are stepping out into a void. But if we can make this leap into the unknown, Jesus told us that all the fragments of our life will come together on a higher level and we will be transformed forever. He said that in the temple of the heart the Presence was like a Shining Angel, casting its Light into every corner of our being. And when we merge with this Angel we will enter a Light brighter than we have ever known, and catch an echo of unimaginable bliss. Then at last our pilgrimage through the realm of darkness will be over, and we will have come home safely into the Light. All the scattered fragments of our being will be gathered up into wholeness, and all limitations will fall away, leaving only love and peace and oneness, and harmony, and joy.

We found this part of Daniel's account very powerful and moving. Daniel heard Jesus talk both to people in the villages and to smaller Essene groups. In those groups he could have spoken much more openly at an esoteric level. The breadth of Daniel's contact with Jesus has enabled many fascinating insights to emerge.

Part Ten:

The Essenes Disperse

And the bud of the shoot of holiness

of the Plant of truth

was hidden and was not esteemed;

and being unperceived,

its mystery was sealed.

Thanksgiving Hymn 18 from
The Complete Dead Sea Scrolls in English
by Geza Vermes

29

After the Crucifixion

We were curious about what happened to Daniel after the crucifixion, and made some inquiries about this.

Joanna: After this time you lived in your community?
Daniel: Yes, for a while.
Joanna: Was it difficult for your communities after the crucifixion?
Daniel: Yes, it became very difficult for all the communities. Some were just harassed, but others were completely overrun. The crops and buildings were destroyed and they had to move on. It was a sad time for our people. The conventional Jews saw that we were weakened then. We had lost our main focus, and we'd poured much of our strength into this one effort. We were like a spent force after that. Many of our leaders were dispersed, and some of us were weak and ill.
Joanna: What happened to the core group after the crucifixion?
Daniel: They split up and went their various ways. Sometimes we got word of our friends in distant places

from Essene Brothers passing through, but not often.

Joanna: What happened to Joseph's sister Mary?

Daniel: I heard that a little while after Joseph had to leave, Mary, Martha and Mary Magdalene set off across the central sea to try to reach the Celtic lands, but I never heard any further reports of them. The movements of the core group especially were known only to a few. Much confusion was deliberately spread to cover their tracks, and there were many conflicting rumors.

Joanna: Do you know what happened to your friend Joseph?

Daniel: Yes, he went to Britain. Word of his sudden departure reached me almost at once, but I only heard much later that he had reached Britain safely.

Joanna: Did you ever hear from him again after that?

Daniel: I never saw him again, nor had any word from him.

Joanna: So the whole core group dispersed at that time?

Daniel: Yes, and most of us did not know where they went. The first few weeks after the crucifixion were a time of turbulence and chaos. There were many rumors but very little was known for certain about the core group. We knew they had other work to do, and their safety had to be considered. In a sense the very presence of Jesus had been protecting us. The Pharisees and Sadducees did not know the extent of his powers. I think they were frightened of him. When he was with us it was as if he was protecting his people, but the crucifixion changed all that. The persecution intensified from that time and it became more dangerous, especially for the core group.

Joanna: So after the crucifixion it soon became difficult for Joseph?

Daniel: Yes. The Pharisees were busy talking amongst themselves and wondering about Joseph. They were beginning to work out that he was more deeply involved in the Essene communities and the group around Jesus than they had thought. Because of his wealth and power he had not been probed into before. Now they were looking more closely at him, and all those journeys he was making. And it reached a point where the Sanhedrin questioned him, but he wouldn't answer, and then he had to leave hurriedly on one of his ships.

Joanna: So that must have been a confusing and anxious time for many of the Essenes?

Daniel: Yes, there were many rumors and much contradiction in them. This was partly because to cover our tracks we had deliberately spread many rumors ourselves in the towns!

Joanna: After Joseph fled, was any of the resentment against him turned upon you as his friend?

Daniel: Oh yes. (He chuckled.) *It was not a popular thing to be Joseph's friend at that time! They did not understand. They said he used his wealth to escape from the difficulties we all faced, but he could not have stayed. There were so many questions the Pharisees wanted answers to, including the location of our communities and who our real leaders were. He was protecting his Brothers, and especially the core group and the elders, by leaving our land. It saddened me to hear anyone speak ill of Joseph, for he had helped so many people. Many young scholars had free passage on his ships to continue their studies in Britain, for example.*

Joanna: Was one of these a scholar called Nathan, a brother of Mary Magdalene?

Daniel: Yes, I met Nathan several times.

Joanna: Tell me about him.

Daniel: Nathan was torn between being a scholar and being a merchant, and it was difficult for him to resolve this. Joseph became his patron and enabled him to continue his studies in Britain. My friend Joseph was a shrewd judge of men. He could see where Nathan's real path lay, and helped him to find it.

Of course we were interested in Joseph's perspective on these events, and during a separate session I was able to question him.

Joanna: So after the crucifixion you traveled and came to Britain?

Joseph: Yes, I had to leave quickly. There was no time to take Mary with me, for the servants of the High Priest were hot upon my heels. I hurried to the coast, boarded one of my ships and left in great haste.

Joanna: This must have been an anxious time for you.

Joseph: We lived through such dramatic times. It was very emotional, but we had to hold ourselves together. (Joseph gave a sigh). *We went through everything, every emotion, within just a few days...because there was so much to do, there was a certain numbness...but then* (here the voice broke as if on the very edge of weeping)...*how can you be that numb* (weeping) ...*experiencing at the two levels of my being. There was the human...the human part of me...he was my pride and joy...I have not talked of these things...*(weeping and the voice almost breaking and very hoarse)...*there was too much to do. I had to keep myself together...I had to stay within the Light.*

Joanna: And you had to be strong for Mary, too, to keep her

going. She must have had a difficult time then.

Joseph: Yes...there was a mixture of emotions because I knew I might be parted from them (here Joseph meant Jesus and Mary) *and from many that I loved, and yet what was done was in one sense joyous and awe-inspiring, and my heart rejoiced for that, but there was the heavy sadness of the parting. They were part of my family* (meaning Mary and Jesus) *...and surely they have not forgotten me!* (His voice became blurred as he wept.)

This had been one of the most difficult sessions for Rowena in her life as Joseph. When she came out of the regression she was still in a highly emotional space, and the energy from the session was clearly still working itself out in her consciousness. This is what she said at that time:

Rowena: It was as if they came, both Mary and Jesus, and said, "We have not forgotten you. How could we forget what you did for us? And now we are come to help you for the time that you helped us." (Weeping)...And yet again I am sad for I cannot be with them. We had to leave them and come again to do this work. I had not remembered how difficult it can be on this plane. We have forgotten so much and it vexes me that I could forget so much. (Weeping again).

Rowena felt a very real link with the energy of Mary and Jesus. Her voice was full of emotion when she reached the realization that they had not forgotten her. This was one of the most moving moments I can remember in any past life regression that I was involved with. The link with Mary and Jesus, and the energy of the past was so strong that it seemed to transcend time, reaching out to connect with, and bless Rowena. For a while the consciousness of Rowena (in her everyday awareness) and Joseph were able to fuse and unite, releasing a healing flow of cathartic energy. I will always remember her voice, quivering with emotion, as she said, "We have not forgotten you."

Comment by Stuart: The dramatic effect of the crucifixion on Joseph and Mary may strike some readers as strange, considering how carefully the Essene Brotherhood had prepared for this. However, theory and practice are two different things, and even these leading Essenes could not be fully emotionally prepared for the impact of these events.

Part Eleven:

Joseph of Arimathea

Joseph of Arimathea...was one of the wealthiest men in the world, not just in Jerusalem. He was a metal magnate controlling the tin and lead industry...Joseph's world control of tin and lead was due to his vast holdings in the ancient tin mines of Britain.

Dolores Cannon,
Jesus and the Essenes

30

Joseph in Perspective

When we began the regression sessions we knew very little about Joseph of Arimathea, apart from knowing that he had asked for the body of Jesus. And when we came to do the research for this book (right at the end of the regression process) we found that there are only a few Bible references to him. In Matthew's gospel (chapter 27) he is described as a "rich man", who "also himself was Jesus' disciple". According to this account he obtained Jesus' body from Pontius Pilate, wrapped it "in a clean linen cloth" and laid it "in his own new tomb, which he had hewn out in the rock". Mark (chapter 15) calls Joseph "an honorable counselor". Luke (chapter 23) also calls him a counselor, adding that "he was a good man, and a just". John (chapter 19) says he was a disciple "secretly for fear of the Jews".

In various non-biblical sources Joseph is referred to as Mary's brother or alternatively as her uncle. If you consider the age point the latter is unlikely, as he would then have been over 70 when he went to Britain after the crucifixion. Since many traditional accounts indicate that he was very active in Britain at that time, it is much more likely that

Joseph was Mary's brother, which would then put him in his fifties at the time of the crucifixion.

During our time working on this book we gathered much information about Joseph, and he came into much clearer focus for us. Much of this information came from Daniel, because Joseph remained cautious and secretive, guarding his answers and never expanding beyond the area of the question as Daniel did.

Joseph never boasted of his wealth, and indeed boastfulness was not in his nature. It came as a big surprise to us to learn during the research stage that Joseph was one of the richest and most influential men of his day.

The source of his wealth and power came from his dominant position as a supplier of tin. Tin was a metal of great domestic and military importance in the world of Joseph's day. It was a major component in the production of bronze, and bronze played a vital part in the Roman military system. The Roman army could not function properly without a dependable supply of this essential metal.

Joseph, thanks partly to the work of his father but also due to his own efforts, had built up a dominant position as the controller of most of the tin mines in Cornwall in the West of England. At that time Cornwall was the only known source of major tin deposits. Joseph's near-monopoly of the world supply of tin gave him a position equivalent in the modern world to that of a Carnegie or a Rockefeller.

Joseph's genius lay not only in the efficient mining of tin, but also in his ability to deliver tin reliably. He achieved this by building what was arguably the largest merchant shipping fleet in the world at that time. Joseph's ships were constantly making the voyage to Cornwall and delivering tin smelted into ingots to all the ports of the Roman empire. In this aspect of his work, Joseph can only be compared to a modern shipping tycoon like Aristotle Onassis.

Joseph's position as the dominant force in supplying and shipping tin gave him influence far beyond the commercial sphere. He became an important member of the Sanhedrin (the Jewish judicial council) and a legislative member of the provincial Roman Senate. He even had a title as a controller of metals within the Roman system: Decurio. This position was greatly prized, as it gave its holder considerable local influence. It also gave Joseph valuable contacts within the Roman power-structure. Joseph thus had power and influence within both the Roman and Jewish systems, something that was most unusual at that time.

Despite all this massive wealth and influence, once he had angered the Sanhedrin (as we have seen in the previous chapter) his power-base in Israel ceased to exist, and he had to flee the country, not because of any danger from the Romans but because the armed militia maintained by the High Priest was a real threat to him. As an international merchant of vast wealth and power this only meant that from that point on he could no longer operate within Israel. However Joseph still had considerable power in other countries, and large estates in Cyprus and elsewhere. So although the loss of Israel as a base was a blow to him, it would not have seriously damaged his economic power.

In George F. Jowett's book *The Drama of the Lost Disciples* there is an account of Joseph, Mary, Mary Magdalene and several disciples being cast adrift by the Romans in an open ship without sails, oars or a rudder. The Mediterranean had a reputation for uncertain currents and sudden storms, and in normal circumstances this would have amounted to a death sentence. However in this particular case a current took the ship safely to the coast of France. This account comes from an interesting source – Cardinal

Baronius, one of the leading historians of the Roman Catholic Church.

Clearly the Sanhedrin wished to be rid of Joseph (who they now regarded as a traitor to the "true" Jewish cause), together with the "trouble-makers" who had followed Jesus. The "castaway" scenario does seem to solve this problem, but it has one major flaw. The tin which Joseph controlled was a strategic material, and the Romans would not have endangered the supply of this vital military resource just to please the Jews in the Sanhedrin. If the Romans had been responsible for Joseph's death, his large and loyal staff (motivated by revenge) might have diverted the supplies of tin. In military matters the Romans were not fools, and they would have foreseen this danger.

What then is the alternative? We had the opportunity to ask Joseph about what happened to Mary after his sudden departure, and this is what he said:

Joseph: There were many who were loyal to me. I left instructions with those I trusted most so that Mary would go secretly on one of my ships. It was all planned well in advance. Do you think I did not know what was going to happen? (Said indignantly with a touch of anger.) *Everything had to be done in great secrecy and the sooner I left the safer it was for the followers of Jesus. I went first to Cyprus and took another ship from there, but I knew that Mary would be safe.*

Joanna: An account reached Rome that Mary, Mary Magdalene and other followers of Jesus had been cast adrift in a boat without oars or sails. Did you know about this account?

Joseph: (He chuckled). *Oh yes, because I constructed it with*

214

a Roman friend of mine, a high-placed official who I had known for many years. It was a way of safeguarding Mary and the closest followers of Jesus. Once the Roman officials had listed them as "castaway, presumed dead" they would take no further action, whatever the Sanhedrin might say. All this was planned ahead, for I knew that it might become very dangerous for the whole group around Jesus.

Joanna: And the Romans were willing to send this false report out?

Joseph: They were amenable to this arrangement, as I told them it would safeguard the future supplies of tin. That was their main concern.

So here we have an entirely different scenario; a neat arrangement in which a bogus report was constructed and sent to Rome, a report that was eventually picked up by Vatican sources. All the people mentioned in this report would have been able to make their own way quietly out of Israel without Roman interference. They would still have had to avoid the minions of the High Priest, but that report would have made their lives much simpler and safer.

Joanna: And all these arrangements were made in great secrecy?

Joseph: Yes, the very greatest secrecy. We had to safeguard the core group and those close to Jesus who would go out into the world and spread the word about the new Way. It grieved me to think that some might feel I had let them down, but I could not ensure the safety of all, and those who would be active in teaching the Way had to have priority.

So perhaps Mary, Mary Magdalene and other followers of Jesus did indeed reach the southern coast of France, but more comfortably in one of Joseph's many ships.

Towards the end of this session I was thinking back over our dialogues with Joseph and trying to get our contact with him into some kind of perspective. So I finished the session with a general question to encourage him to look back over his life. His reply was typically brief and to the point – he would never expand at length on any theme as Daniel often did – yet his answer was still quite revealing.

Joanna: And how would you sum up your life?
Joseph: I created a ripple in a big pond, but I could not guess the full effect that ripple might have over time.

When this session was completed we were able to review our contact so far with Joseph, and reach a much deeper understanding of him than we could get from the Bible account. Joseph of Arimathea emerges from the regression process as cautious but also courageous, intelligent, capable, shrewd and deeply loyal. His ability and integrity inspired trust in people as diverse as the Romans and the Jews. He trod a fine line between the Roman, Jewish and Essene worlds, but was able to balance these worlds with remarkable skill.

Joseph was a person of immense wealth, and he could have been seduced by this wealth, but that did not happen. He remained true to the Essene Order and to Jesus, the nephew he loved and served so well.

216

Part Twelve:

The Celtic Connection

Jesus' message of love, truth and forgiveness was totally compatible with the core of Druidic thinking and practice.

Michael Poynder,
The Lost Magic of Christianity

31

The Druids

We were interested in Joseph's contact with the Druids, and hoped he might provide some practical information to correct the popular misconceptions that have arisen over the years. The historical account of the Druids as brutal barbarians has a suspect source, as it came from their Roman conquerors. Any history written by a conquering people is not known for its unbiased views.

When there was a revival of interest in Druidism in the nineteenth century, they were seen as mystical bards, skilled in seership and poetry but rather dreamy and impractical. Over the centuries there have been many theories about the Druids, but little hard information on them, and certainly one reason for this is the fact that their culture was an oral one, and so they left no written record for us to assess.

It is in this kind of situation that local tradition can provide some clues: the English Westcountry is full of sites which are said to have links with the Druid past, and some sensitives have even picked up a Druid connection with our own site in the Burn valley. All this clearly put the Druids on the agenda for us, and we were curious about any dealings

Joseph might have had with them. Knowing how discreet and secretive Joseph could be we decided to start by asking Daniel about this.

Joanna: After Joseph visited Britain I expect he came back and told you about the Druids. What did he say about them?

Daniel: *Yes, Joseph told me much about them. They seemed to be a branch of the same tree as ourselves but some of their customs and ceremonies were different. They too had a cosmic view of things, and were interested in the stars.*

The Druids had their own teachings, although for them it was more of an oral tradition. We saw the strength in that; it was flexible and could change with time. But we also knew there was a danger that it could change too much, and fall into corrupt practices. In the oral way the teacher was the living book, whereas in our case the teacher was important but the book had a life of its own.

Joanna: Did the Druids store some of their knowledge in crystals?

Daniel: *Yes, they had great faith in crystals as record keepers. We mainly used scrolls for this purpose. We believed that only the most important and secret knowledge should be stored in crystals. Again, we saw that as a strength and as a weakness. If the skill in reading the crystal is lost, then the knowledge is lost also, at least for a time.*

Joanna: So both the Essenes and the Druids were taught by the Kaloo?

Daniel: *Yes, but the two streams developed in different ways.*

Joanna: But there was enough similarity for your people to talk about the things of the Spirit with them and feel reasonably at home?

Daniel: Yes, it was quite possible. They were certainly at ease with Joseph.

Joanna: The Druids would also have been interested to learn about Jesus.

Daniel: Yes, they also had a tradition of great Teachers. They believed in a Teacher who would come to reform the hearts of human beings, yes. They considered it possible that the Teacher might come from another branch that had been founded by the Kaloo.

Joanna: Did the Druids have knowledge of the Teacher's coming by studying the stars?

Daniel: Yes, they knew the time of the Teacher's coming was at hand, so that made them more open, yes. Although from what Joseph told me their system was already beginning to decay...but then (he laughed) *who am I to say that our system was without decay? Are not the Pharisees and Sadducees the sign of a system in decay? We felt that we had preserved the knowledge of the Kaloo more accurately than any other branch, but perhaps this was our illusion. Perhaps we were not as open as we could have been to the creative development of our tradition, yes.*

This was interesting because it showed Daniel beginning to probe the limits of the Essene system. Perhaps his interest in a cosmic perspective enabled him to take a broader view than those Essenes who were simply immersed in the Torah, the Judaic Law. We were certainly beginning to see the Essenes as less of a consistent, homogenous group with one perception and one aim, and more of a loosely-knit group, sharing much but having major differences of perception.

Our intuition proved right about Joseph being reluctant to talk much about the Druids. Perhaps much had been said to him in confidence, but when we asked about this he replied only briefly.

Joseph: My tin trading took me to Britain on a number of occasions. My ships were making regular visits to the tin mines in the western part of the country. From my very first visit I made it my business to contact the Druids, and traveled to Avalon to see their leaders. I discovered that they had an advanced learning system with many hundreds of students on a number of sites. I established a good understanding with them, so that should we need to flee from our land we would have a home there also. It was necessary to plan ahead in this way, because the situation was becoming ever more difficult for the Essenes.

Joseph's reference to "my ships" helps to emphasize his importance in the social structure of his time. He was a merchant of power and influence with a number of ships at his disposal, and as a member of the Sanhedrin he had a place within the Jewish power structure. But Joseph was also a Decurion, an official within the Roman system responsible for controlling tin and other metals within that region. It would have been most unusual for a non-Roman to hold this office, which was coveted as it gave much local influence and prestige. This gives us some idea of Joseph's quite remarkable character and integrity, and his ability to impress the ruling Roman elite with his efficiency and his administrative powers. The Romans would not have given this important office to anyone unless they had good reason to think he could carry it out effectively.

No wonder the Sanhedrin could not believe that Joseph was playing an active role in the support group around Jesus. He would have far too much to lose to get involved in anything so risky. Hence his wealth, position and prestige acted (for a time at least) as the perfect shield against suspicion. After the crucifixion, events moved too fast even for Joseph, and he was forced to leave in some haste.

32

Joseph in Britain

So what happened to Joseph when he settled in Britain?
I had the opportunity to follow this up during another
session.

Joanna: What was it like living in Britain when you went
    there after the crucifixion?
Joseph: My old bones did not like the cold and the damp,
    but it was good to feel more at ease, to feel safe.
Joanna: Was it easy for you to settle in Britain?
Joseph: The Druids helped us. We were given some land, so
    that enabled us to build and settle.
Joanna: Was the land at Avalon?
Joseph: Yes.

We also had confirmation of this from Luke's account.

Luke: I went to Avalon with Joseph after the crucifixion. We
    landed along the northern inlet. The southern coast
    was always watched and it was not safe to land there.
    The Druids helped us; we had arranged that we should

stay with the Druids on a previous visit. Britain was a distant country and suited us well as a remote place to disappear into. The land seemed very green to us, many trees and much water compared to our land. But we didn't like the cold and damp – our bones objected.

It was difficult for us to appear as ordinary ones due to our extra-ordinary skills, but there was no language problem. We had learnt the language on our previous visits, and could also communicate through the inner mind with the Druid elders. We left something behind in Britain to be rediscovered later by us when we returned in a future life.

The leaving of something for future discovery piqued our curiosity – perhaps it is a crystal, but only time will tell. When Luke said "the northern inlet" I think he meant the Bristol channel. The journey from there to Avalon (the modern Glastonbury) would have been quite easy.

I had now established that Joseph had been given land in Avalon, and was curious as to what he had done with this land. I realized that he might not understand the word "church", and I would have to phrase the next question carefully.

Joanna: Did you build a church or temple at Avalon?
Joseph: No!

This was said very emphatically, and it puzzled me as it contradicted local tradition that Joseph had built a simple wattle-and-daub church on the site where centuries later Glastonbury abbey was constructed. I decided to ask him what he *had* built.
Joanna: Then what did you build at Avalon?

225

Joseph: A simple structure; a place of sanctuary and healing. This served also as a meeting place.

Joanna: Were the Druids sympathetic to such a place being built?

Joseph: Yes, they had such places also.

Joanna: So it was not like a church, a temple?

Joseph: No. Why would we build a temple? Jesus did not ask us to build temples.

I was finding this quite difficult to handle. According to the historical account Joseph had been an early pioneer of Christianity, helping to establish the Church in first century Britain, long before the later pioneers such as St. Columba. I had just assumed that part of his work had been to build and establish churches. Surely the followers of Jesus who gathered around Joseph would have needed a church? I decided to pursue this point.

Joanna: But when those who followed the teachings of Jesus gathered, did they not need some kind of church or temple to meet in?

Joseph: No. If the day was fine we met in the open air. There were special places ringed by great trees that were nobler than any temple. But when it was cold and wet – and my old bones endured many such days in Britain – we met in the place of healing.

Joanna: But when you had built your place of healing, did you not go on to build churches or temples?

Joseph: Of course not! (He sounded quite indignant here). *Why should we build a temple? What purpose would it serve?*

Joanna: Well, it could be a place for people to meet for ceremonies.

Joseph: We had only the simplest ceremonies, and these took place in the home, or wherever we happened to be. Why should we build a temple for this purpose? Jesus taught us that it is what happens in the temple of the heart which is important, and that love in the heart makes the body into a sacred space. Knowing this, we had no need to build temples. Each one of us has a temple in the heart, and love is the flame upon the altar there.

This last sentence sounded like a quotation, but from whom, we wondered. Could it be that Jesus had said this? If so, one can well imagine the anger of the priests in Jerusalem should it ever have reached their ears. Emphasis on a temple in the heart would shift attention away from temples of brick and stone.

Joanna: So you had no need of a building of prayer and worship?
Joseph: These things were a part of our lives from moment to moment. Why should we separate them off into a different space?

This did not seem to tie in with the traditional picture of Joseph as an early Church Father, teaching and founding churches — even if they were just little wattle-and-daub buildings. Could Joseph and the other first century followers of Jesus really have been setting up sanctuaries and healing centers? And if that was what Jesus wanted, where does it leave the vast church and cathedral building program extending from the middle ages right down to the present day?

In another session with Daniel he shows how close his

227

thinking was to Joseph on this point:

Daniel: Buildings decay, hierarchies crumble and doctrines
change. But the love in the hearts of the people is
eternal, for love is the nature of God, and all things of
God endure forever.

It seems appropriate to include here Rowena's comments on the Abbey at Glastonbury. "After reliving my life as Joseph I went to Glastonbury on a quiet day in late autumn. I went into the Lady Chapel on my own, and was overcome with sadness. What had happened to the simple healing sanctuary? What has the Church done with a teaching that was simple, compassionate and unstructured – a teaching of unconditional love? It was a long way from the simplicity of our lives all those years ago."

33

The Mother
of Mary and Joseph

When the manuscript of this book was beginning to take its final shape, we went to Totnes to meet Sylvia Moss and Maggi Fielder. From this meeting came a further vital piece of information: that some traditional sources identified Mary's mother as a Celtic princess. Lionel Smithett Lewis' book *St. Joseph of Arimathea at Glastonbury* recalls (on page 63) a Breton tradition that Mary's mother came from Cornwall and was of royal blood. After our meeting in Totnes we went back to the regression process to get Daniel's perspective on this.

Joanna: What do you know about the mother of Mary and your friend Joseph?

Daniel: She was a very special person, a princess from a Celtic family in Britain. She was a very wise and graceful person, but also a person of authority. We recognized her as someone of real ability, a high Initiate.

It is important to understand that attitudes changed over the generations. In the generation of Joseph's father it was quite acceptable for rich Jews who could afford to travel widely to marry into the noble families of other countries. But by the time Joseph had reached marriageable age all this had changed and the burden of Roman rule was bearing down heavily upon us. A hatred and distrust of foreigners was common throughout our land, and it became more and more important to be Jewish – I mean entirely Jewish – in one's ancestry.

Joanna: What was the name of your friend Joseph's mother?

Daniel: She was called Anna, but amongst the family it was pronounced in a different way, so that it sounded more like "Ayna".

Comment by Stuart: This could well be a Celtic version of the name. For example, the Irish Gaelic form of Ann is Aine.

Joanna: And how did Anna come to your land?

Daniel: Joseph's father began the trading in tin, and he went to the western part of Britain. When he went there he was already a rich merchant and he impressed those in that country with his wealth. The Celts there were looking to make alliances with other lands, and so this match seemed good to them.

Comment by Stuart: I think there is much more to it than Daniel's simple statement indicates. There is some evidence that Joseph was descended from the House of David. Hence as his father was of royal blood this would have been seen as the alliance of two royal houses.

Joanna: Was Joseph's father an Essene too?

Daniel: Yes, but he did not play such an active part in the Brotherhood as Joseph did. His time was mainly spent in trading and making contacts with the Druids in Britain.

Joanna: What was the name of Joseph's father?

Daniel: He also was Joseph.

Joanna: Presumably the Essenes and Druids would look at the star charts before a marriage and see whether this was appropriate.

Daniel: Yes, and in this case they realized that this was a match blessed by heaven, a match of destiny. When she came to our land Anna made a big effort to adopt our customs and ways, so as to become one of us, and I think she was wise in that. But with her blue eyes and hair that had a reddish tinge in it, she would never look entirely Jewish.

Joanna: How did having such a mother affect Joseph?

Daniel: It made him cautious. He realized that any suggestion of foreignness might become dangerous, and was very careful to present himself as Jewish in his clothes and customs and speech. He said to me privately that sometimes he felt like a stranger in his own land, and this added an extra layer of anxiety to his life in having to appear to be always perfectly Jewish when he knew he was not. It was as if he was playing a part, but he also played the part of the innocent conventional Jew who knew nothing about the Essenes. Having to play these two parts at the same time imposed a great burden upon him.

Looking back, I think that Joseph's Celtic blood gave his consciousness a subtlety which helped him in dealing with people. He could sense deeply into people and that was useful when dealing with dangerous situations. He

231

could sense when people were beginning to doubt him, and would know just what to say to reassure them. This was most valuable to him, and came from the Celtic side of his nature.

Joanna: Did Anna outlive her husband?

Daniel: Yes, but after Mary was married she returned to Britain. By then she was frail and wished to end her days with her own people. I always knew she was an advanced being, and it did not surprise me when I asked about her in the Interlife and was told she had ascended at the end of her life.

Comment by Stuart: The Breton tradition seems to bear this out, for it records that her body vanished when she died. Sylvia Moss has also drawn my attention to the fact that Anna is represented in Chartres Cathedral, where at the south-east entrance there is a door for Initiates of the New Covenant. On the pier of the central doorway Anna is portrayed as the Supreme Mother, and she is seen again in the middle window, next to Melchizedek. But to return to our session with Daniel:

Joanna: And were Jesus' grandparents important to him?

Daniel: Yes, and the contact with Britain was important too. He learned much upon his visits, with Joseph and sometimes traveling on his own. In a way I think his contact with the Druids made his wisdom more rounded, more universal.

All this information about Celtic links casts new light on Joseph's tin trading. His choice of Britain as his final home now also makes much more sense if he had relatives there, and extensive contacts among the Druids.

34

Connections between the Essenes and the Druids

We still wanted to pursue the connections between the Essenes and the Druids, and began by asking Daniel about Druid visitors to Qumran.

Joanna: Did you ever meet any Druids who were visiting Qumran?

Daniel: Yes, several over the years. One in particular impressed me, a scholar who was interested in history, so we could discuss the development of both streams of knowledge. The Celts were indeed a most subtle people, and I did not realize this fully until I talked to this scholar. Joseph had spoken of hundreds of students in Britain, but I discovered that in truth there were thousands of scholars there in dozens of centers of learning, where people would stay five, ten, even twenty years to absorb the most advanced knowledge that was available anywhere.

Students came from all over the area around and to the north of the central sea. They taught a range of knowledge and skills which taken as a whole would be difficult to find taught openly anywhere else. They taught to high levels and they taught openly. We were able to teach many of these things in our communities, but never openly. The Druids had the support of their own people for these large places of learning, and we wished we had such support from all of our people. We could have taught wonderful knowledge, but our people as a whole were not ready for that. They were too narrow, too suspicious, too hostile. So I rather envied the freedom which the Druids had. And they had developed a whole knowledge based upon trees which was not in our teachings.

Joanna: But then, you didn't have many trees to study.

Daniel: No, our soil was poor and dry and would not support the largest trees. The Druids had many kinds of tree that were quite new to me, and as my heart warmed to all trees I was fascinated to hear my visitor talk of them. He told me of how a whole knowledge had gradually developed around them. The tree had great symbolic significance in their whole system of thought. Their knowledge was the knowledge of the natural world, and how that world related to mankind.

Joanna: Perhaps Joseph sometimes brought back an acorn or two from the trees of Britain?

Daniel: Yes, sometimes he would bring me back the seed of Celtic trees and I would try to grow from these, but in our climate they did not prosper for long.

Comment by Stuart: Even the name "Druid" has a tree association, as it is said by some writers to derive from the word "dru" meaning the oak tree. The oak was one of their most sacred trees, and oak groves were central to Druid ceremony and practice.

Joanna: So this Druid scholar who came to Qumran helped you to extend your knowledge of the Druids?

Daniel: *Yes, very much. He told me how subtle their consciousness was. I had not realized that they had such high levels of skills. Nothing that Joseph said to me prepared me for that. But of course Joseph was always busy when he went to Britain, always going from one place to another, and never had much time to sit in their great places of learning and imbibe their wisdom. This scholar told me how extensive their knowledge was. They had skills similar to many of our skills and that surprised me. Even the projection of consciousness, which I saw as one of our highest skills, was known to them, and that surprised me.*

Joanna: Did the Druids ever talk about connecting with the star people?

Daniel: *Oh yes, for these would be like our Watchers. In the case of the Watchers they seemed to communicate mainly with the Kaloo, but the Druids seemed to have more direct contact with them. Perhaps they put more emphasis on star beings in their knowledge, and this drew them into contact more.*

Joanna: What else did this Druid scholar tell you?

Daniel: *That they learned from many of the sources we learned from. The sage Pythagoras was known to them, for they had many contacts in Greece, and there were many Pythagoreans who lived in Greece and elsewhere, and saw the Druids as a sister teaching. That the Druids had accepted the Pythagorean knowledge I considered to be a mark of how open their system was.*

Joanna: It sounds as if you had a fondness for Pythagoras.

Daniel: *Yes, I had great affection for the sage Pythagoras and all his wisdom, for I found him to be the most excellent of all the Greek philosophers of whom we had knowledge. He put more emphasis upon individual effort in rising towards the Light, and I found that most appropriate.*

Joanna: And how did you see the knowledge of the Druids developing over time?

Daniel: Because the Druids had a long and continuous line of teaching they were able to attract teachers from other lands to come and share their knowledge. By doing this they were able to extend the original narrow base of their studies until it embraced mathematics (including the sacred application of numbers), geometry (including sacred geometry on which the Pythagoreans had much to say), and astronomy (including cosmology and astrology). They also studied many other things, including the practical knowledge of the natural world and the subtler gifts of prophecy and seership. They tried to find sacred aspects to most of their knowledge, bringing the sacred into everyday life so that it became a vital part of that experience, and this was one of their great strengths.

Joanna: The Druids seemed to be regarded as the best teachers of their people, whereas as Essenes you were never the teachers of all your people.

Daniel: Yes, that is true. We had a very different position within our land than they had within theirs. Their wisdom was much more widely accepted, both by the people as a whole and by those who ruled. We were always a minority, and sometimes a rather suspect minority, within our own land, and that was sad for us.

Many writers have commented on the extensive Druid teaching system which was centered upon organizations that Julius Caesar called "colleges" and modern writers tend to call "universities". Nora Chadwick in her book *The Druids* concludes that, apart from the Greek and Roman world, the Druids were the most advanced intellectual group in ancient Europe.

It is also becoming clear that there was much more interchange of ideas between the Druids and the rest of the European culture than had previously been recognized. Gordon Strachan in *Jesus, the Master Builder* emphasizes the Greek influence upon Druid education, especially their extensive adoption of Pythagorean concepts. Strachan also cites R.W. Morgan's assertion in *St. Paul in Britain* that there were forty Druid universities in Britain with a total of 60,000 students. According to Morgan, a typical student would spend twenty years there, studying a range of subjects including natural philosophy, astronomy, geometry, poetry and medicine.

35

The Significance of Joseph's Work in Britain

As we approached the end of this section of the book, we wanted some kind of overview of Joseph's work in Britain, and began moving towards that in our questions.

Joanna: So the obvious place for Joseph to go to after the crucifixion would be the land of his mother?

Daniel: *Indeed, a land where he had many relatives and many friends amongst the Druids.*

Joanna: And it was his task to take the teachings of Jesus to the Druids?

Daniel: *Yes. Because they believed in a Creator, a Preserver and a coming Savior called Yesu, many Druids were open to the teachings of Jesus. That land was perhaps more fertile soil for these truths than our own land, and it saddened me that our own people were not so open. But our land was in turmoil from the time of the crucifixion. There was a great determination to rise up and throw the Roman invaders out of our land — if that was at all possible. This resulted in many years of unrest. It is difficult to establish a new way, a way of love and peace and forgiveness, when the whole land is in ferment around you.*

Joseph had a message to spread in Britain, and he trained others to spread this message also. When he went out to Britain to teach the message of Jesus in a sense what he was doing was reforming and reviving the Druid path. He was not replacing it, but bringing their knowledge to its fullest flowering. He was showing that the Druid prophecies were being fulfilled, so that the Savior they had been waiting for had now come in the form of Jesus. So in a sense Joseph completed the cycle for the Druids as Jesus completed the cycle for the Essenes.

Joseph completed what had been laid down by the Druids. Their work had been done and they could retire with honor. This was the inner purpose behind Joseph going to Britain.

The Druids were not defeated or diminished. They completed the whole cycle of teaching, and then they laid down their staffs to make a clear path for the new way that had been established by Jesus. They recognized that the new way was the continuation of their way, and would now lead on to other things.

Only someone who was partly Celtic could have completed the cycle of the Druid system in this way. Joseph was the Meeting of the Ways, a blending of the Celtic and the Jewish spirit. He was like the confluence of two great rivers, and had to be so in order to do this work.

I had no idea what Joseph's work in Britain had been until I could talk to him in the Interlife, and put it all together in my mind. As Jesus completed the main energy of Essenism, opening up a new way for all who followed him, so Joseph in Britain completed the main

239

energy of Druidism, opening up a new direction for spiritual development in that land. Essenism continued beyond Jesus, and Druidism beyond Joseph, but the main energy of these systems now went on in a new direction.

Comment by Stuart: Here Daniel is making it clear that the Way which Jesus taught does not invalidate either Essenism or Druidism, but simply offers a radical and more direct alternative to both systems.

Daniel: As I talked to Joseph in the Interlife it became clear that when in Britain he had presented the teachings of Jesus, not as something new and alien, but as the very peak of Druid knowledge, the summary and fulfillment of all their past efforts. The fact that the Druids believed in a Savior called Yesu helped Joseph greatly. The love and forgiveness which Jesus taught were seen by them as a simplification, a summary, of all that had gone before in the Druid system.

The teachings of Jesus were entirely consistent with Druid teachings, and were received by many Druids as the peak of the knowledge which they had built up slowly over the years. Joseph told me that not all the Druids were open to this new direction, and some clung to the old complexities, but many accepted the teachings of Jesus as the new way forward.

This underlines the significance of Joseph's work in Britain, and explains why so many Druids welcomed the first arrival of Christianity in Britain, rather than opposing it.

Part Thirteen:

A Deeper Understanding

In the language of their time, the authors of the Dead Sea Scrolls offered a world view that considers a holistic and unified relationship between the earth and our bodies... The principle states, without exception, that we are a part of, and intimately enmeshed within, all that we see as our world... All rock, each tree and mountain, every river and ocean is a part of us. Perhaps most important, you and I are reminded that we are a part of one another.

Gregg Braden,
The Isaiah Effect

36

The Projection
of Consciousness

I now felt ready to ask Daniel to project his consciousness into the future. I realized that his training in projection was a great gift to us, and might open areas that we could not otherwise reach. I decided to be bold and take a really big leap forward in time as our starting point.

Joanna: I know you have been trained to project your consciousness forward in time. I would like you to scan far into the future to the end of the planetary cycle. Could you do that for us?

Daniel: *Yes, I will try to do that.* (A deep sigh and a long pause.) *Yes, at first it is dark and continues in darkness for many centuries...then there is a change in the energy. It starts to get lighter and the Light increases steadily...and towards the end of the whole cycle it is much lighter still, yes. All this hidden knowledge can be brought out just before the end of the planetary cycle. Then there will be no universal fear, but a great manifestation of Light.*

Joanna: So who is going to help with bringing forward the

Light at that time?

Daniel: Jesus is in the center of it all, yes, and around him many ones who linked with him in my time. And also many ones I do not know, angels and ones from the other worlds. It is as if the heavens have opened up and there is Light streaming down upon the Earth. And then we are free of all the fears which have clung to us for so long.

Joanna: So can you see how this plan of Light is going to work out?

Daniel: Yes. It is like a second chance for many who have turned away from the Light. They can leave behind all their fear, and violence, everything that has distorted humanity and kept us in darkness. That can all be left behind and we can climb up into the Light together.

After Daniel said this we ran out of tape, and after I put a new tape into the machine he started off again without prompting, but in a different direction. Once again I was to discover that Daniel was full of surprises.

Daniel: Because I have projected my consciousness far forward in time, I can now draw back and see the group consciousness of your time. I see that you do not have the fear of persecution that we had. There are still some patches of darkness around the world, but compared to my day where you sit now there is much Light, and it gladdens me.

We feared that the darkness would cover everything, that all the knowledge would be destroyed. That there would be thousands of years of despair and that no minds would be free. We sought to counter that as much as we could, by spreading the knowledge and working for the Light, but we feared the ages of darkness and ignorance, the capacity of stupid people to destroy knowledge. If they did not understand something they would destroy it. Destruction came so easily to them. We feared that would result in a terrible darkness and that even the Kaloo, who were by my time a dying race, could not prevent this. And then there would be a great age of darkness, with no knowledge, no wisdom, no harmony, no peace, and no love between human beings.

But by projecting my awareness forward I have seen that the Light was not extinguished. No doubt much was lost, but in a sense the knowledge is not important. What matters is the Light within each heart, because the Light will go forward, will go on to the next cycle. So if every piece of knowledge vanished and only the Light went on, that would be enough. But we feared that if all the knowledge was destroyed then the Light would never shine in the hearts of the people, and at the end of the cycle it would be a great disaster, and only a handful of shining ones would ascend, and the rest of humanity would be doomed to living yet another cycle on some other world. And then planet Earth would be regarded as a failure.

Joanna: How do you mean, a failure?

Daniel: It would have failed to fulfill its primary purpose.

Joanna: And how do you see that purpose?

Daniel: To be a platform for the spiritual development of beings. Not only human beings, but our younger brothers in the animal kingdom and other kingdoms. This planet was intended to give us experience of living at a very dense level, so we could move through that experience and reconnect with our own Divinity. By

245

doing that we would raise not only our own vibration, but the vibration of the whole planet. Spirit and matter would merge, and the Earth would move into a new state of being.

Joanna: So with that in mind, the knowledge was only a means to an end?

Daniel: Yes, it was a way of keeping the people awake, increasing the harmony and peace within them, so that at the end of the cycle they could ascend into the greater life. Think of it as an Infinite Garden. The people are the plants, and the Light in their hearts is the seed. Through applying the water of knowledge we kept the plants alive as best we could, but at one point the plant puts all its strength into the seed, and then, assured of survival in future seasons, it crumbles into the ground and is gone. As the plant is only important until the seed appears, so the knowledge is only important until the Light shines in the heart.

This passage above all others helped to put the work of the Essenes into a bigger perspective for us. What emerges here is not a picture of dry and pedantic scholars, preserving knowledge for its own sake, but rather a people dedicated to the idea of spiritual evolution. They used the knowledge to help in that evolution, but they had a very long term and cosmic view of things. How backward and primitive many of their orthodox Jewish neighbors must have seemed to them, and how impossible it must have been to bridge that gap in consciousness.

At that point, Daniel gave a deep sigh and fell silent. I decided not to ask another question, but to let Daniel continue if he wished in his own time. I realized that he might be scanning forward into what was to him the future, and thought I should give him all the time he needed to do this. And sure enough, after a long pause, he started to speak again.

Daniel: We hoped that as Jesus had gained a great victory for humanity, there would be a period of great Light immediately. But I can see it was not like that. Jesus was misunderstood, I think. I see his message being forgotten, but his image being worshiped. He would not have wished that. Why did they worship him so?

Joanna: Because he could do things that they couldn't. He was something to hold on to, a bit of Light in the darkness.

Daniel: Yes, but they twisted the Light, and made a cage of darkness out of it. How sad. Why couldn't they just let the Light shine?

Joanna: It was too simple.

Daniel: It was only the Light in the heart that mattered, but they had to build structures around it, imprison it, and limit it...(He gave a groan.) ...So much suffering, so many terrible things done in his name...(He sighed.) ...and yet at the end of the cycle there is so much Light. I begin to think it is more Light than we deserve.

Joanna: What will happen at the end of the cycle?

Daniel: All beings will be assessed according to their vibration, according to the brightness of the Light within the heart. Those who are capable of going on to a higher spiritual level will go. And those who have not learned their lessons, who have not risen in vibration, will be set aside for continuing at the same level in another place.

Joanna: You mean, on another planet?

Daniel: Yes, on another physical planet. They will continue

247

until they have learned all the lessons of that level, and learned to live with love in the heart.

Joanna: And what do you see at the very end of the planet's cycle?

Daniel: I see a time when human beings and angels will work together again, when there will be greater understanding. Also the Watchers will come into closer contact with us.

Joanna: And the Watchers are beings from other solar systems who observed human life?

Daniel: Yes, they came from other star systems and observed human progress, or usually the lack of it. Their wisdom was deeper than that of the Kaloo in that they had a profound understanding of the Divine Plan for the whole universe, and saw our little dramas on planet Earth in a much wider context.

Joanna: Yes, I can understand that. And did any of the Watchers ever visit your community?

Daniel: No, although I could feel their presence, observing our consciousness and checking to see that we continued to walk upon the Path of Light. I think their contact was mainly with the Kaloo.

As Essenes we knew that our origins were of the stars, and that at the beginning of things we were star people. Our wisdom was star wisdom, for it saw far out into the cosmos. We were star people, but also Earth people as human beings. We lived in Earth reality and in star aspiration, and in that balance we found the key to many things.

Stuart took some time to come out of this regression space, as this had been a very powerful session for him. I was glad it had ended on a positive note, as Daniel had been quite emotional about the way Christianity had developed. And from what he said about knowledge being only a means to an end I began to see what the Essenes were really about. They were not in the business of producing enlightened literature, but enlightened beings. The scrolls were precious in helping them to do that, but what really mattered was the people, and how they could be helped in their spiritual development by the knowledge which the scrolls contained.

The whole process of projecting consciousness goes some way towards explaining the Essene gift of prophecy, something that is well documented in historical accounts of the period. According to Josephus, Herod excused the Essenes from swearing an oath of loyalty because Menahem the Essene, had predicted a long reign for Herod. However this projection process evidently had its limitations. The Essenes were not able to use it to determine when the planetary cycle would end, as a later chapter makes clear. But since observation and accurate dating are two quite different skills one can understand that.

37

The Balance of Priests and Lay Essenes

Towards the end of his sessions in the Interlife Daniel made a statement about the balance between priests and lay Brothers which enabled us to reach a deeper understanding of how the Order functioned.

Daniel: From this perspective I can see how much the Essene priests contributed to the process of change. While I was alive their rigidity often irritated me, as they seemed so out of step with what the lay teachers were doing, but now I see things differently. Now I can see that the priests were like a central sun to us. The secure and fixed foundation of our world, around which we lay Essenes could move freely, like planets sweeping out a new path through the heavens. Had the priests not been so securely fixed, we would not have been able to be so creatively movable.

Comment by Stuart: This statement on the role of the priests answered a question which had been lingering in my mind. I could see how a rigid Judaic priesthood might have sprung up in the early years of the Essene movement, but why would they allow it to continue when they started to absorb a broad range of ideas from Zoroastrian and Pythagorean sources? Surely they would have found a priesthood with a single focus too restrictive in these changed circumstances.

Yet from this part of Daniel's account it seems that the Essene priesthood continued to fulfill a vital purpose. It was the still center around which the storm of transformation whirled. Without such a stable and unchanging priesthood, with all its rigid rules and detailed ceremonies, the whole organization might have fragmented and dispersed long before the arrival of Jesus. The Essene priesthood provided a static axis around which the lay Brothers were able to move and develop freely.

This balance between the static and dynamic elements in Essene life is a key to understanding how the whole Essene Order functioned. Without this understanding the role of the priests may be exaggerated, and may seem incompatible with change and the Essene contribution to the rise of Christianity. Judging from the scrolls alone the priests appear to be the enemies of change, and one can understand why many scholars have focused on their stiff and unyielding rigidity. But seen within the larger context of balancing forces, the Essene system as a whole was able to demonstrate far more elasticity of thought than the rabbinic group (the Pharisees) of that period.

A failure to understand the balance between priests and lay Brothers leads to a distorted perception of Essenism based upon confusing the part with the whole. Yet it's easy to see why this situation should have arisen. The written evidence presents the position of the Essene priests in some detail, but hardly touches upon the interests and concerns of the lay Brothers. Since Daniel and many other lay Essenes were studying dangerous and subversive texts (from the rabbinic point of view) they would have transmitted information orally to people they trusted, and committed very little to any written form. This underlines the importance of the regression evidence in enabling us to get a more complete picture of the Essene movement in a way which is simply impossible through the written record alone. The ability to see the Essenes in this more complete form should prevent future generations of scholars from confusing the part (the Essene priests) with the whole (the Essene Brotherhood). It may also generate a new sense of respect for an organization set up in such a far-seeing and balanced way.

But did this subtle system of balance arise accidentally or was it planned? We were curious about its origin and asked Daniel about this.

Daniel: It was the Kaloo who insisted that our priesthood must be unchanged and unchanging, like fixed stars in all the whirling movement of the heavens. While I lived I felt the priests took their unyielding rigidity to unnecessary extremes, yet now I am able to see how much they contributed to the Essene Way. Without these fixed stars to guide and stabilize us we might have lost our way in the vast reaches of Universal Thought. We were like eagles soaring in the blue sky, while they were like trees drawing strength from deep roots.

The fluid freedom of the lay Brothers was continually anchored by the unchanging presence of the priests. Without them we would have split apart and scattered our strength. Only now I understand the full wisdom of the Kaloo in this matter. Perhaps during my lifetime I was too much caught up in the process of change to appreciate the role of the priests, but now I can see just how great a gift they gave us, and how wise the Kaloo were to set up the Order in this way.

The two halves of the Essene Order both contributed to change and development, but in very different ways. The priests confined themselves to Judaic sources, while the lay Brothers were more interested in Universal Law and Eternal Truth, from whatever source it came. In the work of the Essene lay Brothers we can see the roots of nascent Christianity, especially in its Gnostic form, but the inflexible priesthood also played a key part in this process as the secure central axis around which the whole vortex of change revolved. Both priests and lay Brothers contributed to change, but the priests were essentially passive whereas the lay Brothers were active agents of change. Without the priesthood as a fixed point in the Essene system, the process of rapid movement and transformation might have been too chaotic and unstable to have led to lasting change. This balance of the static and dynamic created the perfect climate for the fluid ideas of Christianity to gather and crystallize.

Part Fourteen:

The Coming of the Light

Man is in process of changing
to forms that are not of this world.
Grows he in time to the formless,
a plane on the cycle above.
Know ye, ye must become formless
before ye are one with the Light.

The Emerald Tablets of Thoth the Atlantean
translated by M. Doreal

38

Stepping into the Light

We were aware that there were many ways of looking at the life and work of Jesus, and wanted to get some kind of overview from Daniel.

Joanna: When you look back at the work and teaching of Jesus now, where do you see this all leading to? What do you think he was really trying to do?

Daniel: *Above all, Jesus taught love, but why did he teach this? Expressing love in our lives may make us better human beings, but I think there's more to it than that. I think Jesus could see the direction which humanity was taking and knew that at some point we would reach the end of the planetary cycle. At that point every human being will be challenged to complete their learning process down here on Earth and move on. We move on by going through an ascension process, because that allows us to access new areas of growth and higher levels of consciousness and being. The energies of love flowing through the heart make this process of spiritual transformation and ascension possible. And if someone's heart is closed, and they are unable to love God and love themselves, then ascension is impossible for that individual. So love is the key to ascension, and I think that's the reason why Jesus taught love.*

He also taught forgiveness, because that is the best way to clear any obstacles we may have to ascending. Forgiveness constantly clears our energies and lifts us out of hurt and separation. So the work of Jesus was all focused in that one direction. I see it all as preparing us for ascension.

Joanna: And can one ascend and still keep the physical body?

Daniel: There are many levels of ascension. At the first level which is spiritual ascension you can continue in a physical body for a while, but when your task on Earth is completed you go forward into physical ascension. At that point the physical body dissolves into Light, and from then on as an ascended being you live within your Body of Light. If you are an immortal being, living an Eternal Life in harmony with God, why would you need a physical body? The whole point of ascension is to move into limitless and eternal being, beyond the constraints of physical form.

Joanna: So resurrection and ascension are different things?

Daniel: Yes, very different things, although they are often confused. Resurrection allows you to continue in physical form, but it does not enable you to enter Eternal Life, whereas ascension does. In the case of Jesus, resurrection from a death-like state would have been followed by ascension, but I don't know when that occurred. It is said that at the end of her life Mary also ascended. We assumed that where these two great beings led, many would soon follow, but perhaps it did not work out like that.

Joanna: This is all most interesting, Daniel. Where did you get this information on ascension from?

Daniel: When I visited our community at Alexandria I studied a number of Egyptian texts. Ascension was part of the esoteric tradition in Egypt, and was well understood in the inner schools there. Our Brothers at Alexandria had much knowledge of this subject and I learned as much from them as I could. The Egyptian texts spoke of the Merkabah, the Body of Light through which we become travelers upon the higher planes of being and citizens of the universe. The Egyptians knew that the universe was built upon sacred geometry and sought to unite this with our own inner Light-structure in order to complete our journey as star-beings. So I learned much in Egypt, and my meetings with the Kaloo also helped to add to my knowledge.

Joanna: What did the Kaloo tell you about ascension?

Daniel: That it was the Great Completion of which the ancient sages spoke. Spirit and matter merge and become one, and the body is raised into a higher realm. They said that a human being may attain ascension at any time, but in the Divine Plan for this planet it was intended that the great bulk of humanity should achieve it at the end of the planetary cycle.

Joanna: Did all the Essenes believe in this ascension process?

Daniel: No, it was an individual choice. The more practical ones were very skeptical, but for myself I saw it as the very peak of our knowledge. To ascend is to become one with the Light, and as we are Children of the Light I regard this as most fitting and logical.

259

Jesus told us that when we go through the doorway into the ascended realm, we would be changed forever, and have bodies made of Light. All our littleness would fall away, and we would be one with God. I regard this as a fitting goal and destiny for all the Children of the Light.

Joanna: Did Jesus actually teach about this ascended state?

Daniel: Of course — but only with his disciples, or when visiting our communities. When he was talking out in the towns or villages he would cloak his words, and call the ascended state "The Kingdom of Heaven", for it is a separate realm with its own laws and ways of being. And the words "Eternal Life" were also used to signify this state, for the Body of Light which we shall then wear is immortal and does not decay or die.

Even amongst the disciples there was disagreement on this. Some thought that such a path was not practical, saying that human beings can only progress a little at a time. But a few, like John and James, and Thomas and Mary, and Mary Magdalene, were at one with Jesus on this. They said that if you do not put the Completion stage before people they will not be able to aspire to it, and may spend many lives at lesser levels. If the idealism, the Sacred Fire in the heart, is not kindled, many ones may sleep their lives away within the home, the market or the temple.

Joanna: Is it a very difficult thing to ascend?

Daniel: It has been, certainly, and those who have achieved this in the past did so with great difficulty and after many lives of struggle. But Jesus came to change that, and to make the way clear and straight. He told us that ascension is a transformation of the heart. A brilliant mind will not help you to ascend, but a loving heart will.

Joanna: You make it sound almost easy!

Daniel: As the cycle progresses it will get ever easier. When you reach the end of the cycle it will just be like stepping into the Light. Yet it is important to see ascension always as the Completion stage of our existence. Jesus said that we should aspire towards it in our lives, but from day to day, moment to moment we should focus upon our area of service, our self-appointed task. He also said that when our task upon Earth is completed, we should be ready to ascend into the realm of Light.

Jesus told us that there comes a point in the development of every human being when the soul is filled with a great longing for the Light. At that point everything that the world can offer seems hollow and worthless. The only thing that will then satisfy the soul is to return to the Light from whence it came, and merge with that Light and become one with it. This state of Oneness with the Light is what we call ascension.

And for ascension, the heart alone can open the door. It is unconditional love working through the heart which makes ascension possible. This is a simpler and more direct way than was practiced before, and will enable many ones to ascend who could not master the complex procedures I found described in the Egyptian texts. But to move forward in this way, we will need to give up every little hatred we harbor in our hearts. In this I separated myself from many of the priests, who held that hatred of wickedness and the sons of darkness was a virtue, even a duty for the Essenes. I could not agree with this, for I saw the destructive effect hatred had in people's lives. And when I heard Jesus talk always about love and never about the need to hate, this only confirmed me in my view that love uplifts and purifies whilst any form of hatred destroys and defiles. Those who hate are denying themselves their birthright, their right as Children of God to ascend into a state of Limitless and Eternal Life.

The joy of limitless being is the very core of what Jesus taught us, and he demonstrated it first by rising from the tomb, and later by ascending from physical form into the glory of the formless state. But Jesus knew from the beginning that many people would not be able to accept his teachings. They would cling to the outer husk and reject the inner seed which gives Eternal Life. How can life be eternal if we do not live it as ascended beings? The principle of ascension makes sense of all that Jesus said, and without this key he would seem to be speaking in riddles. Yet we saw how difficult it was, even for Essenes, to accept this inner seed, for this teaching was so profound and subtle. It requires a great leap into the unknown, and many people would be too fearful to make this leap.

Many would prefer to think of a comforting heavenly space, a warm and homey place filled with friends and loved ones. But this Interlife state, this space between lives, always leads us back into another life upon Earth. It is part of the cycle of life and death, and for that reason cannot be an eternal state. Only through the ascension process can we move out of this cycle and know the freedom of endless life as ascended beings, dwelling in Eternal Joy.

Joanna: So you saw the work of Jesus as being focused on the future, a preparation for what was to come?

Daniel: Of course. The wise see what is to come and prepare for it. Jesus was wise indeed, and he had wise teachers. He revealed to us the limitless joy of the ascended state and turned our hearts and minds towards Heaven. Jesus opened up the way and turned a narrow and difficult path into a broad road into the Light. In doing so, he saved us from continuing in a series of limited physical lives. He saved us from spiritual poverty and spread before us all the abundance of Eternal Life, for that is truly what the ascended state is.

Once again, Daniel had surprised and challenged us. The whole of this testimony gave us a new perspective on the life and work of Jesus. Seeing him as a leader in spiritual transformation and ascension certainly puts him into quite a different context.

Altogether this was one of Daniel's most remarkable statements, and it gives practical expression to the words of the Community Rule: "Eternal joy in life without end, a crown of glory and a garment of majesty in unending Light." When we realize that this passage in the Dead Sea Scrolls refers to the ascended state, it becomes much easier to understand. Words which might have seemed extravagant or poetical suddenly become a factual description of a real state of being.

Daniel had focused us on the whole subject of ascension, a fascinating and controversial area. In the Jewish tradition both Enoch and Elijah are recorded as having ascended, and non-canonical texts speak of the ascensions of Abraham, Moses, Isaiah and Ezra. Clearly the idea of ascension is firmly established within Judaic culture, whereas Christian tradition limits ascension to Jesus and

Mary. As these great Beings are perceived as infinitely beyond us, this has the effect of discouraging any later generation from even attempting to follow where they have led.

We realize that this statement by Daniel has vast implications, and although we cannot provide answers perhaps we can begin to frame some of the questions:

Was Jesus, in secret at any rate, teaching what we would now call Ascension Classes? Did Jesus really want his followers to follow him on a path of ascension rather than worship at his feet? Does this mean that we have misunderstood the real purpose of Christianity? And if most people were not ready for this teaching two thousand years ago, are they ready for it now?

Do all the New Testament references to Eternal Life and the Kingdom of Heaven really refer to ascension? Was this the secret message at the heart of the Gospels, the "inner seed" which gives Eternal Life?

Physicists are now talking about the existence of many dimensions. How could we begin to understand ascension before we took on board the idea of a multi-dimensional universe? Is ascension simply stepping into the next dimensional reality in order to access another stage of our spiritual growth? Is it a natural step in our development rather than a rare and bizarre event? If so, is it possible for mass ascensions to occur, as the traditions of many Native Peoples suggest?

If the Earth is moving towards Transition soon, will mass ascensions occur during the next decade? And does that mean ascension will be an option at that time for all people of goodwill, not just exceptionally wise and holy Beings? Does this really mean that many people now living have a unique opportunity NOT to die, but instead to enter immortal life as part of the Endgame of linear-time humanity?

The Christian Church associates ascension with only two people: Jesus and his mother Mary. As Jesus is perceived within the Church as the Only Son of God, this effectively exalts and marginalizes ascension into something that no mere mortal could ever hope to aspire to.

The regression process which forms the core of this book makes it clear that the Essenes had a very different view of things. They saw Jesus as an advanced human being, an Elder Brother who has simply traveled further along the spiritual path. And Daniel's account in particular makes it clear that ascension was the central platform of Jesus' teaching, and the ultimate goal which he encouraged all true believers to aim for. If this perception becomes widely accepted, it will revolutionize the theory and practice of Christianity, through restoring the lost foundation upon which it was built.

Jesus, the remote godlike figure, is receding into history: Jesus, the advanced human being leading us into ascension is just beginning to come into focus.

Part Fifteen:

The Melchizedek Heritage

Thou art a priest for ever after the order of Melchizedek.

Psalm 110:4

39

The Order of Melchizedek

Comment by Stuart: In July 2001, at the invitation of Anne MacEwen, President of the Essene Network International, I gave a talk at the Network's Summer Gathering in Kent. By that time it looked as if most of the research for this book had been completed, but even at that point there were still things Daniel would not speak about.

In the areas that concerned the Essenes, and only the Essenes, we had obtained a rich harvest of material, but in those areas where the Essenes overlapped with the Order of Melchizedek we could get no information whatever. It looked as if we were dealing here with shared vows of secrecy at the very highest level.

Little pieces of information about the Melchizedeks had already come our way through the books we read as part of running the Starlight Centre, and we were aware that the Order of Melchizedek was a powerful and highly secretive organization which was said to have had members right across the ancient world. The references to the Order in the Bible are quite brief, starting with this in Psalm 110:1, 4:

The Lord said unto my Lord. Sit thou at my right hand...The Lord hath sworn, and will not repent, thou art a priest for ever after the order of Melchizedek.

Here the identity of "my Lord" is not clear, but the later reference in Hebrews chapter 6:20 is more specific:

Whither the forerunner is for us entered, even Jesus, made an high priest for ever after the order of Melchisedec.

The curious thing about both these references is the phrase "for ever". How can any Order be "for ever" if it is limited by the normal constraints of space and time that rule our lives on Earth? The next chapter in Hebrews, 7:3, which describes "Melchisedec, king of Salem" enters even stranger territory, saying that he is:

Without father, without mother, without descent, having neither beginning of days, nor end of life; but made like unto the Son of God; abideth a priest continually.

This makes it quite plain: we are dealing here with a powerful, immortal and Ascended Being, and by implication his Order belongs to God's kingdom and the realms of Light, and thus transcends the space-time continuum which governs planet Earth. In this context "for ever" begins to sound more rational.

But the main question still remains: are there links between the Order of Melchizedek and the Essenes? We had heard rumors to that effect, but that's all they were, just rumors. This was all very frustrating, because a link between the Melchizedeks and the inner founder of the Essenes would have taken us into a most interesting area for research. The outer founders – the Kaloo – were very well documented, but any questions about the inner founder were met with a consistent wall of silence. This had so discouraged us from proceeding that by the time I went to the Essene Network's Gathering I was resigned to accepting the inner founder and the Melchizedeks as areas that sadly we would never be able to get information on through the regression process. By that point we were ready to settle for the remarkable material that we had already obtained.

However, my time at the Gathering convinced me that it was worth while making one final effort to break through this wall of Essene secrecy. So when I returned to Devon we prepared for another round of regression. Joanna asked Daniel to go back to "the Brotherhood as a whole", and request that this vow of secrecy be released, allowing information on the Order of Melchizedek and the inner founder of the Essenes to be brought out in what was to him "future time". We emphasized that as our group was in this future time, there would be no danger to the Essenes in Daniel's time if this information was brought out, and furthermore as humanity had evolved spiritually we felt it was now appropriate.

From that point on it became much easier. Daniel succeeded in obtaining the consent of the Brotherhood, and after his vow was released we were able to access the information.

Joanna: Are you now able to tell us, please, who the inner founder of the Essene Brotherhood was?
Daniel: Yes. My vow has been set aside and it is possible for me to speak of this. It was Melchizedek who

founded the Essene Brotherhood, that is, the being who is known by this name in the Jewish tradition. There are always two names for any Melchizedek, and the Melchizedek of the Jewish tradition was actually called Aleph-Etz Melchizedek. The word "Aleph" is related to "alpha" and means "the beginning". The word "Etz" means "tree", and the whole name means "the beginning of the tree of Melchizedek". So the Tree of Life was planted at that time by this great Teacher within the Melchizedek Order.

Joanna: This is not the name given in many traditional accounts.

Daniel: I know. There are inner and outer names; this is the inner one.

Many years later this same Teacher returns as Jesus, and Jesus is Elohenu Melchizedek. "Elohenu" is literally "the glory of God", but it could also be translated as "the Divine creative flowering". Hence his name means "the Divine creative flowering (of the tree of) Melchizedek". So this great Teacher plants the Tree of Life, and returns again at the culmination of this whole process, when the Tree reaches its full flowering. In that sense Jesus can be seen as the overlighting and presiding spirit of our Order, guiding and directing the whole Essene impulse.

Joanna: And the Melchizedeks are found in many places apart from this planet?

Daniel: Indeed. They are a universal Order of service, and work in many parts of the galaxy. According to the Kaloo they have made a major contribution to the development of consciousness upon this planet.

Joanna: Could you please tell us something of the qualities of the Melchizedeks?

Daniel: The Melchizedek Order is vast, and contains a wide range of beings of different ranks and skills, but I can offer some opinion as to their chief qualities. First of all, I would say compassion, because that is why they are here to help us. That is what keeps them going, to solve so many difficult problems on so many planets. When consciousness is unable to move forward on any planet, then a Melchizedek will be despatched to see what can be done. They are like roving ambassadors of spiritual education and transformation, receiving and teaching the Light. It is the Light which really moves people forward along their chosen path, much more than structures, techniques or ideas. The Melchizedeks also have flexibility and creativeness, because they are dealing with new and challenging and difficult problems all the time. And on many occasions there is no precedent, no rule to follow. I would also say they have detachment. Many of the Melchizedeks come from the angelic line, and much of their work is quasi-angelic in nature, in that they sweep away the problems at the lower levels in order to reach the truth, and connect the ones they are trying to help with the Light. In doing so they penetrate to the heart of things and see them as they are, and not as they seem to be in this realm of illusion.

They are also very tolerant, because often they can be very far from their own planet or star-system of origin, and you need to be very tolerant when you're that far out in the universe dealing with a wide range of different beings. And I should also mention their sense of humor is very keen, and well developed amongst many of the Melchizedeks. They need to be humorous and imaginative if they are to explore all the possible ways of moving people forward.

But there is one important thing I must add about this Order. It is characterized by a complete and rigorous equality, and if you consider their position you will see that this must be so. If you are a member of a service Order that operates across the galaxy, then any prejudice by race or gender will just seem absurd. This principle of equality is seen at work in the group of female disciples around Jesus, led by Mary Magdalene and Mary, the mother of Jesus. This group of women, which included his sister Clare, formed an integrated and dedicated team. Many of the male disciples did not see the profound nature of the heart energies which the female disciples were working with. Jesus could see this perfectly well, however, and that is why he had a special respect for them, especially for his mother and Mary Magdalene. And if you take all of the disciples together, Mary Magdalene was the real star in that firmament, although many of the men did not enjoy being outshone by a woman.

Joanna: And how did Mary the mother of Jesus relate to the group of women disciples?

Daniel: Mary held the focus as the presiding figure of the group. As an advanced Initiate with extensive experience of working with cosmic energies she was able to help the group understand the greater framework and the greater responsibilities within the whole Melchizedekian system. These responsibilities unfolded over time parallel to, but quite separate from, the organization that sprang up to present the teachings of Jesus. I have projected my consciousness forward and investigated this, and it is clear to me that although the energies of Oneness focused by Jesus

274

could be received by anyone, some of their higher frequencies were largely transmitted from woman to woman over the centuries. In particular the frequency of this energy which focuses on peace and peace-making was transmitted almost entirely in this way.

Joanna: So this was passed from generation to generation through the female line?

Daniel: Yes, that is correct.

Joanna: And was a lot of this transmission passed in the form of energy?

Daniel: Yes. Much of it was passed in subtle ways beyond words, and it flowed like a great river from heart to heart down the female line. The beginning of this inner transmission gave the work of the female disciples around Jesus a special quality, a very profound and spiritual significance and a deep level of responsibility. They kept the inner spirit of the Melchizedek teaching alive, and it was passed like a living flame of wisdom from heart to heart down the female line.

Joanna: Thank you for telling us about this, Daniel. I think it's important that many know of it. And what can you tell us about the head of the Melchizedek Order?

Daniel: The head of the Order is Melchizedek Melchizedek, that is, Melchizedek of the Melchizedek Order. He sends out emissaries of Light to many parts of the universe. His work is founded upon sacred geometry, and he is responsible for the development of the Light throughout the universe. How the Light, moving through the processes of spiritual unfoldment, transforms consciousness and reconnects us with the Source of that Light. In that sense the Order of Melchizedek may be considered to be responsible for administering the gifts of the Spirit.

Joanna: And the Kaloo worked under the guidance of the Melchizedeks to set up the Essene Brotherhood?

Daniel: Yes, exactly so. That guidance came first from Aleph-Etz Melchizedek, and from that time there was a succession of Melchizedeks who held the focus, one succeeding the other, until the time of Jesus. There was always this central figure, this leader who held the focus, with a number of Melchizedeks working under his direction, and they guided the Kaloo to set up the communities. The Melchizedeks taught the wisdom of the Spirit, which the Egyptians called the "Ka". That is why the Kaloo are so named: the word means "People of the Spirit".

Comment by Stuart: Even at this stage we were learning things about the Kaloo. Now we knew at last what their name means. The "Ka-" component also occurs in the word Mer-Ka-Bah, which translates as "Light-Spirit-Soul" (ie: the Light Body which, when empowered by the Spirit, becomes the vehicle of the Soul.)

Joanna: What would you say is the most useful thing you learned about the Melchizedek teachings?

Daniel: The teaching about movement and repose. This was considered to be a key balance for any being with a physical form in order to maintain a healthy and harmonious life. Too much, or too little, of either destroys the harmony of the being and undermines the health.

Comment by Stuart: The phrase "movement and

repose" also occurs in *The Gospel of Thomas*, a text in the Nag Hammadi Library.

Joanna: And how would you sum up the work of the Melchizedek Order?

Daniel: I think the work of the Melchizedek Order is about drawing the dispersed parts of creation back into Oneness. That is why the Melchizedeks are sent to the areas of greatest separation, greatest conflict, because this is precisely where their healing and unifying talents are most needed.

The Melchizedeks understood that, despite the illusion of manyness, many beings and many levels, the universe is not divided in its fundamental Reality. In this Reality, which is the deep truth of things, the universe is integrated into Oneness. This Oneness lies at the heart of our Brotherhood, and the whole of the Essene Way flows from this central cosmic fact of Oneness. And the origin of our deepest knowledge of Oneness is the Melchizedek tradition and the work of the Kaloo who taught within that tradition.

40

The Way of Oneness

The information on the Order of Melchizedek was certainly fascinating, and there was one aspect that I wanted to follow up.

Joanna: You said that the origin of your deepest knowledge of Oneness is the Melchizedek tradition. Could you comment on this please?

Daniel: Yes. *I always thought the teaching about Oneness was most profound, but I saw that it was also very challenging. The Melchizedek teachings tell us that Creation began in Oneness, began in Light, and though we journey through darkness and chaos we will return again to the Light. So the journey of humanity is seen as circular. Starting in the Light of Oneness, moving through all the darkness of this world and returning to the Light of Oneness as we connect again with the*

Spirit within.

As Essenes we believe that Heaven and Earth are linked together in the Oneness through balance. The whole of our lives depend upon many balances such as that of Spirit and body, inner and outer, movement and repose. Each side of these balances is dependent on the other, nourishes the other, and is sustained by it. The balance of inner guidance and outer fellowship is a good example of this. The stronger and clearer our inner guidance becomes, the more natural it is to share this with our brothers and sisters. And the more we share, the more we are encouraged to trust our guidance and to live our lives according to it. The two parts of any balance are like the two sides of a coin, facing in opposite directions and yet closely linked. Thus Oneness is sustained by forces pulling in opposite directions, and yet these energies merge in effect to form a synthesis of joint action and united power.

Joanna: And did all the Essenes understand the Melchizedek teachings on Oneness?

Daniel: By no means. I felt the teachings sometimes had an uphill struggle, especially in the minds of the priests. In the training and focus of our priests the Judaic element dominated, and although this was necessary, and approved by the Kaloo, I could still see the dangers in it.

The main danger lay in too narrow a focus, leading to intolerance and a tendency to exclude and reject people. The Essene priests, for example, could be quite obsessive about the issue of purity. Of course purity is important to us, and we took it seriously, but I saw that excluding people due to impurity, rejecting and condemning them, was a dangerous process, and one

279

that is difficult to control once it is set in motion. It led so easily to extremes and I think our main complaint with the priests was that their positions were often extreme ones. In any extreme position we lose sight of that balance which is the heart of the Melchizedek teaching.

In the case of Jesus, because he understood the Melchizedek teachings so profoundly, he never took extreme positions, and he never judged and condemned people. He might condemn their wrongdoing, but never the man or woman who had done that wrong. I think that was why the disciples felt safe with him. They knew that however much they erred, he would never judge or condemn them. He would often be strong in condemning error, yes, but not in condemning people.

In that respect I thought he demonstrated the Melchizedek teaching in his life much better than our priests, because he understood it much better. In many of the scrolls beloved by the priests there are strictures against the sons of darkness, and all the doers of wickedness in this world. I never heard Jesus mention the sons of darkness at all. He focused much more upon Light and the path to the Light. The whole direction of his mind and heart was profoundly positive, and in that he reflected the Melchizedek teachers very well, for all their teachings are positive and full of faith in the Triumph of the Light.

Those priests with extreme views were often driven by fears for the future of our Order and our people, and their visions were often dark and apocalyptic. I preferred the Light, and the gentler, broader and more positive view of the Melchizedek teachings, with their deep roots in star wisdom and a knowledge that stretched out into the far reaches of the cosmos. To them the universe was a known and friendly place, full of beings progressing in many different ways towards the one Light. That they had worked and taught in so many places in the universe inspired me with confidence in their ability to guide us, and their reliability as spiritual teachers.

Comment by Stuart: This is a remarkable statement, for it puts the Dead Sea Scrolls (with their narrow focus and strictures on purity) and the teachings of Jesus (which reflect a broader and more accepting tolerance) into a larger perspective. This perspective is illumined by Daniel's reference to the Melchizedek teachings which underlie Essene wisdom. From his account it becomes clear that Jesus was a more accurate presenter of these teachings than the priestly scribes who wrote the Dead Sea Scrolls. Both form part of the Essene spectrum, but Jesus, through understanding and reflecting the spirit of the Melchizedek teachings more accurately, was able to draw upon deeper wisdom and set out a more durable pathway into the Light.

Daniel's remarks about the balance of Spirit and body are also highly significant. In the West we tend to separate the soul (which is seen as spiritual) and the mind (seen as potentially spiritual) from the body (which is seen as either neutral or even as potentially bestial). This perception distorts our experience and pulls us out of balance. It lies at the root of our alienation from nature and our tendency to pollute and despoil the Earth.

The Essenes, unlike many modern traditions which emphasize the spiritual side but ignore the body, consciously promoted a balanced process. Balance has a deep resonance for us as we try to reconcile the demands of the modern world with the needs of the inner life. Restoring the balance between the Heavenly and Earthly aspects of our being may prove to be an essential part of the journey into wholeness. But to return to the session with Daniel:

Joanna: So you saw the path of humanity as a rising in consciousness into the Light?

Daniel: Yes. Our teachers told us that when we rise into the joy of expanded consciousness, we will look back and see our present level of awareness as small and limited, like the mind of a child. If we are to fulfill all our potential as human beings, we must surrender to the greater consciousness of the Spirit. We cannot do that if we cling to all the fears and limitations of the child self. We have to let go of this lesser self if we are to rise in consciousness and enter Eternal Life.

Comment by Stuart: This passage reminded me of the words of Anne Hughes, a spiritual teacher who has inspired our group:

In the surrender of the little me the Eternal I is born.

Joanna: You have told us about Oneness and how it leads to Eternal Life. Did Jesus teach forgiveness as a way of moving towards these things?

Daniel: Yes. Forgiveness is a vital part of embracing Oneness, and that is one reason why Jesus taught this. When you completely and utterly forgive someone, what they have done to you or those dear to you ceases to exist in your consciousness. It is not that you stop holding this event against them, but that for you the event doesn't exist any more. As it no longer exists, it no longer separates you from the doer of this deed, hence it is not an obstacle to unity. This level of forgiveness is hard to achieve, but Jesus told us it is a key to entering Oneness, and it should be the aim of all those who follow the Way.

Comment by Stuart: We now live in a divided world where it is all too easy to think in terms of revenge and punishment, rather than forgiveness and Oneness. Unity and forgiveness are hard lessons for us, yet they are a key to releasing the past. Only when the past is released can we begin to live at peace with ourselves, and with our neighbors.

Many people face tragedy and trauma in their lives, and the use of forgiveness in dealing with these events is now becoming more widely recognized. Forgiveness enables us to reclaim our freedom of action, so that a single event does not define our lives. New therapies are now emerging based upon this principle, and the books focused on it include *The Journey* by Brandon Bays.

But to return to our session with Daniel, there were further aspects that we wanted to explore.

Joanna: And forgiveness was part of the Melchizedek teachings?

Daniel: Very much so. Through forgiveness the Melchizedeks constantly cleared their consciousness so they were always flexible, balanced and able to move forward. In this state there are no obstacles to Oneness.

Joanna: I can see the benefits of focusing on Oneness, but how can we do this amidst all the confusion of everyday life?

Daniel: By listening to the Heart, for the Way of Oneness is also the Way of the Heart. Even though the mind can be deceived, and swept away by the drama of the world, the Heart can see beyond this. That is why the Heart, which is sensitive to the promptings of the Spirit, can lead us back to the One Source from which we came. Through the Deep Knowing of the Heart, the seeds of the Spirit, scattered throughout the universe, are brought together and made whole again. Then the universe, which was One, shall be One again, and all hurts shall be healed.

Joanna: And why is this teaching about Oneness so challenging?

Daniel: Because to apply it, to enter Oneness, we have to let go of everything: our past, our hopes for the future, even the precious little self that we cling on to so tightly. All this has to go, if we are to enter Oneness. But it is all worthless baggage, compared to the treasure of Eternal Life. Those who experience the level of Spirit encounter the deep Mystery that embraces all in Oneness. At this level there is no separate self, only the joy and wonder of limitless Being.

Joanna: And your teachers taught about Oneness as part of the Mysteries?

Daniel: *Of course. Oneness is the Mystery of Mysteries, where diversity dissolves into Unity and many beings into a single, all-embracing state of Being. There is a loss of focus as a small, self-contained and separate self, but a great gain of joyful life which has no boundaries or ending.*

Comment by Stuart: This reflects the text of the Dead Sea Scrolls which talks of "eternal joy in life without end". It also sounds like a description of Gnosis, a state in which Oneness moves from a mere idea to the reality of a lived experience.

41

The Diversity of the Melchizedek Teachings

By now I had reviewed the information which Daniel had given so far on the Melchizedek Order, but I still had the feeling there was more to come in this area. I had prepared a list of questions which had emerged from the earlier material, and now began to work my way through this list.

Joanna: Did the Melchizedek teachings always follow the same form wherever they taught?

Daniel: No. The Melchizedeks were very thorough in adapting their teachings to the needs of the particular civilization they were dealing with. They saw all civilizations as having strengths and weaknesses, and something beyond this; an orientation in a specific direction of consciousness which gave that civilization unique abilities. It was their aim to develop the strengths of each civilization so it reached its full potential, its full flowering as they would say, and was thus able to offer its unique gift to the greater Consciousness.

Joanna: And were the Melchizedeks critical of a civilization's weaknesses?

Daniel: *They never blamed a civilization for any weakness, preferring to concentrate on developing its strengths, its unique gift to the greater Whole.*

Joanna: And the Melchizedek teachings when applied resulted in a system of great balance?

Daniel: *Yes, a very profound balance, and this went far beyond what the conventional Jews could accomplish. We saw their system as top-heavy, and lacking adequate grounding. It did not go down far enough into the Earth, or up far enough into the Heavens. We saw it as a tree with shallow roots which were unable to support tall growth. Those who followed that way looked to us like stunted trees, imprisoned within their own limitedness, and determined to force those limitations upon others.*

Joanna: And how did the Melchizedeks regard these conventional Jews?

Daniel: *They had compassion for them, and told us they were locked into a rigid system which would not allow them to develop their full potential as Children of the Light. They said we should also have compassion for them as brothers who had gone down a dark and narrow road, shuttered in upon both sides with the walls of their own fears and prejudices, and unable to see the Light enjoyed by the many star systems which benefitted from the Melchizedek teachings. I could see that to regard the Pharisees and Sadducees in this way was a path of high wisdom, but I must confess it was not always easy. When they seemed so intent upon opposing us at every turn, persecuting our Brothers whenever they could, it was hard to look upon them with pity and compassion. I could see why our priests hated them so, and called them sons of darkness, for they seemed such enemies of the Light. Yet I knew this was not the Melchizedek way, and hence I tried to regard them with compassion. This was not easy, and I fell from grace often in failing to sustain my compassion for them, especially when I heard they had caused one of my friends to suffer.*

Joanna: So the Melchizedeks adapted their teachings, but were there always common elements?

Daniel: Yes, of course. There was always an emphasis on a healthy physical life, and on study, meditation and prayer. We saw that the conventional Jews in the towns treated prayer like a mere mumbled formula of little real significance, but we knew it was much more than that. The Melchizedeks told us that prayer was one of the most powerful forces for change, but sometimes that change was not manifested outwardly, but in great changes within our own consciousness and being. Yet the outer changes brought about by prayer could also be most wonderful. They told us that if large groups of people ever learned to harness the true power of prayer, they would be able to heal from great distances, and even stop wars and prevent many natural disasters. We were told that God works through many angels in the process of Creation, but upon the Earth he has given humanity a creative process of great power and that is the process of prayer. It is a pity that outside our Brotherhood it is so little understood, for it is so great a force for good in the world.

It was only after reading Gregg Braden's book *The Isaiah Effect: Decoding the Lost Science of Prayer and Prophecy* that I began to understand a little of what Daniel is saying here. It seems we have seriously underestimated the power of both individual and group prayer. Perhaps prayer, practiced as a specific technique as this book indicates, is a way of transforming consciousness and creating a new reality.

42

The Triumph of the Light

Although Daniel had talked about the Melchizedeks adapting their teachings to a number of civilizations, it was not clear whether these were on Earth or on other planets, so I came up with a question to clarify this point.

Joanna: When the Melchizedeks visited the Earth, did they confine their contact to the Essenes and the Druids?

Daniel: *By no means. They had contact with many civilizations, but some were more open than others to such a contact. And of course, there were contacts which fall outside the human level.*

Joanna: I do not follow that – please explain it for us.

Daniel: *The Melchizedeks recognized the whales and dolphins as advanced beings, but having a different quality of consciousness to humans. Whilst human beings communicate through words or symbols, the whales and dolphins communicate mainly through sound. A single note can convey a vast amount of subtle information to beings who are attuned to picking up all the qualitative contents of that note. There are overtones and undertones, and the presence – or lack – of these can be very revealing. A single tone can express the totality of your being to creatures who operate in these subtle ways. Human beings generally don't have this level of skill, although some part of it can be developed through training.*

Joanna: Many human beings find it difficult to believe that dolphins can have anything like as advanced a consciousness as ours. We are so very different.

Daniel: Only at our present level. As human beings rise in the ascension of consciousness they come together with dolphin consciousness.

The Melchizedeks taught us that there are three stages in the process of rising into the Light:

Deep Knowing, *in which the boundaries between ourselves and other forms of life begin to dissolve.*

Integration, *in which we learn to live upon the level of Deep Knowing every day, and become aware of our own true nature.*

Ascension, *in which we move beyond Earth reality and merge with the Light.*

Comment by Stuart: In modern terminology these stages would be seen as:

1.   Gnosis.
2.   Becoming a self-realized (or God-realized) being.
3.   Ascension.

Joanna: And the dolphins are concerned with the ascension of humanity?

Daniel: The dolphins are as much concerned with the

*ascension of the Earth as the ascension of humanity,
because both of these are linked.*

Joanna: So are the dolphins very much our brothers?

Daniel: *Yes, our lost brothers, the brothers from whom our
consciousness has at one point in our history diverged.
However, as we ascend, we ascend closer to each
other, for all forms of consciousness are needed to
create the Harmony of the Whole.*

*Our teachers have told us that when we ascend we
will discover that we have overvalued some aspects of
consciousness, and undervalued other aspects. Both
human beings and dolphins need each other to fully
enter the wholeness and Oneness of the Greater
Consciousness. Together, both streams of being can go
forward into the totality of the Light, which is Eternal
Joy. Joy is a special form of wisdom which gives rapid
and easy access to Deep Knowing. Without Joy, Deep
Knowing is hard to access, and difficult to sustain. The
dolphins are masters in the understanding and
experience of Joy.*

*The whales and dolphins are also important because
they remind us of our deep connection with the Earth.
Through the process of our creation, human
consciousness and the consciousness of the Earth
became joined. We are the result of a sacred merging
of the Spirit of the Heavens and the substance of the
Earth. The Spirit gives life, and the Earth gives form,
a physical presence. In the Melchizedek teachings
consciousness and energy are not two separate things,
but form one single ebb and flow of being. So when I
say, "The consciousness of the Earth", I mean that
entire system of consciousness and energy which forms
the integrated whole of the Earth's life and being.*

Because we are linked to the Earth through our creation, the consciousness of humanity as a whole affects the Earth profoundly. When human beings developed a selfish separateness from each other and from other creatures, this deviation from the Light caused a deep sickness in our consciousness. As we are so closely linked to the Earth, the energy system and consciousness of the Earth also became sick.

The song of the whales calms the Earth in its sickness, and soothes it so that this sickness is bearable. If the sickness became unbearable and overwhelmed the Earth, the tilt of its axis would become unstable. If that happened, the Earth would not be able to sustain its orbit. It would move rapidly towards the sun, or out into the far reaches of space. In either case, life on Earth would cease.

When human beings experience the Oneness of the Spirit and rise in awareness, that will heal our consciousness and will also heal the sickness of the Earth. Then the Earth will produce a new note, not the discordant tone of a being in pain, but the joyful tone of a healed and reborn planet. When she sounds out this new note she will join her sister planets as all of Creation moves upwards into the Light and the Greater Harmony. Humanity will rise upwards in consciousness, and we will be able to live in the Eternal Joy of which our scriptures speak. That is what we call the Triumph of the Light, and this is the whole process which the Melchizedeks have been guiding and supporting here and elsewhere in the galaxy over countless centuries.

Comment by Stuart: This is a remarkable part of

Daniel's evidence, because it puts the whole of the spiritual struggle of humanity into a larger perspective. In this context the words of the Dead Sea Scrolls no longer seem so obscure or extravagant. In speaking of "Eternal joy in life without end", they are simply describing one of the stages in the development of Creation. A stage at which humanity has risen far beyond its present limitations.

This insight was one of the key parts of Daniel's evidence. It was only at this point, after all this dialogue, that we were beginning to understand what Daniel meant by the term he had used much earlier, "The Triumph of the Light".

This statement underlines how vast the Melchizedek operation was, and how long the time-span of their work. Here we have a sense of the cosmic sweep of Creation rising upwards, and the Melchizedeks – and their pupils the Essenes – playing their parts within this great process of spiritual evolution.

Now that we had so much information on the Melchizedek Order and its teachings, there was one more question I wanted to ask Daniel.

Joanna: Were the Melchizedek teachings a special interest of yours?

Daniel: *Yes, over time they became so, but they only formed a tiny part of my original training. They were never taught as a separate subject at Qumran or in any other community I had contact with, yet I came to see this as a very important study. It was central to our understanding of the great sweep of spiritual development on this planet, and I found that it also opened up a deeper understanding of our Teacher of Righteousness and what he was trying to do.*

Much of what Jesus said would make very little sense if you did not know about the tradition from which he drew his deepest knowledge. He was so firmly rooted in the Melchizedek wisdom that he was able to transcend the limitations of this planet and connect with the deep knowing and profound Oneness that lies at the heart of the Universe. All that he taught about love and forgiveness makes perfect sense when you know about this Oneness which is the deep reality of things. Yet if you did not know about this, much of what Jesus said would baffle you. It would be like studying a tree while remaining ignorant of the roots which sustain and nourish it.

Part Sixteen:

Towards Completion

The flow of history is made up of impulses expressing themselves through human souls and groups. The greatest and most all-inclusive of these is the Christ Impulse, that release into the human life stream of the Divine Energy of Love and Unity...It appears that the Essene movement protected and guarded the nascent Christ Impulse and that Jesus himself was a leading initiate and believer. In our age of the Second Coming is it not likely that this group will reemerge to continue the work?

Foreword by Sir George Trevelyan
to *The New Essenes* by Sophie Edwards

43

The Final Gathering

Joanna: Were there any big meetings after the crucifixion?
*Daniel: There was one final gathering of the elders, again
in the cave to the north. Joseph's sister Mary was the
only member of the core group present. Joseph had
already left, and the others in the core group were
scattered. How difficult it must have been for Mary at
that time. I could see the lines of strain etched upon her
face, but her dedication held her steady and when she
spoke to welcome the elders her voice was as calm and
clear as ever. She thanked us for our presence and
acknowledged that these were difficult times for many
within our Order. She introduced two members of the
Kaloo who were present, an unusual thing for they
normally visit the communities one at a time, and in
any case do not come to meetings such as these. I
knew as soon as she spoke of these Kaloo that this was
a very special meeting indeed, and even as she spoke
the thought crossed my mind that this might be the last
time we would all gather in this way.*
Between the Kaloo sat a most impressive person of

quiet dignity and noble bearing. Mary introduced him as the senior member of the Melchizedek Order upon our planet, and asked him to address the meeting. When he spoke he gave out this sense of calm and quiet authority, and I recognized him as a high Initiate. His voice was sonorous and each phrase was measured and deliberate.

He thanked each one present for all the efforts that had been made, asking the elders to thank all those in the communities on his behalf. He said that this meeting marked the end of the Essene Order's outer and visible role in the world, and it was time to gather ourselves and take stock of what had been done. And the achievements, he said, were considerable. The communities had been well founded and well run, and had given several generations of Essenes an experience of Star Wisdom. Many souls had been helped upon the path to the Light, and much knowledge had been gathered and circulated. The Teacher of Righteousness had been helped by an excellent supporting organization, making his task much easier. That task had now been completed, despite a much more substantial opposition than had been foreseen at the planning stage. The cosmic energies had been gathered and brought into synthesis, ending one great cycle of human development, and the new love-energy had been firmly established upon the Earth. All these achievements had culminated in a great leap forward in the spiritual consciousness of humanity. Whatever happened in the future this achievement could not be overturned. The harvest of it might be delayed for some time, but it could not be swept aside. The Triumph of the Light was now assured, very largely due to the work of the Teacher of Righteousness and those who supported him.

After he had finished speaking there was a long silence, as we absorbed what had been said. During this time I felt the blessing of many angels being showered upon us.

Then Mary spoke again. She thanked each one of us on behalf of the core group, and said that our Order was now moving into a new phase. She asked the elders to stop the search for scrolls, and to make arrangements for the sending out of non-Judaic texts, and Judaic scrolls of an esoteric nature, to the libraries of Alexandria and Damascus. She also asked the senior elder from Qumran to arrange for the great crystal to be sent to Alexandria. She said that the two Kaloo here present would oversee the dismantling of the model of the solar system, and its dispatch to a place of safety.

She said that the Order must now prepare for a difficult time when the scrutiny of those who did not wish us well would bear down heavily upon our communities. Families with young children should be encouraged to leave the communities and settle in safer places where they had the support of relatives, or good contact with nearby town Brothers. Teachers with special knowledge should consider leaving their communities and traveling to Alexandria or Damascus, so that the knowledge they had gathered would be available to the next generation of students.

It was likely, she said, that the communities would be destroyed, not immediately perhaps, but over a period of time. We should run down the scale of our work, and make plans to evacuate the few remaining Brothers at short notice.

Joanna: This must have been a shock for you. How did the elders take this announcement?

Daniel: *Remember we were still reeling from the shock of the crucifixion, and our land was in turmoil. Joseph's departure had been a shock too, for his wealth and influence had protected us all, and he had seemed so secure, so invulnerable. Now indeed we felt like orphans, and we could feel a great storm coming, a storm which might engulf the whole Brotherhood. Some of the elders were anxious, but others heard all of this with calm resignation. For myself, I realized that the golden days of our Order were gone indeed, and in the days to come we would be much diminished.*

Yet I knew that always when a Teacher of Righteousness departs, the tents are folded and the caravan moves on. We had taken part in a great drama, but now it was over and we must prepare for a different sort of existence. At this point I was glad that I was getting old, and had seen the high point of our Order when I was young and full of vigor. How much more difficult it must have been for the Essenes who were young still, and full of hope for the future, to see everything we loved dispersed and dismantled in this way.

My life course was already largely run. What happened now would only be of passing interest, compared to the life upon the high peaks of achievement that I had witnessed.

Joanna: As you were a teacher "with special knowledge", did you consider leaving your community and going to Alexandria or Damascus?

Daniel: *No. By then I was too old and frail, and knew that my time was soon coming. I was too old to begin again in a new place, and was determined to stay in the community I loved for as long as I could. Besides, I had already passed on what I knew to others who were younger and would be able to continue the work.*

Comment by Stuart: The process of dispersing the scrolls seems to have been carried out with typical Essene thoroughness. This is why no Egyptian, Pythagorean or Zoroastrian texts were found among the Dead Sea Scrolls. For the same reason no Mystery School or Kabbalistic material was found in any of the caves around the Dead Sea. The Essenes, with Kaloo and Melchizedek guidance, had foreseen the problem and taken action long before Qumran was overrun.

One important principle emerges from this: what we have in the Dead Sea Scrolls is not the totality of Essene knowledge, but only the fragments which the Essenes chose to leave behind, the less important and less dangerous texts. The fragments are interesting, certainly, but they do not represent the totality of what the Essenes knew. More significantly they over-represent the Judaic element at the expense of all the non-Judaic material which the Essenes certainly studied, but which would have presented a real problem for them if their communities had been raided by the militia maintained by the High Priest in Jerusalem. This non-Judaic material was simply too dangerous to keep in the communities once the period of wind-down and dispersal had begun.

If the Essenes excelled at anything, it was foresight and effective planning. Daniel's account of this final meeting shows how carefully they planned the final phase of winding down their operations and dispersing their possessions and their people.

There remained one other question that we wanted to get an answer to.

Joanna: And what happened to the history of the Essenes on which you worked for so long?

Daniel: As I completed each main section the original was sent to Alexandria, with a copy to Damascus. A further copy was sent to Qumran for dispatch via the Kaloo to a place where the Kaloo would keep it in safety. As time passed I could see how wise all these precautions were, for the land was in turmoil and many were moving against us. The safe and settled life I had known when I was young was over, and such times would never return again for us. As I finished work upon my history I had a sense of a complete cycle of development. The seed had been planted, the plant had flourished and now the seeds were being scattered.

44

Completing the Process

Throughout the sessions with Daniel and Joseph we were aware of a greater picture into which the individual accounts fit, and this became steadily clearer as the project continued. There was also a sense of the Essene Brotherhood as a whole, energizing and working within the individual experience, and that gave these sessions a unique and distinctive quality.

In the case of lives in other areas there was often a sense of completion, or at least the feeling that it was time to acknowledge the past experience and let it go. Yet all seven people who went through this regression process with us reported having the same feeling about it: *that the Essene work was not yet finished.* And we all had − to varying degrees − the feeling that we had some part to play in this completion process.

We also had the feeling that clarity would come from collaborating with others as we put together the pieces of the Essene jigsaw. What was less clear at this stage was where this collaboration might lead. For example, would it be possible, or even desirable, to revive the old Essene process of community living today? Fortunately we were able to get some insight on this during a session where Daniel talked about time-cycles.

Joanna: Did you believe in great ages of time?

Daniel: We understood that there were great cycles in the heavens, and lesser ones of just over two thousand years. But when the whole planetary cycle finishes, that time we did not know.

Comment by Stuart: The Essenes were clearly not aware of the Mayan Calendar, a system that identifies the 20 years which find completion in 2012 as the key time of change. If it is true that the Earth's dimensional shift or Transition into the Light is coming this soon, then leading up to that point we can expect major geophysical changes. There may be unusual weather patterns and intense seismic activity. Fluctuations in the Earth's geomagnetic field may also trigger changes within us right down to the cellular level. Gregg Braden's book *Awakening to Zero Point* and chapter 18 in *The Ancient Secret of the Flower of Life* by Drunvalo Melchizedek explore the principles of this planetary shift.

Daniel: When the cycle does come to an end we knew there would be a regathering of those ones who were our people. The energies set in motion would be brought into balance, the harvest would be gathered and then it would be time for a new cycle, a new life for this planet.

Joanna: So at the end of the cycle the people who worked

with Jesus will be drawn at a vibrational level to meet?
Daniel: Yes, they will feel a strong connection. The past for them will also be the present as the cycle comes round.

We had wondered why the Essenes had suddenly become news again, and were so visible in books and articles, and on television and many websites. We had reached a similar point in the cycle and the energies were coming round again.

Daniel: They will relive their experience with Jesus in order to draw strength from his strength and go forward into the Light with him. From the energy point of view, the group gathers and goes forward into the Light together. We go forward as a soul family, and there are many other soul families, so all these families will be reconnecting and renewing their energy links at that time also.

The soul family reconnects in essence, but not in the reconstruction of our communities and customs and way of life. All that was rooted in a certain place and a certain time, and will soon be gone forever. The spirit of the Essene Way will endure, for we are all linked into the Essene Consciousness. That link, once made, can never be broken, and those who were our people will be able to tap into this Consciousness. It will be a beacon in times of confusion. If they reach out with their hearts they can feel the presence of our Brothers still, and this will hold them in the Light. The Light is strong in the hearts of our people, and as one united soul family we will follow our Teacher of Righteousness into the realms of the Greater Light.

Joanna: So have all the Essenes made a vow to return to Earth together at the end of the cycle?

Daniel: Some have gone on to work upon higher levels, but many will return. Old friends will recognize each other, and many a tear of joy will be shed as we meet again. The sufferings of the past will be behind us and we will meet again in joy.

Once again, Daniel had surprised us. We had assumed that he would have liked to see the establishing of new communities on an Essene basis, but Daniel was more subtle in his approach. His understanding of time-cycles was clearly prompting him to look to the future of the "soul family" as he described it, rather than merely trying to repeat the past.

45

Farewell to Qumran

By this time Daniel had become like an old friend, and I was aware how great a gift he had given us through this extended and detailed contact. This section is about the process of withdrawing, starting after the crucifixion with Daniel as an old man.

Daniel: My community has been raided by those who wish to destroy our way of life. I have escaped, but now we all have to go our separate ways. We cannot go to Arad or Ein Gedi as we know these are under threat too. I am old now, and go to my cousin in Samaria to see out my few remaining days. (At this point Daniel's voice sounded very old and tired.)

Samaria was the name of the northern Israelite capital and the land around it. The capital lies about 40 miles north of Jerusalem. Samaria was considered as a separate administrative area during part of the Roman occupation period, as were Judaea to the south of it, and Galilee to the north.

Joanna: Did you visit Qumran on your journey north to Samaria?

Daniel: *My northward path took me near to Qumran and I decided to call in one last time and see the place where I had spent so many happy hours. I had not been there for a long while, and I found the whole place sadly changed. In the library only a few scrolls were left upon the almost empty shelves. I saw that even the writing materials and new scrolls for copying had been taken away, so I knew this was no longer an active, working library. The few scrolls that remained were like the debris which the sea leaves behind upon the shore after a high tide. And I felt in my bones that the high tide of our Brotherhood was now long past, and as each month went by we got weaker as the tide ebbed away from us, never to return.*

Comment by Stuart: This explains why so few writing materials were found by the archaeologists at Qumran. When the scholars and scribes went, these things went with them. But to return to Daniel's account:

Daniel: *The great crystal had long since gone, of course, and all the beautiful machinery of the Kaloo. The place had a sad and almost deserted air about it, and I saw very few faces that I recognized.*

When I walked around the gardens for the last time, where now weeds competed with the few remaining flowers, I knew that the sweet dream of our Order was over. A few Brothers might linger for a while, here or elsewhere, but the dream would never be sweet again, and these gardens would never echo to the eager talk of old friends and the happy laughter of the children.

310

When I took up my staff and resumed my journey I resolved not to hold this sad, depleted memory of Qumran in my mind. Instead I would remember it as it once was, full of joy and vibrant life, with many hands working together in happy harmony. For even the ordinary everyday tasks seemed lighter when shared by Brothers and Sisters who knew and loved the Essene Way. I determined that my mind should echo still with the happy conversation and joyful laughter of those earlier days, so that I should remember Qumran in this way. For as long as one soul carries this sweet memory, the spirit of Qumran will always live, and will never be forgotten.

This had been a difficult session for Stuart, and I could feel Daniel's emotion as he talked about seeing the place he loved now so much changed. I could see why he would not wish to linger there, as that would have brought up too much sadness for him. And I was glad he had found a happy thought to comfort him as he resumed his journey to Samaria.

46

The Last Days of Daniel

We rejoined Daniel as he moved into the final stages of his life. He was now an old man, living with relatives in Samaria. His voice sounded very old and tired at this point, and there were many pauses when he would stop and sigh before continuing.

Daniel: There is just the view of the hills now, and I'm towards the end of my life. I am staying with my cousin and his family, and I'm looking down from the hills, yes, and wondering if my old friends are all right. I have time to reflect on things now. So many things happened in my life...such an eventful life. We spread the Light as much as we could, yes...(he gave a deep sigh)...*and now my time is running out.*

Joanna: And in a way you achieved much, didn't you?

Daniel: Yes. It has been a good life, but also an anxious one. (Here he sounded very old and weary).

Joanna: What do you remember most?

Daniel: Traveling around with Jesus. I had duties as an elder which kept me in my community some of the time, but I did as much traveling as I could. Going from village to village, yes, I remember that. Hearing him speak and watching him heal. I will always remember that.

So many things I remember...the gathering in the cave and focusing the energies in our community...the meetings with my old friend Joseph, and others, yes, friends in other communities...the long road, the hot sun, the winding path, but at the end a light, and friends, a good meal, a little wine, and talk into the night. Yes, I remember these things.

When we next encountered Daniel we found him in the Interlife, still reviewing his life, but now taking a larger and more detached view of things.

Daniel: I only survived a few years after the crucifixion. I was glad to go: many of my friends were dead or had to leave. It became very difficult for us. Our community was overrun, and I had to leave. I went to be with my cousin, but it was not the same. The great days of the Essenes were over, and even Qumran was going through difficulties. It was a sad time for our people.

Joanna: Did you make any vows at the end of your life?

Daniel: I vowed to continue striving towards the Light, yes, and to bring what I knew to those who would listen.

Joanna: Did you have any regrets looking back over that life?

Daniel: I regretted the process of getting old, perhaps (he chuckled). *I would have avoided that if I could, but real regrets, no. It was sad that I could not see my old friends again. One can accept that this is for good reasons, but one can still be a little sad that you do not see the face of an old friend, yes.* (Here he gave a sigh).

Joanna: And what was the main lesson you learned in that life?

Daniel: *The power of love working in the heart, how strong this could be, and how this love could be a blessing to all who touched it. Our hope was to see this love spread out until it would cover the Earth, like a planet carpeted with flowers.*

Joanna: And when you look back now, how do you see your life fitting into the overall Essene pattern?

Daniel: *I can now see that I was born at a time when the pattern of Essene thought was about to change and develop more rapidly than at any time in our history. That development increased in speed during the period when Jesus was at the height of his powers. That was an exciting time for us, but also challenging because Jesus was confronting us with new ideas, a new way of looking at the relationship with God. What had seemed to us so securely settled after a long period of turbulent development, suddenly became fluid again. It needed great courage to go forward in trust into the unknown. When Jesus changed the focus from God in the Heavens to God in the Heart, only some within our Order could fully accept this. Many of our Brothers found this too challenging, and so they clung to the traditional form of the Essene Way.*

This process of change and transformation swept through our communities like a tidal wave, fragmenting and eventually dispersing the Brotherhood, but this had to be so in order for the new Way to be established. Looking back over it all, it is now clear to me that this was all part of the necessary pattern of things. In the

Infinite Garden the old always has to give way and die a little, so that the new growth can come forth and flourish.

Having got to this stage in Daniel's account we can see his process of transformation reaching a climax as he moved towards a new understanding. He was letting go of the complexity of the mind and moving ever closer to the concept of "God in the Heart". Daniel the Essene was gradually becoming Daniel, the Gnostic follower of Jesus.

Joanna: What do you remember most about Jesus?
Daniel: How he made everything simple. His teachings were so simple: love, forgiveness, and seeking the truth within. When he spoke, all the complexities of the past dissolved into the simplicity of the Way of the Heart. He just loved and accepted everyone as they are, without judging them.

At this point in the session with Daniel there was a long pause, and when he spoke again the voice seemed to come from a distant place of calm insight and remembrance:

Daniel: This life was so intense, such a special time...
Joanna: And what do you see when you look down at the Essenes still living on the Earth?
Daniel: I can see that our main task is completed now. The main reason for us all coming together – to provide support for Jesus and his work – all this has been accomplished. We will continue to preserve the knowledge, but our main task is done. (Here he paused and gave a long sigh).
There are cycles in many things, and the cycle of

our movement is drawing to a close. The Essene tree is beginning to die. Its seeds continue in the hearts of those who shared in its beauty and its joy, and it may flower again at the end of the cycle, one brief and final flowering. And then it will be time for the completion of all things.

Part Seventeen:

Summation

Make me an instrument,
Lord of thy peace,
as I let go,
as I release;
make me an instrument
humble and free,
as I awaken
the living Christ in me.

An extract from a chant by Anne Hughes,
inspired by the words of Francis of Assisi

47

New Light on the Essenes

The Essenes have been a mystery, an enigma, and a real understanding of them has taken a long time to emerge. This is largely due to their obsession with secrecy, but the Essenes had also become marginalized to the point where they were considered to have had very little influence on Western culture. For many people this meant that the Essenes were simply an obscure Jewish sect of no real importance which could safely be forgotten.

However since the discovery of the Dead Sea Scrolls the Essenes started to come back into focus again. When put together with previously known texts, a picture of the Essenes began to emerge, and this picture may be summarized as placing them into three main categories:

1. **The Religious Group**: A severe ascetic priesthood, living in rigorous monastic seclusion. The aim of this priesthood was greater purity and righteousness through following Judaic Law and building a new and more perfect Temple. (This Group is represented by the Community Rule, the Damascus Document and the Temple Scroll, texts within the Dead Sea Scrolls).

2. **The Social Group**: An esoteric brotherhood, sharing property, and living in a state of communal cooperation. The aim of this brotherhood was personal and social harmony and peace through following Universal Law. They respected human culture and the natural world, and followed a strict vegetarian diet. (This Group is represented by *The Essene Gospel of Peace* translated by Edmond Bordeaux Szekely. The first volume in this series was published in 1928, predating the discovery of the Dead Sea Scrolls by almost two decades).

3. **The Political Group**: Militant political activists who lived in wilderness camps in desert areas and saw themselves as part of an Army of God. Their aim was the violent overthrow of Roman rule. They had a radical and apocalyptic view of Judaic Law, and their position was close to that of the Zealots. (This Group is represented by the War Scroll, a text within the Dead Sea Scrolls, and the writings of Robert Eisenman).

These three Groups have sharp areas of incompatibility. Although the Religious and Political Groups share an interest in Jewish texts, the orientation of the former was peaceful and the latter violent. The universal focus of the Social Group (embracing Greek, Persian and Egyptian texts as well as the Jewish Law) would have been offensive to the other two Groups. And the meat-eating habits of the Religious and Political Groups would have offended the vegetarians of the Social Group.

For a long while the Essenes were perceived by many scholars to fit into the Religious Group, with several writers suggesting that Qumran was run on celibate lines like a medieval monastery. A number of Essene texts do seem to support this. However this view proved untenable after the emergence of the Damascus Document, with its regulations governing husbands and wives, and the discovery of skeletons of women and children in the graveyard at Qumran.

In the face of this contradictory evidence many scholars are now beginning to wonder whether we have really understood the Essenes at all. Certainly an excessive reliance upon the written word can be misleading when dealing with an Order as obsessed with secrecy as the Essenes were. To add to the confusion the Essene story (especially that part of it dealing with the Dead Sea Scrolls) has been adapted and reinterpreted by scholars with their own agendas – pro-rabbinic or pro-Christian. Various attempts have been made to absorb the Essenes within the greater Judaism or the greater Christianity, despite the Essenes' history of fierce independence.

Into this cauldron of confusion and conflicting views there now emerges a new perspective in the form of past life regression. The first breakthrough came with the publication of Dolores Cannon's book *Jesus and the Essenes* in 1992. This gives a detailed description of the community at Qumran, with a number of families as well as single teachers and priests. The presence of children indicates that Qumran was certainly not an austere monastery.

Our own work which forms the basis of this book confirms that general view of Essene communities. Although Daniel lived in the Hebron community, life there had many parallels with life at Qumran, and he presents the picture of a diverse group of people. He mentions the austere priests, but also talks about craftsmen, lay teachers and other men and women who were simply absorbed in

321

family life.

The regression evidence, started by Dolores Cannon and continued in our own researches, indicates that the Essenes as a whole were too diverse to fit neatly into any of the three Groups cited above. This evidence presents a complex picture of communities and Essene families living in towns, together with a secret layer of Essene activity which focused around the Teacher of Righteousness. There were certainly many Essenes including Joseph of Arimathea and others in the Core Group whose sole aim was to support and protect Jesus. These Essenes worked within the framework of the Essene communities, but their allegiance was to the Teacher of Righteousness, and not to the communities or the Essene movement as a whole.

But the evidence we have uncovered goes much farther than this in investigating the roots of Essene values and philosophy. It now seems clear that, for the lay Essenes at least, there was no centrally-enforced dogmatic platform of Essene belief, but a framework which encouraged individual research and direct knowledge of the truth. Each one was free to choose his or her own perception of God. This freedom contrasts sharply with the rigid restrictions accepted by the priests, their minds being focused intensely upon Yahweh.

The balance of a rigid priesthood and a lay element which was open to change and transformation is a key factor in Essenism. This balance of the static and the dynamic created the perfect climate for the birth of Christianity. An understanding of this balance solves the riddle of how an inflexible Judaic system focused upon the past and the scriptures of the past could produce a great stride forward into the future like Christianity. The lay Brothers among the Essenes had so freed themselves from the heavy hand of the past that they were able to form a crucible of change in which the ideas of Jesus, their Teacher of Righteousness, could take root and flourish.

However the written record still presents obstacles to understanding the processes underlying these changes. There is a great gulf between the rule-bound restrictiveness of the Dead Sea Scrolls and the tolerant openness of the Nag Hammadi Library, and it is difficult to see how any system could have evolved from one to the other. The work of lay Essenes like Daniel provides the missing link between these two systems of thought, casting light both on how the Essene Way developed, but also on the earliest origins of Christianity. In the light of this knowledge it is possible to see the birth of Christianity as a natural process of evolution rather than a sudden and inexplicable leap into the unknown.

The regression evidence makes it clear that the Essenes were a complex and diverse group, with some Essenes on the fringes of the movement having much in common with the Zealots. This is confirmed by the discoveries of Essene texts at the Zealot stronghold at Masada. The experiences of Suddi Benzahmare (walking a more conventional Essene path) and of Daniel Benezra (some of whose statements have Gnostic resonances) were very different, and indicate the extent to which the lay Brothers encompassed very disparate points of view.

This diversity is also reflected in the four key areas which formed the core and foundation of the Essene system:

Source	Location	Key concepts	Savior-Hero
Egyptian	Egypt	The Sun, ascension	Osiris
Judaic	Israel	Light, Yahweh	The Messiah
Zoroastrian	Persia	Duality of Light and darkness	The three savior-sons of Zarathustra
Pythagorean	Greece	Enlightenment, self-perfection	The individual initiate

The process of moving through these four systems of thought was a continual broadening, retaining the central symbol of Light but shifting gradually from the god-like savior-hero towards a focus upon the individual, who is seen journeying from darkness and ignorance up into purity, enlightenment and ascension.

One can see at once the need for secrecy. Only literature associated with the Judaic source would have been acceptable to the Pharisees and the High Priest in Jerusalem. All the other three sources would have been considered heretical. As the lay Brothers studied quietly in the library at Qumran they must have known they were reading banned material.

If the more esoteric and controversial (and therefore more dangerous) texts have not yet been found by archaeologists, this may indicate that they were better guarded, or hidden with greater care. Before Qumran was finally overrun during the Jewish uprising against the Romans in 66-74 CE the most precious texts might have been taken out of the area. Their absence among the scrolls so far discovered is no proof that they did not exist.

In any case, if the Essenes sprang from Judaic sources

alone why were the Pharisees and Sadducees so disturbed by the depth of Essene knowledge? If the sources had been purely Judaic these groups would also have had access to them, and they would have presented few surprises. It is far more logical to suppose that it was the extra-Judaic element in Essene sources and Essene thinking that was the core of the problem. To many Jews of that period, such literature would have seemed alien, heathen and heretical, and they would have regarded any who chose to study it as a dangerous and subversive element in Jewish society.

Essenism presented the orthodox Jews with a direct challenge. The wide-ranging wisdom of the Essenes and their grasp of Universal Law undermined that sense of uniqueness to which the conventional Jews clung with such tenacity. Curiously enough it is also the question of uniqueness – the uniqueness of Jesus – which makes the Essenes seem so challenging to some Christians. The uniqueness of Jesus in their view is based upon his emergence as a great spiritual Teacher with no major antecedents. In this view, Jesus springs miraculously from a spiritual void, and single-handedly establishes the Truth upon Earth. The reality which emerges from the regression evidence is very different. The Essenes had a long tradition of Teachers of Righteousness, and Jesus fitted within this tradition. Some of the basic concepts were already in place by the time he came to take up his work, and so were many of the ceremonial customs, including baptism, drinking wine from a communal cup, and the ritual meal.

What *was* unique about Jesus was the way he shifted the focus from "God in the Heavens to God in the Heart". This radical change must have been difficult enough for the Essenes, but for orthodox Jews whose perception of the Father was much more rigid and specific, this shift from the

God around us to the God within must have seemed quite impossible. It would have felt like a betrayal of a personal relationship established by their forefathers and hallowed by time.

The regression evidence has revealed a good deal of the background to Jesus' life and work from the Essene viewpoint. What is clear from this evidence is the extensive structure of support which existed around him. This is not the story of a lone Teacher but an integrated spiritual family focused on Jesus. The whole Essene movement revolved around their Teacher of Righteousness, and the unfolding story presents a picture of careful planning, dedicated teamwork and wise coordination. The ground had been well prepared for Jesus and he had the backing of a committed and dedicated team.

Joseph of Arimathea also emerges as a key member of this team. The regression evidence makes it clear that Joseph was a figure of major significance within the Essene Brotherhood. Being a man of wealth and position within the greater Jewish community, Joseph was well placed to protect the Essenes' interests at times of crisis.

The Essenes emerge here as much more complex than earlier accounts have suggested, and this complexity has many aspects to it including a multi-faceted philosophy and an elaborate security structure. The Essenes are often described as being tolerant, dedicated and idealistic, and these elements of Essene life are present in the regression evidence. But in this account the Essenes are also practical, emotional and humorous. These are real people with human feelings and emotions. It is this aspect more than any other which lifts them out of history and brings them to life for us.

Part Eighteen:

Overview

Dare to think the unthinkable.
Dare to question the unquestionable.
Dare to consider different concepts of life and death.

Dolores Cannon
Jesus and the Essenes

48

The Continuing Story

When we began the past life regression process in 1994 we had no idea it would open out to this extent. As our research developed it became clear that the information we were receiving ran parallel with the work of Dolores Cannon in her book *Jesus and the Essenes*. However Suddi (in that book) and our main subject Daniel proved to be very different characters. While Suddi gave much time to a description of the customs and details of Essene life, Daniel focused more upon ideas and the underlying philosophy. They were talking about the same experience, but from different viewpoints.

Looking back now we can see why Daniel was always surprising us. He turned out to be a complex and subtle character with a restless spirit and an ever-questing consciousness. He was prepared to go to the very limits of what he knew, and one of his great strengths was that he was always searching for subtler insights and deeper perceptions.

It took us some time to realize the most significant difference between Suddi and Daniel. Suddi studied and taught the most traditional aspect of Essenism, the Jewish

Law, and perhaps because of this he remained permanently rooted in the established Essene Way. Although Suddi actually taught Jesus when he was a young boy at Qumran, he never had the opportunity of spending time with him during his ministry as Daniel did. Hence the possibility of absorbing the new Christian ideas was much greater in Daniel's case.

Daniel stands at a unique point in history, when Essene ideas were beginning to merge into nascent Christianity. While Suddi always remained firmly within the Essene tradition, Daniel formed a bridge between Essenism and Gnostic Christianity. It is this transitional position of Daniel that is one of his greatest gifts, as it allows us to see the very earliest aspects of the Christian impulse starting to emerge from the creative crucible of Essenism.

Those who had the closest and most profound relationship with Jesus – like John and James, and Mary and Mary Magdalene – seemed much more in tune with Gnostic ideas than the more conventional disciples. And as the regression process continued it became obvious that Daniel's sympathies were very much with the Gnostic group.

In the end we realized that in many ways Daniel was the perfect complement to Suddi in *Jesus and the Essenes.* While Suddi was a brilliant communicator of the fundamental structures of Essene life, Daniel was much more fascinated by ideas and principles. Suddi told us about the physical appearance of Qumran, and how the community was governed and lived from day to day. These things were not Daniel's main interests. He was more focused on why the communities had been set up, what the Essenes believed in, and where all this process was leading to. Suddi was a master of practical things, and Daniel was a master of the bigger perspective. Together they gave us a more complete picture of Essene life than we could have dared to hope for. In both cases they leave a strong impression that they were speaking with the approval of the Essene Brotherhood so that the truth could be told. This was confirmed by a statement which Daniel made quite late in the regression process:

Daniel: Some of the information I have given goes beyond what I managed to gather myself. The Brotherhood as a whole has valued this dialogue and has considered it important to give as full an account as possible, so I have had access to the accumulated knowledge of the Brotherhood. That is unusual, and at first it surprised me that the Brotherhood should wish to make all this knowledge available.

Joanna: You said, "at first". Did your opinion on this change?

Daniel: Yes. When I grew accustomed to our dialogues and to the idea of your group being in future time, I realized this process posed no danger to us, and might have benefits for the whole Order. Gradually I began to see these dialogues, and others like them, as being a bridge into the future for us, an opportunity to tell the truth about our Order.

If our communities continued to flourish they would in future time be able to speak for themselves, and correct any false notions about our Order which might have sprung up over the years, but by projecting my consciousness I have seen that all our communities will soon be extinguished.

When the last Essene community disappears from the Earth, our direct contact with future generations will vanish with it. That is why we value these dialogues, and why so much information has been given.

It is important to understand that the situation has changed greatly for us over just a few years. Whilst the Teacher of Righteousness was working in our midst we were not concerned with anyone outside our Order understanding us. Indeed, if all other people were totally ignorant of our work that would have served us very well. But now the main work of the Teacher has been completed, and the Brothers have been scattered like seeds. At this point the Brotherhood has begun to look to the future.

We can see a day coming when the secrecy that has served us so well will no longer be needed, and the true story of our Teacher of Righteousness and those who helped and supported his work can be told. As you stand in future time, the Brotherhood considers these dialogues as part of that process. A process that may well continue with other contacts, for we have an important and complex story to tell. Many worked within the Order, and there are many viewpoints within the main story.

Comment by Stuart: As we worked upon this project we became more aware of these "many viewpoints" within the Essene Order. In this book we have only been able to tell a little of this story, and much about the Essenes remains to be revealed. Both Daniel and Suddi were lay Brothers, and neither was married. What would it have been like to be a husband or a wife living in an Essene community? How would an Essene parent view the process of bringing up children? And what was it like to be an Essene priest, or a craftsperson, or a Town Brother, or one of the Essenes who traveled constantly in the search for ancient scrolls? Although Daniel's evidence has greatly extended our knowledge, and opened a new window on the Essene world, there are still many aspects of Essene life that are waiting to be explored.

49

Conclusion

When we thought that the whole of this manuscript was thoroughly completed, something quite extraordinary happened, something that led to one final and unexpected gift. At the end of a routine past life session with Stuart, the energy suddenly changed, and he felt a strong connection with Daniel. As there had been a gap of many months since our last session focusing on the Essenes, this turn of events surprised us, but it seemed that Daniel had one more piece of information to deliver. As what he had to say forms a fitting conclusion to the whole regression process, we have included it here.

Daniel: When our dialogues were drawing to a close I realized that I had not well understood the world which you experience in your future time. The gap between my time and yours is vast. That, at any rate, I realized when I projected my consciousness forward. And I felt I had not done enough to bridge this gap. Through the process of projection I had caught glimpses of your world, but they were only fleeting glimpses. I wanted to understand your world more thoroughly, and so I approached the Brotherhood as a whole for help.

I have already spoken of the consciousness which unites all who have ever lived as Essenes. Those who were our people are joined forever in this consciousness, which is like a great river of energy. I asked the Brotherhood that I might be given the opportunity to observe this river of consciousness as it flows on through time, and my request was granted. I was given special guidance to help me, and now I am able to report to you the results of this endeavor.

I was able to stand, as it were, upon a high place, and see the individual threads of consciousness rooted in Essene lives. But when I became fully attuned to this process, it was more than just seeing: whatever these individuals knew, I also knew. I watched as our people came back time after time to work within the Way that our Teacher of Righteousness had established. The original simplicity of the Way only lasted for a little time. Too many minds were at work to change and codify and "improve" it — where no improvement was needed. Our people tried to keep the Way simple, but events overwhelmed them. And as I watched, the structure grew ever more complex, ever more rigid.

I saw that over the centuries Jesus became misunderstood, until most people believed that he came to establish a religion in the Greek fashion, descending like the son of Zeus to save the world entirely on his own. What a lie that is! What an unjust lie, removing from the record all the work and efforts and suffering of the Essene Brotherhood in support of our Teacher!

And Jesus taught such powerful and simple things.

He taught us to unite with the Spirit and go into the Light — that is all! Nothing else — no elaborate ceremonies, no building of temples, no great hierarchy of priests, no formulas to learn or doctrines to master.

So simple his teachings were: unite with the Spirit, be open to the Kingdom of Heaven that is the world of Spirit, and let the energy of the Spirit flow down into us and wash away all heaviness, all fear, all doubt, and all the littleness within us that is uncomfortable with the Light. And when we are full of the Spirit, how easy it is to step into the Light which is our Source and the very nature of our being. How easy to lay aside the body that has served us well, and in the formless world become one with the Light. And he taught us that the nature of the Spirit is Truth and Love and Freedom, and when these three are present in our hearts then indeed we may feel the Kingdom of Heaven close to us.

And he taught us always to keep these things simple, and clear, and not muddied up with elaborate words and rigid formulas, for in simplicity he said we would see the Truth of things. And when that simplicity, that Love and Truth and Freedom flowed through us and blessed us, then indeed we felt that God was with us, carrying us upwards on the wings of the Spirit.

But there was such a contrast between the simplicity of the Way and the vast and rigid structures which I saw accumulate around it. And when I saw all the complexities that time had heaped upon this simple Way, all the doctrines and formulas and ceremonies, my heart became sad for my Brothers.

Only the Light at the very end of the planetary cycle gives me any hope for a better outcome. Perhaps then simplicity will return again, and the path of the Spirit shall shine before us and lead all humankind into the Light.

Comment by Stuart: This remarkable material summarizes where Daniel stands in relation to the teachings of Jesus. Our ability to be changed by the Way which Jesus established seems (according to Daniel) to be more concerned with the energy of the Spirit than any intellectual understanding or ritual ceremony.

Whilst the Spirit may be able to function in any circumstances, our openness to it seems to diminish when we are confronted with complex structures, and try to deal with these structures through using our minds. In contrast to this, simplicity forms the ideal environment for the Spirit to transform our lives and our consciousness.

We live in a fragmented and complex world, whose complexity increases every day. Against that background, a return to spiritual simplicity is starting to emerge as one of the great challenges of our time. That need is being reinforced by the very wealth which technology has delivered to us. We are now richer and live easier lives at the physical level than our great-grandparents could ever have imagined. Yet this wealth and physical ease have been accompanied by a great rise in stress and mental illness, and an acute sense of spiritual loss.

Could an answer to these problems lie in the profound simplicity of the Way as originally taught by the Essene Jesus?

But to return to our final session with Daniel:

Joanna: Thank you for making this effort to bridge the gap between your time and our time, but one thing still puzzles me. You say that Jesus taught only uniting with the Spirit and going into the Light, but surely he also taught love and forgiveness.

Daniel: Of course. Uniting with the Spirit and going into the Light are the aims of his teaching, whilst love and forgiveness are the methods he puts forward to achieve these aims. Both love and forgiveness are processes of the heart, and uniting with the Spirit and ascension are breakthroughs at the heart level. When we receive the energies of the Spirit, these energies transform and transcend our previous state of being.

Joanna: So it is really a question of receiving?

Daniel: Completely. One of my teachers at Qumran once wrote:

> *Fill the chalice of the soul*
> *with the living waters of the Spirit,*
> *and step into the Light.*

But before the chalice can be filled, it must first be emptied of all the littleness and anger and hurt, all the rubbish we carry around inside us. Love and forgiveness help us deal with the rubbish, and keep the chalice empty of the little self. All this is simple to say, and Jesus was a master of saying it simply, but the doing of it may be difficult. Many prefer their limited self which contains very little to the great ocean of the Spirit which contains everything. If they are unwilling to give up the little self, they can never enter the eternal joy of the Spirit. And the mind only locks them deeper into complexity and littleness. Out of this maze, only the simplicity of the heart can find a way.

Even after all the sessions were completed, we were

still reeling from the impact of all this information, some of it quite unconventional and deeply challenging. It was only with the passing of time that we could begin to put all this into some kind of perspective. That applied particularly to the material concerning what Jesus had taught. When we looked at the whole spectrum of information contained in this research, certain principles of the Way started to emerge:

1: No temples
2: No priests
3: Only the simplest ceremonies
4: Reliance on the Spirit, not upon scripture
5: Love and forgiveness in our hearts for all beings

The Way is a path of the Spirit, a path of the heart and not of the head. The heart simply follows the Spirit and moves towards the Light. In that direct yet profound process we catch an echo of the Essene Jesus, living and teaching long before the New Testament was written.

It was in the communities of the Essene Brotherhood that the Way was first taught, and perhaps in that setting it was most fully understood. The Essenes did not try to elaborate the teachings of Jesus into any kind of ceremonial or doctrinal structure. The simple and profound fellowship of lives lived close to Mother Earth had taught them the power and beauty of simplicity.

From this unique perspective, they understood that the forgiveness and love demonstrated by their Teacher could transform the Children of the Light, lifting them up in the power of the Spirit so that they could ascend into the Kingdom of Eternal Joy.

Glossary

AD/BC: These terms are disliked by many non-Christians and the modern equivalents have been used in this book: CE (Christian Era) and BCE (Before the Christian Era).

Ascension: Jewish tradition records the ascension of Enoch and Elijah and (in the non-canonical texts) four other ascensions. Ascension is a process in which the physical body is absorbed into Light.

Dead Sea Scrolls: About 500 mainly Hebrew and Aramaic scrolls (or scroll fragments) discovered from 1947 onwards in the caves of Qumran and in other locations near the Dead Sea.

Druids: The teachers and leaders of the Celtic peoples. The Druids had contact with both the Kaloo and the Essenes.

Essenes: One of the three main groupings within Judaism at the time of Jesus. (See also Pharisees and Sadducees).

Gnosis: A state of Deep Knowing in which the knower and the known merge and become one. In this state of being there is neither self nor other.

Israel: In this book Israel has been used rather than the traditional term Palestine, because there is some doubt about Palestine being used by the Romans (in the form of Palaestina) for any area larger than Gaza before 135 CE. The Jews disliked this term as it comes from a root word meaning Philistine.

Jeshua: see Yeshua.

Jewish Law: The system of religious, moral and ethical law which shaped the lives and customs of the Jewish people. Also called the Torah.

Judaea: One of the three administrative areas of Israel under Roman occupation, the others being Samaria and Galilee. At various times during the occupation Judaea was used to indicate:

    (a) Judaea only

    (b) Judaea plus Samaria (4-41 CE)

    (c) Judaea plus Samaria plus Galilee (from 44 CE).

Kaloo: The founders of the Essene communities who worked under the direction of the Order of Melchizedek.

Lay Brothers: The progressive and open-minded Essenes who acted as a counter-balance to the rigid and inflexible Essene priesthood.

Light: Light in the spiritual sense (with a capital L) is the boundless and eternal Divine Light (the Ain Soph). This is quite distinct from the common light of star systems (with a small l), although some translations do not observe this distinction. In *The Gospel of Thomas*, a text in the Nag Hammadi Library, Jesus makes it clear that Light is the Source from which we came, and thus we are children of the Light.

Melchizedek, Order of: A service order of advanced Teachers working on many planetary systems throughout the galaxy.

Merkabah: The Egyptian name for the Body of Light which is used after ascension. Also called the Garment of Light in Biblical texts.

Mystery Schools: Esoteric teaching groups within many Western and Middle Eastern systems. The outer Mysteries allowed all to take part in rituals and celebrations, while the inner Mysteries put aspiring Initiates through a series of tests and trials.

Nag Hammadi Library: Gnostic texts discovered in 1945

near the town of Nag (or Naj) Hammadi in Upper Egypt. These 13 codices are 4th century copies of 2nd or 3rd century scriptures and commentaries.

Palestine: see Israel.

Pharisees: The rabbinic group which controlled the education system operating through the synagogues. When the Sadducees and the Essenes disappeared, the Pharisaic group was left as the mainstream of modern Judaism.

Priesthood, Essene: The rigid and inflexible Judaic priesthood which was the source of the Dead Sea Scrolls.

Sadducees: The wealthy land-owning group of Jews who were mainly priests and who controlled the Temple in Jerusalem.

Sanhedrin: The supreme judicial council of the Jews, which met regularly in Jerusalem.

Torah: see Jewish Law

Town Brothers: Essenes who lived in towns and had a less strict and dedicated lifestyle than those in the communities.

Watchers: The Essene name for ET teachers (including Melchizedeks) who supervised and monitored the work of the Kaloo.

Yeshua Benjoseph: The Essene name for Jesus, another form being Jeshua. Jesus is the Greek form of this name.

Zealots: A group of extremist Jews who saw themselves as Warriors for God, and who focused on an apocalyptic war in which the Romans would be expelled and Israel reclaimed and purified. Some Essenes had sympathy for the Zealot view.

Further Reading

In the area of Essene studies, one writer – Edmond Bordeaux Szekely – stands out as the author of over 30 books on Essenism. Szekely showed there was life within Essene philosophy, its roots could be traced beyond Judaism, and the practical application of Essene ideas could address present-day concerns and needs. His bold and creative approach focusing on the timeless inner spirit of Essenism continues to inspire many people throughout the world. As Sir George Trevelyan wrote: "Szekely's presentation is exciting. It makes the whole vision come alive."

If we take Essene studies in general as they stand now, new information continues to emerge. The first Dead Sea Scrolls Cave 4 material, for example, was only published in 1993. The archaeology of Israel is still developing, and with the emergence of regression evidence a whole new window has opened on the Essene world. A new generation is now exploring this world, and that may lead to many fresh insights to enrich and extend the Essene heritage.

Allegro, John, *Dead Sea Scrolls: A Reappraisal,*
> Penguin Books, London, 1964. A thorough and interesting survey, though some of his conclusions are controversial.

Baigent, Michael and Leigh, Richard, *The Dead Sea Scrolls*

Deception, Cape, London, 1991. An interesting analysis of the academic controversy surrounding the scrolls, but the idea that all the Essenes were Zealots is a maverick one taken seriously by very few scholars.

Bays, Brandon, *The Journey,* Thorsons, London, 1999. A profound and liberating book which focuses on forgiveness as a technique of great power.

Braden, Gregg, *Awakening* to *Zero Point,* Radio Bookstore Press, Bellevue, WA, 1997. A helpful guide to the science underlying the planetary shift.

Braden, Gregg, *The Isaiah Effect: Decoding the Lost Science of Prayer and Prophecy,* Three Rivers Press, New York, 2000. A fascinating blend of science, vision and scholarship which opens up a perception of prayer as a powerful technique for changing our reality.

Cannon, Dolores, *Jesus and the Essenes,* Ozark Mountain Publishing, Huntsville, AR, 2000. (Originally published in 1992 by Gateway Books, Bath.) The first big breakthrough on regression material from Essene lives. Gives a detailed account of Qumran and much insight into the reality of Essene life.

Cannon, Dolores, *They Walked with Jesus,* Ozark Mountain Publishing, Huntsville, AR, 2001. (Originally published in 1994 by Gateway Books, Bath.) Regression material focusing on the life and work of Jesus.

Cooper, Diana, *A Little Light on Ascension,* Findhorn Press, Forres, Scotland, 1997. A refreshingly straightforward and practical guide to the principles of accelerating spiritual growth. Makes a good introduction to the whole area of ascension.

Edwards, Sophie, *The New Essenes,* self-published in 1983. A good book for the beginner in Essene studies. Direct and simple in approach (see Note 3).

Eisenman, Robert H. and Wise, Michael, *The Dead Sea Scrolls Uncovered,* Element Books, Shaftesbury, Dorset, 1992. The first translation of 50 documents of Scroll material. The authors were key figures in breaking the long silence imposed on the Scrolls. Controversially this book presents the Essenes and the emergent Christian church as being militant and political in a Zealot-like way.

Freke, Timothy and Gandy, Peter, *Jesus and the Goddess: The Secret Teachings of the Original Christians,* Thorsons, London, 2001. A powerful and well-researched book revealing the hidden teaching at the heart of the gospel story.

Fritsch, Charles, *The Qumran Community: Its History and Scrolls,* Macmillan, New York, 1956. A scholarly and detailed account of the background to the scrolls.

Hilarion, *The Letters of Paul: A New Spiritual World View,* Triad Publishers, Ashland, OR, 1989. A remarkable series of letters channeled by Sylvia Moss-Schechter. This book puts the life and work of Paul into a completely new perspective. Informative, lucid and full of insight.

Hodge, Stephen, *The Dead Sea Scrolls: An Introductory Guide,* Piatkus, London, 2001. An easy-to-read modern guide to the discovery and significance of the Scrolls.

Howlett, Duncan, *The Essenes and Christianity,* Harper, New York, 1957. An interesting study of the effect of Essene ideas on the emergent Christian religion.

Hunt, Teresa (writer and producer), BBC Horizon documentary *Resurrecting the Dead Sea Scrolls*, 1993. Focuses on the original cartel of scholars and the causes of delays in publication, the controversy surrounding the dispute of Eisenman versus Schiffman, and the archaeology of the Qumran site.

Hurtak, J. J, *The Book of Knowledge: The Keys of Enoch,* The Academy For Future Science, Los Gatos, CA, 1977. A profound and esoteric book which is widely regarded as the ultimate source-book on the metaphysical universe and the transformation of consciousness. Chapter 52 in Joshua David Stone's *Hidden Mysteries* provides a good introduction to Hurtak's text, and the video *Merkabah: Voyage of a Star Seed* by Dr. Hurtak and Jean-Luc Bozzoli gives a visual overview of it.

Hurtak, J. J, and Hurtak, Desiree, *Pistis Sophia: A Coptic Gnostic Text with Commentary,* The Academy For Future Science, Los Gatos, CA, 1999. Fascinating Gnostic material from the Askew Codex, discovered in Egypt in 1773. This book is a remarkable Gnostic dialogue on consciousness, Light and the spirit of wisdom.

Jowett, George F, *The Drama of the Lost Disciples,* Covenant Publishing, London, 1961. The remarkable story of Joseph of Arimathea and the disciples in Britain and France.

Larson, Martin, *The Essene Heritage,* Philosophical Library, New York, 1967. Gives a concise overview of the development of the Essenes based on historical sources. Contains tables which compare Essene concepts and customs with those of other groups.

Lewis, Lionel Smithett, *St. Joseph of Arimathea at Glastonbury,* James Clarke, Cambridge, 1922. Gathers together most of the traditional accounts of Joseph, and the legends concerning his mother St. Anna.

Melchizedek, Drunvalo, *The Ancient Secret of the Flower of Life* (2 volumes), Light Technology Publishing,

Flagstaff, AZ, 1998 and 2000. The best modern text on relating sacred geometry to the process of spiritual transformation and ascension.

Meurois-Givaudan, Anne and Daniel, *The Way of the Essenes: Christ's Hidden Life Remembered,* Destiny Books, Rochester, VT, 1993. (Originally published by Editions Arista, Plazac, France). This book is based upon reading the Akashic Record. Vivid, gripping and full of atmosphere.

Pagels, Elaine, *The Gnostic Gospels,* Penguin Books, London, 1990. A scholarly but very readable account of Gnostic material from the Nag Hammadi Library.

Picknett, Lynn, *Mary Magdalene: Christianity's Hidden Goddess,* Robinson, London, 2003. A controversial and fascinating book which identifies Mary's birthplace as Magdala in Ethiopia, and describes her as a leading disciple and the wife of Jesus.

Poynder, Michael, *The Lost Magic of Christianity: Celtic Essene Connections,* Green Magic, London, 2000. The Wisdom Tradition, Essene links and Celtic Christianity.

Robinson, James (editor), *The Nag Hammadi Library in English,* HarperCollins, San Francisco, 1990. The ultimate reference-book for many gnostic sources, with complete translations of all the Nag Hammadi Scrolls.

Schiffman, Lawrence, "Essenes" in *Encyclopedia of Religion,*edited by Mircea Eliade, Macmillan, New York, 1987. A historical survey presenting the rabbinic view of the Essenes as a sect derived from mainstream Judaism.

Schonfield, Hugh, *The Essene Odyssey,* Element Books, Shaftesbury, Dorset, 1993. A reappraisal of the significance of the Essenes and their symbolism.

Steiner, Rudolf, *The Fifth Gospel,* Rudolf Steiner Press, London, 1995. Contains much information on the Essenes from Steiner's unique viewpoint.

Stone, Joshua David and Parker, Janna Shelley, *A Beginner's Guide to the Path of Ascension,* Light Technology Publishing, Sedona, AZ, 1998. One of a series of books on ascension which gather information from a wide range of sources.

Strachan, Gordon, *Jesus, the Master Builder: Druid Mysteries and the Dawn of Christianity,* Floris Books, Edinburgh, 1998. Uncovers many connections between the Celtic world and Mediterranean culture. Also emphasizes the influence of Pythagorean knowledge on Druidic thinking.

Szekely, Edmond Bordeaux, *The Teachings of the Essenes from Enoch to the Dead Sea Scrolls,* C.W. Daniel, Saffron Walden, Essex, 1978. A key text which contains the Communions and the basic Essene philosophy. This is recommended as the best book for the beginner in this area of study.

Szekely, Edmond Bordeaux, *The Essene Gospel of Peace,* International Biogenic Society, Nelson, Canada. First edition published in France in 1928. This is the first part of the classic text which forms the foundation of modern Essene studies. (Book 1 of a 4-book series).

Trevelyan, George, *Summons to a High Crusade,* Findhorn Press, Forres, Scotland, 1986. Chapter 8, "The New Essenes" is full of insight by this writer who brought a new understanding to the study of Essenism and inspired a whole generation of readers.

Vermes, Geza, *The Complete Dead Sea Scrolls in English,* Penguin Books, London, 1997. The best English translation of the Scrolls, with a good introduction putting the Scrolls into perspective.

Yadin, Yigael, *The Temple Scroll: The Hidden Law of the Dead Sea Sect,* Weidenfeld and Nicolson, London, 1985. The severe and priestly end of the Essene spectrum, focusing on building the perfect Temple.

Note 1: Some of the books cited above (especially the more esoteric titles) may be difficult to source from general bookshops. They can be obtained from Arcturus Books at www.arcturusbooks.co.uk, phone 01803 864363 or from Aristia at www.aristia.co.uk, phone 01983-721060 or Cygnus Books at www.cygnus-books.co.uk, phone 01550 777 701. The Szekely titles published by I.B.S. can be ordered direct from: International Biogenic Society, P.O. Box 849, Nelson, B.C. Canada V1L 6A5.

Note 2: The book by Gaura Devi from which we quote in Chapter 9 may not be widely available through bookshops. It can be obtained from the publishers, the Nymet Press at: info@nymetpress.co.uk.

Note 3: The book by Sophie Edwards, *The New Essenes,* from which we quote in Part Sixteen is now out of print, but some copies may still be available through the Essene Network International. The Network's website may be found at www.Essenes.savethisplanet.com.

Index

A

Akhenaten-45
alchemy, spiritual-76
Alexandria community-36,37,45,79,
    105
Allegro, John-343
almonds-59
Amon-Ra, Amun-45
angels-33,67,115,244
Anna, St
    ascension of-232
    as a Celtic princess-229
    how she came from Britain-230
    return to Britain of-232
Apocryphon of James-198
Arabic texts-106
Arad community-37,41,71,72
archaeology and archaeological
    sites- 38,40,60,343
Archangel Michael-165
Armitage, John, a regression subject
    see also Luke-40,41,70
ascension see also eternal life:
    as a Completion-261
    Jesus taught-260
    the Kaloo on-259
    levels of-258
    love is the key to-261
    makes sense of what Jesus
        taught-262
    more direct way of-260,261
Ascension Classes-264
Ascension Rite of the Sun-44
Ashe, Geoffrey-135
astrology see also star charts- 62,236
astronomy-236
Atlantean:
    continent, sinking of the-25
    technology, advanced-25,
        162
Attunements-98,99
auras-80,90
Avalon-136,224

B

Babaji, Haidakhan-75

Baigent, Michael-40,344
balance:
    between movement and
        repose--60
    of priests and lay Essenes-250
balsam, fragrant-47
Banus, Essene Master-19
Baronius, Cardinal-214
Bays, Brandon-283,344
Belsey, Ashian-145
Berlin Museum-22
blind man healed-151
Body of Light see also
    Merkabah-260
Braden, Gregg-102,241,289,306,344
Breton tradition-229
Britain:
    Druids in-219
    Joseph's work in-238
    landscape of-136
    visited by Joseph and Jesus-135
Browning, Robert-193

C

Caesar, Julius-237
Cannon, Dolores-ii,21,22,24,36,77,
    78,117,123,209,321,329,344
Carol, a regression subject-139,142
cave:
    final gathering in the-299
    meeting in the-155
Celts and Celtic lands-112,204,229
center of balance, shifting the -122
Chadwick, Nora-237
children-62
Children of the Light-42,96,111,112,
    113,259,327
Christianity-87,124,183,253,264,
    322,323,330
Clare, sister of Jesus:
    healing Jesus in the tomb-171,
        172
    with Mary Magdalene-183
Clough, Judith-41
Columba, St-226
communities:
    central foundation-36
    crafts practiced in-46

different functions of-50
diversity of people in-45,50
Father House-36
grouped in threes-37
harassed and overrun-203,309
inner core on which founded-56
location of-35
main stem-36
map of-39
Mother House-36
in remote areas-36
size of-42
  *seealso*Alexandria, Arad,
  Damascus, Ein Gedi, Hebron,
  Jenin, Mount Carmel, Mount
  Horeb,Qumran, Rama
Community Rule, the-319
Cooper, Diana-344
Core Group:
  description of the-124
  members of the-125
Cornwall-229
counseling and advising-66
crafts and craftspeople-46
Crucifixion:
  Archangel Michael at the time
    of the-166
  Daniel describing the-164
  Joseph and Mary during the-
    167
  Luke and Roberta during the-
    168
  sacrifice of others during the-
    167
crystals-71,74,109,155,161
Cyprus-213,214

D

Damascus community-3,36,37,79,
  102,106
Damascus Document, the-4,60,319
dances, circle-60
Daniel Benezra:
  areas of study-86
  as a bridge between Essenism
    and Christianity-330
  as a complement to Suddi-330
  complex and subtle character-

329
Credo of-110
friendship with Joseph-17
friendship with Luke-72
interests of-27,294
summing up Joseph-16
training of-27,78
transitional position of-330
Dead Sea:
  communities to the west of-ii
  other communities in relation to
    the-38
Dead Sea Scrolls:
  cave 4 material-343
  reinterpreted by scholars-321
  text of-47,48,60
  see also the Community Rule,
    the Damascus Document, the
    Temple Scroll and the War
    Scroll
Decurio, Joseph as a-222
Devi, Gaura-75,349
diet-58
Divine Light-341
Divine, many perceptions of the-110
Divine Presence within-192,196,199
dolphins-290
Donceel-Voute, Pauline-47
Doreal, M. (translator)-255
Druids:
  advanced learning system-233,
    236
  at Avalon-136
  connections between the
    Essenes and-233
  description of the-233
  Joseph contacts the-220
  oral tradition of the-220
  savior called Yesu-238,240
  stars, interest in-220
  Teachers, tradition of-221
  visited by the Kaloo-23
  visiting Qumran-233

E

Earthly Mother-95,113
Earth's dimensional shift-306
Edwards, Sophie-297,345,349

Egypt and Egyptian knowledge-36, 41,44,324
Ein Gedi community-37,40,71,72
Eisenman, Robert H.-320,345
Elohim-100,110
energy system:
  described-158
  map of-160
equality-274
Essene:
  belief, foundation of-113
  children-62
  Consciousness-307
  councils-53,56,120
  elders-16,53,56,299
  Father House-36
  gatherings-120,299
  gift of prophecy-249
  ideas and knowledge-95
  lay Brothers-250
  libraries-104
  Mother House-36
  prayer-196
  priests-250
  secrecy-10,119
  structure, inner-34,127
  system, key areas in-324
  teachings and texts-95
  town Brothers-43
  work not yet finished-305
Essene Brotherhood as a whole-26, 34,335
Essene communities see communities
Essene Network International-99, 269
Essene Order:
  achievements of-300
  how it functioned-251
  Jesus as the overlighting spirit of-272
  security structure of-128
Essene Way:
  development of the-26,28
  four major strands of the-31
Essenes:
  history of the-304
  main groups within the-319

return of the-307
rewarded merit-56
working day of the-33
eternal life, see also Kingdom of Heaven-197,260,264,282

F
female disciples of Jesus-182,274
Fielder, Maggi-229
forgiveness-197,283
Foundation Prayer, the-195
Francis, St-126,153
Freke, Timothy-185,345
Fritsch, Charles-345

G
Galilee, Sea of-38
Gandy, Peter-185,345
geometry, sacred-236,275
geophysical changes-306
Glastonbury, see also Avalon-225
Glastonbury Abbey-228
Gnosis-285,291
Gnostic Christianity-253
Gnostic sources-181,183,187
God in the Heart-314,325
Gospel of Mary-181
Gospel of Thomas-277
Grace-188
Great Completion-259
Greece and Greek knowledge-44
grounding-103

H
healing-65,88
healing and sanctuary, place of-226
heart-96
Heart, Way of the-284
Heavenly Father-95,113
Hebrews-270
Hebron community-37,59,72
Hengel, Martin-126
herbs and salves for healing-65,71, 72
Herod, King-249
High Priest-206
higher self-vi
Hilarion-345
Hippolytus-42

Hodge, Stephen-345
honey-59
Howlett, Duncan-345
Hughes, Anne-163,282,317
Hunt, Teresa-345
Hurtak, J.J. and Desiree-346

I

inner:
    and outer-100
    groups-146
Interlife, the-iii,35
Isis tradition-44
Israel:
    landscape of-135
    Starlight Group members
        visit-40
    State of-38

J

James, brother of Jesus-181
Jenin community-37
Jericho-159
Jerusalem-155,159,173
Jesus:
    ascension of-258
    bringer of Grace-189
    brings energies together in a
        synthesis-156
    center of all things-188
    character of-132
    completing the cycle for the
        Essenes-239
    cosmic energy, bringing in-156
    disciples of-141
    establishing a new way of
        spiritual development-156,
        199
    far out of body after the
        crucifixion-169
    female disciples of-182
    great victory of-247
    as healer-142,151
    imprints stones with Light-138
    leader in spiritual
        transformation-263
    living in the moment-149,191
    and the Melchizedek teachings-
        280
    ministry of-127,157,162
    refuses to judge-149
    resurrection of-258
    revived by healers-172
    ritual death experience-155
    safety of-52
    stepped out of time-150
    strongest impression of-132
    student, as a-133
    teachings of-111,148
    theories about the survival of-
        175
    as a timeless being-189
    traveling to the villages-146
    the ultimate Essene-134
    visit to Britain by-135
    vortex of cosmic energy around
        -188,191
Jewish:
    ancestry-230
    Law, *see also* the Torah-13,58,
        77,221
    uprising-324
Jews, conventional and orthodox-12,
    32,47,81,246,287
John the Apostle-125,260
Joseph of Arimathea:
    Bible references to-9,211
    as a blending of the Celtic and
        Jewish spirit-239
    in Britain-224
    building place of sanctuary and
        healing-226
    and the burden of silence-122
    completing the cycle for the
        Druids-239
    dealing in tin-10,137,232
    departure for Britain, final-206
    father of-230
    favorite story about the young-
        15
    friendship with Daniel-17
    helped by the Druids-224
    interventions cost him dearly-
        174
    and Mary during the crucifixion
        -167
    mother of-229

questioned by the Sanhedrin-205
relationship to Mary-131,211
shipping fleet owned by-212
significance of his work in
Britain-238
summing up by Daniel-16
training-92
Josephus-19,60,93,249
Jowett, George F.-213,346
joy-292
Judaic sources-324,325
Judas-141

K

Kabbalah, the-100
Kaloo:
as an ancient race-21
came from the west-21
civilization-22
communities founded by-28,36
encouraged a study of the
mysteries-32
at the final gathering-299
forecast a time of intolerance-107
founders of the Essene Way-28
gathered the best knowledge-30
as messengers and teachers-22
other names of the-21,74
storing knowledge-23
as teachers-22
travels of-22
use of crystals-23
Karma Yoga-99
kibbutz movement, Israeli-61
Kingdom of Heaven-184,260,264
Koot Hoomi, Master-126

L

Lake Mareotis-36,105
lamps-71
Larson, Martin-126,175,346
Leadbeater, C.W.-126
Leigh, Richard-40,344
Lewis, Lionel Smithett-135,229,346
leylines-159
Light:
Body of-260
and darkness, duality of-30
Divine-341
expansion of the-111
God manifests as-111
in the heart-247
longing for the-261
pathway to the-263
Plan of-244
realm of-45
Sons of-13
in the spiritual sense-341
stages of rising into-291
as a symbol-13
Transition into the-306
Triumph of the-112,290
we came from the-327
lions of darkness-81
Lord's Prayer-195
Luke:
as a healer-71,72
healing Jesus in the tomb-171
relationship with Joseph-v
remembering Daniel-73

M

MacEwen, Anne-269
Marazion-135
Martha, disciple of Jesus-182
Martha, a regression subject-139,143
Mary, mother of Jesus:
ascension of-265
departure for the Celtic lands-216
disciple of Jesus-182
leader of the female disciples of
Jesus-274
mother of-229
sister of Joseph-211
with Joseph at the crucifixion-167
Mary Magdalene:
disciple of Jesus-184
as the friend of John-186
keeper of the inner mysteries-180
member of the core group-125
power and authority-180

priestess of Isis-179
relationship to Jesus-184
as the supreme disciple-187
Masada-43,323
mathematics-236
Mayan Calendar-306
Melchisedec, king of Salem-270
Melchizedek, Aleph-Etz-269
Melchizedek, Drunvalo-306,347
Melchizedek, Elohenu-272
Melchizedek, Melchizedek-275
Melchizedek:
Order-267,269
teachings of-276,280,286
Melchizedeks, qualities of the-273
Menahem the Essene-249
merit-56
meritocracy, the universe as a-112
Merkabah-260,276
messengers-120
Messiah, the-324
Meurois-Givaudan, Anne and Daniel
-50,347
Montessori, Maria-64,101
Morgan, R. W.-237
Morya, Master-126,145
Moss, Sylvia-229,232
Mount Carmel community-37,50,
106
Mount Horeb community-42,59
movement and repose, balance of-
276,279
multi-dimensionality-vi,264
Mystery Schools and the mysteries-
27,32,156,284

N

Nag Hammamdi Library-181,198
Name, Angel of the-67
names, meaning of-4
Nathan, brother of Mary Magdalene-
205
Nicky, a regression subject-139,144

O

Oneness-197,277,278,295
original sin-57
Osiris-324

P

Pagels, Elaine-347
parables-147,150,183
Parker, Janna Shelley-348
past life regression-i.iv
peace and peace-making-113,275
perfume-47
Persia and Persian knowledge-31,36,
44,106
Peter the Apostle-126,181
Pharisees-13,29,150,171,173,204,
221,251
Philo of Alexandria-1
physical limitations-67
Picknett, Lynn-177,347
planetary cycle, end of the-243,247,
249,257,259,306
Pontius Pilate-9,211
Poynder, Michael-217,347
prayer, power of-288
Prodigal Son-112
projection of consciousness-86,235,
243
prologues, Essene-99
property, donation of-44,48
prophecy, gift of-236
Psalms-267,269
Pythagorean Order-31
Pythagorean knowledge-30,44,235,
324

Q

Qumran community:
as the central community-36
crystal in-109
Daniel's visits to-104,105
depleted state of-309
library in-104
location of-36

R

Ra, cult of-45
rabbi, rabbinic-96,98
Rama community-37
reattunement to one's note-88
records, cosmic/angelic-89
reincarnation, belief in-v,57
resistance-65

retreat houses-50
Robinson, James-347
Romans and Rome-14,55,174,213, 222
Rowena, a regression subject-8,207

S

Sabbath-13
Sadducees-29,204
Sages and Master Souls-44,91
Salome-177,182
Samaria-309,312
Sanhedrin-173,205,213,223
Schiffman, Lawrence H.-347
Schonfield, Hugh-348
scrolls and scroll summaries-16,23, 48,105,106,107,303
secret levels of knowledge-35
seership, gift of-236
sharing-74,75
Shekinah-196
Shewen, Roberta, a regression subject -40,70
Silent One, The-70,125
Silwad-159
simplicity-57
Sinai-42
skills and powers-84
Sophia-185
soul anchored by the age of seven-64
soul family, return of the-307
souls, oldest-55
Spirit and matter merging-246
Spirit and soul-197
Spirit, gifts of the-276
spiritual development-245
spiritual evolution, the idea of-246
star:
    charts-55,67,231
    cycles-306
    wisdom-248
Starlight Center-i,ii,144,269
Steiner, Rudolf-54,64,175,348
Stone, Joshua David-348
Strachan, Gordon-126,135,237,348
Suddi, Benzahmare-77,329
synagogues-44,81,98
Syria-38

Szekely, Edmond Bordeaux-320, 343,348

T

Teacher, great-29
Teacher of Righteousness:
    coming of the-4
    energy system to support the- 161
    to establish a new way-156
    shield to the-44
    supportive framework for the-30
Temple, perfect, building of the-49
Temple Scroll, the-49,319
temples-226
third eye-66,71
Thomas the disciple-181,260
Thoth-255
time and timelessness-188
time-cycles-306
tin, trading in-10,212
tomb, empty-169
Torah, the, *see* Jewish Law
transformation-251
traveling-77
Tree of Knowledge-100
trees, Celtic-234
trees, Druid knowledge based on- 234
Trevelyan, George-33,297,343,348

U

unconditional love-vii,95,148,228
Universe, the-97,100
Universal Law-253

V

Vatican, the-215
Vermes, Geza-129,201,349
vortex travel-86
vows of secrecy-269,271

W

wadis-40
War Scroll, the-320
Warriors for God-42,59
Watchers, the-235,248

water-30,38
whales-290
Wholeness, restoration of-89
Wise, Michael-345

Y

Yadin, Yigael-49,349
Yahweh-110,115

Z

Zarathustra-324

Zealots-42,58,323
Zoroastrian:
    purification rituals-30
    sources and teachings-30,44,
        324

ABOUT THE AUTHORS

Stuart Wilson was born in Exmouth in the West of England. He came from a conventional background and went to a Scottish public school (Fettes in Edin-burgh). However his mother was fascinated by theosophy and the writings of Alice Bailey, and this led to Stuart's lifelong interest in esoteric teachings and the Eastern and Western wisdom traditions.

After service in the RAF on Christmas Island in the Pacific, he entered advertising as an agency copywriter, rising over some years to become an advertising manager for an industrial company. He then retrained as a counselor and set up a small publishing business, which he later sold to concentrate on writing. He wrote two best-selling name dictionaries, including Simply the Best Baby Name Book, and moved in 1990 to help his friend Joanna Prentis with the development of the Starlight Centre in mid-Devon.

He writes of this period: "It was inspiring and fascinating but also exhausting! A stream of visitors came in to the Centre, mainly from the United States and Australia, but some also from Europe. We had an amazing and mind-expanding time sitting at the feet of internationally respected spiritual teachers and workshop leaders. What I remember most about this time was the big gatherings when our friends came in to share a meal and talk about our experiences and all the changes that were happening in our lives. It was a wonderful time, full of joy and laughter, and the special events, like Anna Mitchell Hedges sharing her crystal skull, and the two fire-walks led by Esassani, were simply magical!"

Joanna Prentis: I was born in Bangalore in southern India. When I was two my family returned to Scotland where I spent my childhood and teenage years. After leaving school I traveled exten-sively, married and lived in Hong Kong for two years and then ten years in the Australian bush in Western Australia, where my three daughters were born. It was there that my interest began in alternative medicine and education, organic farming, metaphysics and meditation. With a local nurse, I ran a homeopathic and Radionic practice.

On returning to the UK I trained as a Montessori teacher and educated my two youngest daughters at home for a few years. My daughter Tatanya now lives in America, and Katinka and Larissa in southwest England. I now have two beautiful granddaughters.

I did several healing courses and have a foundation diploma in Humanistic Psychology. I also trained with Ursula Markham and have a diploma in Hypnotherapy and Past Life Therapy.

With my daughter Tatanya, I set up the Starlight Centre in 1988, a center for healing and the expansion of consciousness. She has introduced us to many innovative techniques and interesting people, and she continues to do this from her home in San Francisco.

Working with Stuart and my other regression subjects for this book was the most amazing experience I have ever had with any of my clients. The information that poured forth was incredible and the energies in the room were so blissful and powerful. The happiness of being with Jesus was out of this world and breathtaking, but the sadness and confusion after the crucifixion were a complete contrast. I hope this book will convey some of this. It is an amazing story and one I feel whose time has come.

Feedback From Readers

We hope this book will generate interest in the Essenes and the Essene Jesus. On reading this book many of you may feel "I was there! I want to tell my story too." Well, you can. Please let us know what you feel about our book as that feedback may help us when developing future books in this series. Visit us at our website:

www.foundationforcrystalchildren.com

Other Books Published
by
Ozark Mountain Publishing, Inc.

Conversations with Nostradamus, Volume I, II, III...............by Dolores Cannon
Jesus and the Essenes..by Dolores Cannon
They Walked with Jesus..by Dolores Cannon
Between Death and Life... by Dolores Cannon
A Soul Remembers Hiroshima..by Dolores Cannon
Keepers of the Garden..by Dolores Cannon
The Legend of Starcrash..by Dolores Cannon
The Custodians..by Dolores Cannon
The Convoluted Universe - Book One, Two, Three, Four......by Dolores Cannon
Five Lives Remembered ....by Dolores Cannon
The Three Waves of Volunteers and the New Earth .... by Dolores Cannon
I Have Lived Before...by Sture Lönnerstrand
The Forgotten Woman..by Arun & Sunanda Gandhi
Luck Doesn't Happen by Chance....................................by Claire Doyle Beland
Mankind - Child of the Stars.............................by Max H. Flindt & Otto Binder
Past Life Memories As A Confederate Soldier........................by James H. Kent
Holiday in Heaven..by Aron Abrahamsen
Out of the Archives .... by Aron & Doris Abrahamsen
Is Jehovah An E.T.?...by Dorothy Leon
The Essenes - Children of the Light...............by Stuart Wilson & Joanna Prentis
Power of the Magdalene..................................by Stuart Wilson & Joanna Prentis
Beyond Limitations ....by Stuart Wilson & Joanna Prentis
Atlantis and the New Consciousness .... by Stuart Wilson & Joanna Prentis
Rebirth of the Oracle..................................by Justine Alessi & M. E. McMillan
Reincarnation: The View from Eternity......by O.T. Bonnett, M.D. & Greg Satre
The Divinity Factor...by Donald L. Hicks
What I Learned After Medical School ....by O.T. Bonnett, M.D.
Why Healing Happens...by O.T. Bonnett, M.D.
A Journey Into Being..by Christine Ramos, RN
Discover The Universe Within You...by Mary Letorney
Worlds Beyond Death...by Rev. Grant H. Pealer
A Funny Thing Happened on the Way to Heaven .... by Rev. Grant H. Pealer
Let's Get Natural With Herbs...by Debra Rayburn
The Enchanted Garden...by Jodi Felice
My Teachers Wear Fur Coats........................by Susan Mack & Natalia Krawetz
Seeing True...by Ronald Chapman
Elder Gods of Antiquity...by M. Don Schorn
Legacy of the Elder Gods..by M. Don Schorn
Gardens of the Elder Gods .... by M. Don Schorn
Reincarnation...Stepping Stones of Life ....by M. Don Schorn

Continue for more books by Ozark Mountain Publishing, Inc.

Children of the Stars .... by Nikki Pattillo
A Spiritual Evolution .... by Nikki Pattillo
Angels - The Guardians of Your Destiny ....by Maiya & Geoff Gray-Cobb
Seeds of the Soul..by Maiya Gray-Cobb
The Despiritualized Church...by Rev. Keith Bender
The Science of Knowledge ....by Vara Humphreys
The Other Side of Suicide ....by Karen Peebles
Journey Through Fear ....by Antoinette Lee Howard
Awakening To Your Creation ....by Julia Hanson
Thirty Miracles in Thirty Days ....by Irene Lucas
Windows of Opportunity ....by Sherri Cortland
Raising Our Vibrations for the New Age .... by Sherri Cortland
Why? ....by Mandeep Khera
The Healing Christ ....Robert Winterhalter
Morning Coffee with God ....Michael Dennis
God's Many Mansions .... by Michael Dennis
Ask Your Inner Voice ....by James Wawro
Live From the Other Side ....by Maureen McGill & Nola Davis
TWIDDERS ....by Anita Holmes
Evolution of the Spirit.. by Walter Pullen
You Were Destined To Be Together .... by Tom Arbino
Teen Oracle .... by Cinnamon Crow
Chakra Zodiac Healing Oracle .... by Cinnamon Crow
The History of God .... by Guy Needler
Lifting the Veil on the Lost Continent of Mu .... by Jack Churchward
The Big E - Everything is Energy .... by Jarrad Hewett & Dee Wallace
Conscious Creation .... by Dee Wallace

For more information about any of the above titles, soon to be released titles, or other items in our catalog, write or visit our website:

OZARK
MOUNTAIN
PUBLISHING

PO Box 754
Huntsville, AR 72740
www.ozarkmt.com
1-800-935-0045/479-738-2348
Wholesale Inquiries Welcome